Secret Heroes:

From Holocaust Survivors to Nazi Interrogators

A novel by

Dianne Ogden

In collaboration with
Cynthia Michel

Resources used:
Department of the Interior
National Park Service
George Washington Memorial Parkway
Fort Hunt P.O. Box 1142 Oral History Research Project

ISBN: 9798868333996
Imprint: Independently published

Edited by: Elizabeth Ward
Copyedited by: Ellen Sappington

Cover Design by: Tracie Dailey

Printed in the United States of America

To my love,
Fred

4

For my friend, Cynthia, who entrusted me with the story of
her father and her family. I hope this work honors both.

You honor me,
You honor my father.

Secret Heroes:

From Holocaust Survivors to Nazi Interrogators

Table of Contents

A Knock at the Door   Louisville, Kentucky May 30, 2006

Chapter 1

A Knock on the Door

Louisville, Kentucky
May 30, 2006

Bright spring sunshine is spreading across a tree-lined street on the eastside of Louisville, Kentucky. This time of year, the grass is like a fresh green carpet, hugging the townhomes lining neatly groomed cul-de-sacs.

Cynthia and her mother, Lucille, are finishing a cup of tea outside on the back deck, their favorite breakfast spot during early summer. Her father, Fred, has already gone back inside. Cynthia believes this is the best of quiet suburban life. Morning tea outside while looking out over a forested neighborhood, the *forest* being nothing more than a buffer zone between streets. Still, she finds it soothing.

Cynthia just moved into her new condo down the block from her sister and elderly parents. The location allows her some privacy and the flexibility to be with her parents as much as they need and to spend time with her older sister.

Her sister, Deanna, who the family call Dee, graduated top of her class, went to college, became a physical therapist, and started her family in Louisville. Fred and Lucille moved here a few years ago to be closer to their oldest daughter's family, which is expanding. Dee's two grown children are now having children of their own.

Cynthia, on the other hand, always felt she was a challenge for her parents. After graduating from the Fashion Institute of Atlanta, she spent a decade as a makeup artist for CNN and another decade in production for TNT. Cynthia then decided to leave television and ran a successful wedding venue in the Historic District of Roswell, a suburb of Atlanta. But Dee needed her help, so after her divorce, she sold the business and moved to Louisville to help care for her parents, something she felt was her familial duty.

Her mother, now eighty, is still in good shape, agile, alert, witty and always the conversationalist. Lucille was a ball of fire in her day, and throughout Cynthia's life always kept abreast of current events and politics. Living first in Alexandria, then in Arlington demanded it. Their neighborhood was filled with people who worked for the government. You never knew what politics, initiatives or projects would come up in conversation. Besides, Lucille also had to keep up with her intelligent husband.

Fred, a quiet but brilliant engineer, is not faring as well. He fled Nazi Germany with his family as a youth because they were Jewish. He has accomplished much in his life, but now all the milestones of his 85 years are catching up with him, in his joints and in his mind. Cynthia never thought he was particularly tall, but his quiet, strong demeanor commanded respect and made him a giant in her eyes. Now his shoulders have a bit of a slump, and his receding gray hair does little to bring out the twinkle that used to dance in his eyes.

Fred had become a recluse in self-imposed purgatory, shut up in his office watching TV, the blinds pulled, the commentary of a news anchor his only company. A nagging depression had gotten ahold of him. He had somehow lost his will to live and now seemed to be just waiting.

Strange, Cynthia thinks, *for him to get to this point in life after all he's been through. Surely others who escaped the Nazis and survived the war embraced life and were grateful to have survived.*

Cynthia adores her father and wishes he could enjoy his remaining years. She knows deep down she should be grateful for the relationship they shared and the man her father had been. He is still there, somewhere inside, but now he is simply quieter and a little unsteady.

Their home has plenty of room and a wonderful back deck off the kitchen. There is a French-doored study adjacent to the living room that serves as a perfect refuge for her father. After breakfast, Fred retreats there, a routine that is now all too common, and disappointing.

Cynthia's place is still a pile of boxes and half unpacked clothes, but she knows she will get to it. Right now, she is working to acclimate to her parents' routine, and she sees morning tea on the back deck with her mom as a perk allowing for more quality time together. Once they have finished,

Cynthia picks up both cups from the bistro table and heads to the kitchen.

"You sit for a minute, I got this," she calls to Lucille through the open sliding door. "Be right back."

She deposits the mugs in the dishwasher and glances over to her father's study peeking through the French doors. She thinks he might be on the phone, but who would he be calling? *Maybe he's adjusting his chair*, she thinks. She is starting to get used to her father barricading himself until meals and takes it in stride, heading back to the deck. She will spend a little more one-on-one time with her mom before the visitor arrives.

What an interesting visit this will be, she thinks, *especially considering the twisted path that led to today.*

It was last December, sometime before the holidays, when they had gotten a call from Sandy and Jon Gray, their old neighbors in Alexandria, Virginia. Sandy called Lucille to alert her that she had an encounter with a national park ranger who wanted to talk to Fred about his service at Fort Hunt during World War II.

"Well, my goodness I can't imagine what that's about?" Lucille responded, a little surprised.

"Let me start at the beginning," Sandy tells her, trying to control her excitement.

Just after Thanksgiving, Sandy and Jon had taken a tour of Fort Hunt, part of the George Washington Memorial Parkway.

During the tour, a park ranger asked the group for help. The National Park Service was reconstructing the history of Fort Hunt and needed more information about WWII. The ranger asked if anyone knew someone who may have been stationed there during the war, and if so, they'd like to talk to them.

"They knew about some military activities, but they guessed there was more to the story and that's why they were asking for the public's help," Sandy explained. "The ranger knew it was a shot in the dark, but what could she lose?"

"Apparently her shot in the dark was a lucky hit!" Lucille laughed.

"I remembered you telling me Fred was there during the war so I thought he might be able to help."

"I'll have to ask Fred, but I don't think he'd mind talking to her."

"Great," Sandy went on. "The person Fred can call is Ranger Dana Dierkes," she said as she spelled out the last name so Lucille could write it down. "She's a Public Affairs Officer, I think. She's very knowledgeable about the Fort and the parkway," she added with confidence. "So do you think Fred can talk to her?"

Lucille let out a sigh. "You know Fred. It's up to him. Let me ask. Here, talk to Cynthia. She's here visiting for the holidays." Lucille got up to find Fred and thrust the phone towards her daughter. Cynthia had just taken a sip of hot tea, which stung the roof of her mouth. She took the phone from her mother, swallowed with a wincing gulp, and still managed to compose herself enough to brightly say, "Sandy! How the heck are you!"

That opened a whirlwind of conversation about her impending move and eventually wound back to the topic at hand.

"What does the park service want with dad? You know mom grew up there, so she knows the area like the back of her hand."

"They're doing some historical project, and they're looking for people who might have served there during the war - the *Second* World War," Sandy said with playful emphasis for Cynthia, who was rolling her eyes.

"I wanted to ask Fred if he wouldn't mind talking to them." She thought a minute, then added, "That ranger was thrilled. She couldn't believe her luck!"

"At finding dad?"

"Yes. Apparently, they don't really know exactly what went on at Fort Hunt during World War II. She mentioned something about intelligence, like Fort Hunt was an intelligence center or something. They want to talk to a veteran so they can figure it out and so far, they haven't found any. I think Fred is the only name they have."

"Got it, got it," Cynthia nodded. Fred had worked for the Army as a civilian and she was used to him being involved with confidential work she couldn't ask about. She took Army intelligence in stride. Then she turned away from the doorway and lowered her voice. "Listen, Dad's not been doing great lately. He's been very depressed. Who knows, maybe this will get him thinking about something else?" Then she quickly changed tone as her mom appeared. "Mom's back. Great talking with you," and with that she handed over the phone.

"Sandy?" Lucille began. "It took a little coaxing, but Fred said if Ranger Dierkes was expecting him to call, he'll call her." Then Lucille turned to more social issues. "Tell me what you and Jon have been up to!" and Lucille settled into a comfortable chair for the rest of the conversation.

After the request, Fred sat in his study, conflicted and not sure what to tell this park ranger. It takes almost a week for him to come to terms with what he feels he can disclose and finally calls. When he reaches Ranger Dierkes, she explains the research project and their efforts to find someone stationed at Fort Hunt during the war. The National Park Service, keenly aware that few visitors to the George Washington Parkway fully understand its origin and importance, initiated a project to develop information boards and wayside exhibits for display at each site along the twenty-five-mile route. Fort Hunt was the one location considered the least understood and in need of the most work.

Fred understands the project and chats amicably about the Fort, the grounds and buildings; but when the conversation rolls around to his service he politely declines.

After a few more strategic attempts, Ranger Dierkes feels she has pushed as hard as she can and decides to turn pursuing Fred over to the Cultural Resources Ranger assigned to the project. She tells Fred there is a whole team of people working on this and to expect a call from Ranger Brandon Bies after the holidays. Once she hangs up, she leaves a sticky note with Fred's number on Brandon's desk.

Brandon Bies, a twenty-six-year-old Cultural Resource Specialist, was hired a few months back. Although he was one of the newest and youngest members of the team, he came with good credentials; a degree in archeology, a depth of knowledge necessary to reconstruct the timeline of Fort Hunt, and a keen interest in military history. What set him apart were his interviewing skills and the simple fact everyone liked him.

Cultural Resources Officer Matt Virta hired Brandon as his assistant for all these qualities and that he could take this one large project off his plate. Young and eager, Brandon relished the opportunity to dive head-first into this tailor-made assignment. When Brandon met Chief Ranger Vince Santucci, he found a kindred soul. Both were archeology and World War II buffs and hit it off right away.

Vince Santucci had been with the National Park Service going on twenty years handling assignments in national parks from the Badlands to the Grand Canyon to Yellowstone. He isn't a tall man but has what you would call a firm build. His neatly trimmed beard combined with wire rimmed glasses and professional demeanor adds gravitas to the uniform he proudly wears. Vince is extremely knowledgeable about the workings of the park service and performs his job in a professional and pleasant way. When Brandon comes on board, he sees immediately that Vince is the kind of guy who gets things done.

After Brandon got the assignment, his preliminary research indicated there was more to uncover about Fort Hunt during World War II than anyone realized. Most of the historical information he was given stopped in 1942, the beginning of WWII. Brandon knew he needed deeper and more extensive research. He had always been an organized person and decided to focus his efforts on what he considered the source, the National Archives.

He had recently located declassified documents stating that Fort Hunt was used for military intelligence and interrogating German prisoners of war. The boxes he called up from the bowels of the archives were filled with green folders containing yellowed pages, some crumbling around the edges, some indented with decades old paperclips. He reviewed page after page referencing German prisoners, lists of names and transcripts of interrogations, a declassified summary report on Fort Hunt and lists of soldiers transferred from Camp Ritchie to Fort Hunt. He reasoned any prisoner interrogated at Fort Hunt would have been questioned by U.S. soldiers.

But how many soldiers and which branch of the military? Army, Navy or perhaps both? How many prisoners were held there? He has more questions than answers.

Brandon was given information and resource materials from his boss Matt, and absorbed as much about World War II intelligence as he could. He was also keenly aware of the passage of time. It has been almost sixty years and even though much information has been declassified he wondered why no one knew anything about Fort Hunt. Realizing this, his expectations were low when it came to finding Fort Hunt veterans, who would now be in their mid to upper eighties. In fact, the chances of finding anyone still alive were slim to none.

When he sees the post-it note it takes Brandon by surprise. Fred Michel's name and phone number is his first and only real lead. He hoped Fred could remember what Fort Hunt was like so he could provide enough information to get the exhibits done. Plus, he and Vince would like to know the kind of intelligence work that was conducted and if Fred Michel knew anything about it. Dana had mentioned Fred was a little hesitant, which is understandable when dealing with intelligence. Still, it was something he and Vince discussed. Brandon had the feeling he didn't know what he didn't know about Fort Hunt and World War II.

With the holidays behind them and the calendar announcing it was 2006, Brandon gathered his notes and picked up the phone to call Fred. An elderly gentleman with a pleasant voice answered. Brandon introduced himself, explained how he got Fred's number and outlined the exhibit project. Their conversation was amicable, with few details. Things changed, however, when Brandon started to ask more pointed questions.

"I'd like to find out what went on at Fort Hunt during the war," Brandon said.

"I really can't talk about that, Brandon. There's nothing to tell anyway. Soldiers were stationed in many places and prisoners were moved around during the war."

"But it looks like you were sent *from* Camp Ritchie *to* Fort Hunt."

"I can't comment on that."

Brandon decides on a different approach. "Do you remember Fort Hunt? What it looked like? Can you remember how many buildings there were?"

Fred hesitantly mentioned barracks for the soldiers, literally measuring every word. Undeterred, Brandon smoothly encouraged Fred to talk about the grounds and physical set-up of the Fort, then he invited Fred and Lucille to Washington for an interview.

Fred acquiesced and said he could talk about Fort Hunt and the grounds, but was reluctant to talk specifically about what he did and bluntly told Brandon, "If I haven't told my wife about this in sixty years, why would I talk to you?" He politely but firmly ended the conversation.

Brandon was surprised but still hopeful. He brought all this information back to Vince and they discussed how to proceed. Over the years, Vince had dealt with numerous Washington types, many of whom had opinions on how the George Washington Memorial Parkway, which seemed to sit under a microscope, should be managed or what events should be given special treatment. Through this high-level management of the parkway, Vince developed relationships with the CIA, Senators, Congressmen, and various branches of military intelligence. Vince and Brandon reasoned they may need something official to convince Fred it was OK to talk about the war. Vince had a contact at the Department of Defense and made the call.

The next day Vince sat down with Brandon. "Listen, I got ahold of my contact at the Pentagon. He says there was an oath these guys signed and although they can't be released from the oath, they can talk about what they did if they think it will help training our guys today."

"So, it's kind of a half-way permission?" Brandon said slowly.

"Yeah, that's the Army," Vince shrugged, "and it's the best we're going to get. So, let's see if we can get Fred back on the phone. I'd hate to miss talking to him."

"Me too."

Brandon called Fred optimistically highlighting their previous conversation and saying they would fly him and his wife to Washington for the interview. Fred felt bad for this kid who was just trying to do his job, so he tried to meet him halfway, at least agreeing to talk about how the fort was set up and some of the buildings. Brandon was hoping to get Fred to reveal much more.

When word got out that the Cultural Resources team's combined efforts produced a name which led to a veteran coming to visit, everyone was excited. The whole team was operating under the assumption that Fred was the only soldier they would find, maybe the last and only survivor they would ever be able to talk to and they all wanted to make the most of it.

Brandon gathered a handful of old pictures from his research showing Fort Hunt's grounds dotted with numerous buildings that no longer stood, listening devices that resembled museum relics, and smiling soldiers he had no way to identify. His efforts to understand wartime activities at the camp felt like trying to solve a puzzle with the center pieces missing. This chapter of the Fort's history was turning out to be like nothing he had imagined, and he hoped Fred could complete the picture.

After the travel arrangements were made, Fred had second thoughts. A week before the flight, he called Brandon. "I don't think we can come to see you. I am not feeling well, and I really don't think I should fly." It was an excuse but one he hoped Brandon would buy.

"I'm sorry to hear that Fred," Brandon was genuinely concerned but knew Fred was feigning bad health.

"Yes, it just wouldn't be good to travel now." Fred told Brandon and tried to convince himself this would put it to rest.

Brandon, however, would not be deterred. "Fred, if you can't make the trip then I'd be happy to come to you." Brandon was getting savvy to curve balls and quickly tossed it back to Fred.

Thwarted, Fred came clean. "You see, I just can't talk to you. I took an oath and what I did at Fort Hunt is something I can't discuss."

"Yes, I know about the oath. But this material, the information about Fort Hunt has been declassified. The pentagon said so," Brandon tried to explain. "They say you can talk to me if you feel it might be helpful in training today's soldiers." That left a slight opening and Fred thought about it.

"You may be the last person alive to talk about what happened during World War II, and it's important to have your account on record."

That last argument hit Fred hard. What if he was the last Fort Hunt survivor? What if the story dies with him? *Surely not*, he thought, *but what if?* He mulled it over and finally gave Brandon permission to come.

Brandon said he would get right back to him with travel arrangements, hung up and headed to Vince's office. He quickly laid out the current crisis and asked to use the budget to fly and see Fred. Vince agreed, and Brandon got back on the phone telling Fred he would come to Louisville at the end of May, the 30th and 31st. Fred consented, and the meeting was back on.

Finally, through that serendipitous turn of events last December and after months going back-and-forth, the day of the interview arrived. It's early and Brandon is at his gate at Dulles International Airport. He is carrying all his documentation and an audio recorder stuffed in a bulging case along with an overnight bag. Just then his phone rings. He answers. It's Fred.

"Fred, hey, I'm at the airport. I should be there in a couple hours."

"Hello Brandon, that's what I wanted to talk to you about," Fred slowly starts. "I have thought about it, and I think we'd better cancel your trip. I don't know if I can talk to you."

"What?" Brandon is dumbfounded. "But Fred, I'm *in* the airport, *at* the gate. I can't really cancel at this point."

"I'm not sure what I can tell you," Fred stalls.

"Listen, I can assure you what we'll talk about has been declassified. It will be ok. Seriously, we *can* talk about this." Brandon is trying not to raise his voice but finds it hard to control what is beneath his calm exterior.

"Yes, I know what you said about declassification," Fred is ever so slightly less resistant and takes a long pause. "Ok then, if you are at the airport."

"Yes, I'm boarding now, as we speak. I'll be there in a couple of hours, and we'll talk more then," Brandon reassures. There was silence so Brandon ends with, "Fred I'm really looking forward to meeting you."

"Yes, yes. I'll see you when you get here." With that Fred hangs up.

Unbelievable Brandon thinks. This is going to be a little tougher than he'd thought. There is so much unfolding about the WWII years he finds incredulous, and Fred's reluctance only fuels his curiosity. He has no idea what this impending conversation with Fred Michel will reveal.

Fred was just hanging up the phone when he saw Cynthia out of the corner of his eye. By the time he fully looks her way, she is headed back to the porch to sit with Lucille. He leans back into his chair and lets out a long breath. After all these years he is still conflicted. He can't let it go because his oath is an oath, his word is his word, and his promise is something he cannot go back on. He still struggles with what he can and cannot say. His forehead is moist with a rising level of anxiety. He must decide what he is going to say and be firm when Brandon arrives.

Cynthia has no idea what is going on as she rejoins her mom at the bistro table. She listens to Lucille chat away about planting flowers in their small bed and Cynthia comments about her own favorite choices.

"So what time is this Brandon fellow coming?" her mom asks.

Cynthia glances at her watch. "He should be here at about 11:00, we have some time."

She and her mom fall into a comfortable rhythm, watching eye-catching pairs of red Cardinals and listening to the enchanting warble of South Carolina chickadees as they bounce along the grass. Above them the full branches of maple trees play host to skittering squirrels performing their acrobatics. Cynthia watches and let's her mind wander.

"Did dad ever talk about the war, about what he did?" she finally asks. Her dad was an engineer with an impressive resume of various achievements and awards which, if you looked at it on paper, was rather extraordinary. His contemporaries always referred to him as *Doctor* Michel, even though she knew he'd only earned a Masters. That was the quiet power of Fred Michel. His accomplishments, his work ethic and his capabilities were his calling card, and it earned him the respect of his associates and the industry. He won the SME Gold Award for manufacturing engineering innovation and served a term as that organization's president. But his career successes didn't explain his activities during World War II.

"No, he was always vague, and I knew not to ask. Soldiers could never tell you what they did, usually just where they were stationed. During the war we would meet at the USO. At first, his poor parents didn't know where he was, only that they could write to him at P.O. Box 1142. That's it." She pauses for a minute and shoots Cynthia a playful look," but I figured it out, you know," she said with a satisfied smile.

"I never made a big deal out of it," she continues, "but your dad showed me a picture of him and his buddies at a pool. "I said, 'you're at Fort Hunt!' and he shushed me!" She is indignant with a deep grin on her face. "He was upset and said, 'no one must know!' I told him, *everyone* knows." Here she can't help but laugh at how uptight Fred was. "He was more than a little surprised and told me not to say anything. So, I promised I would keep it quiet, but it was the worst kept secret!" She chuckles, relishing the tease.

Then she says thoughtfully, "He still never told me what he did. Never has. I figured it was classified. You know what they used to say, *Loose lips sink ships!* We took that seriously during the war. Besides, our conversations were about us. You know what it's like to be twenty-something and in love." This was a racy conversation for Lucille that Cynthia finds endearing after 60 years of marriage. She can't help but smile.

Fred was a young Army soldier who was drafted right out of college. Lucille was a United Service Organizations or USO volunteer during the War. In fact, as the family legend goes, that's how they met, dancing at a USO party.

For most of her life, Cynthia felt her father's commanding presence. He was unpretentious, highly intelligent and knew quickly what was going on, whatever it was. He projected a quiet strength and was never showy. She always thought of the phrase, *if you want people to listen to you, you whisper.* That summed up her father.

As do most young daughters, she considered her dad handsome, in an elder statesman kind of way, and could see why her mom fell for him. He had light brown hair back then, kind eyes and could be very charming with a quick, dry wit. As a parent, he had been tough but loving: a guiding force with knowing intuition. Now, in his twilight years, there were few of those traits left.

She remembers her parent's first trip back to Germany and all the emotions it fomented in her dad. Surely after finding out about lost relatives and concentration camps, he had come to terms with what happened during the war. She thought he was beyond the pain of those years. Cynthia admits to her mom it is hard for her to understand her father's worsening depression. A sad terminus to a life filled with daring courage, academic success, and professional triumphs. But what she thought she knew of her father and his history would soon be re-written. Cynthia hears a knock on the front door and gets up to answer.

A national park ranger stands at her door in a full ranger uniform. The gray shirt and green pants are neatly pressed but the shirt hangs a little loose around his slender neck. Cynthia notices the arrowhead emblem on his sleeve as he flashes a broad, clean-shaven smile from under his tan ranger hat. He quickly removes the hat as he says, "Good morning, ma'am. I'm Brandon Bies. You must be Cynthia," and extends his hand. "Nice to meet you."

"Yes, hello Brandon. So nice to meet you too." Cynthia can't help but notice how much enthusiasm accompanies his youth. She warmly takes his hand. "Come in, we've been expecting you."

At least his family is friendly, Brandon thinks, after all he's been through with Fred.

Lucille comes out to make her own introduction. Cynthia motions for Brandon to take a seat in the living room, then turns to get her father. Even at this point, she wasn't sure her father would behave and talk to Brandon, but she likes the young man and wants to help. She knocks on the door of her father's study and opens one of the French doors.

"Dad, the park ranger, Brandon Bies, is here to see you. Can you come out?" she says from the edge of the door. The swivel chair turns away from the TV to reveal Fred, looking perplexed.

"Who is it?" he asks.

"It's the park ranger, from the National Park Service who wants to talk about Fort Hunt. He's waiting in the living room," Cynthia coaxes.

"I already told him, I'm not sure what I can tell him at this point," Fred says as he starts to turn back around.

"Oh, c'mon dad. He came all this way and you said you'd help him out. He seems nice." Cynthia knows she should make it sound simple and easy.

"Yes, yes alright, I'm coming." With that, Fred pushes himself up out of his chair and heads toward the living room. Cynthia turns to follow him, wondering why her father is acting so strangely. Is it the fact that he is old or stubborn or both? Hard to tell at this point. She simply directs him to his favorite chair.

Brandon pleasantly chats with Lucille who is enjoying the company. When Fred enters, they both stop talking and Brandon rises.

"Good morning, Fred," Brandon says with a note of relief that he is finally standing face to face with Fred Michel. He sees a distinguished looking older man who still has most of his hair. His midsection is softly rounded, giving him a grandfatherly silhouette.

For eighty-five he looks pretty good, Brandon thinks. The men shake hands and sit down, then Brandon says, "It's so nice to finally meet you."

"Yes, yes, nice to meet you too, Brandon. As I told you on the phone though, I'm not sure I can help you out." Fred is genial but reserved, and Brandon knows he has his work cut out for him.

"Yes, but I'm simply trying to fill in the history of Fort Hunt. We have a fair idea of what went on during World War II, but I'm looking for a more complete explanation of the activities. Then perhaps we can talk about what the fort looked like, how it was set up when you were there?" He smiles and hopes the change in tactic will get Fred talking. Lucille and Cynthia certainly seem interested.

Brandon decides to jump in. "Can we start with your experiences at Fort Hunt? What were your duties?"

"Brandon, that is something I can't talk about." Fred was matter of fact.

"Dad, can't you tell him anything about the war?" Cynthia cuts in, not wanting to be rude but trying hard to extend the conversation.

"No, I can't talk about this," Fred says resolutely, looking directly at Cynthia. She knows this look and knows not to press.

"But sir," Brandon approaches cautiously, "it's been almost 60 years since the end of the war and this information has been declassified. It's OK to discuss activities at Fort Hunt. In fact, many declassified documents and transcripts point to Fort Hunt being an intelligence hub. Were you part of that?"

"I'm sorry," Fred says resolutely. He gave his word along with his fellow German speaking soldiers. They were never to disclose their actions with other military personnel, friends or even their family - ever.

"If I may, sir," Brandon continues, "I have a transcript of an interview I believe was conducted by you." Brandon digs into his case and pulls out a stack of stapled pages, then hands it to Fred.

"The Pentagon declassified this information in the mid 90's. It's now 2006. That's almost ten years ago. We are just now combing through many documents trying to make sense of the program. An explanation from someone who was there, well, it would be very helpful." Brandon pauses then continues.

"We have a general idea that a military intelligence center was located on the grounds during the war. This would have housed two intelligence branches, MIS-X and MIS-Y. As far as I can tell, MIS-Y was the interrogation branch where you would have been assigned. There are only a few files or records of the wartime activities that still exist. That's why I'd like to get your description."

Fred thumbs through the papers but is overall unchanged. Cynthia looks at him, her interest genuinely piqued and ready to burst with her own questions. Fred quickly realizes as he looks up at his daughter and his wife, that the pressure he is getting from this park ranger will be nothing compared to what he is about to get from his family. So, he deflects.

"If the Pentagon has declassified this information, they can tell me themselves." He looks directly at Brandon. "They can contact me."

"How about the DIA?" Brandon offers. He has Vince's contact at the Defense Intelligence Agency. "I can get someone on the phone now if you like."

Brandon has his phone out quickly dialing. In another moment he asks for an officer.

While he waits Cynthia mouths to her father, "What's M-I-S-Y?

"It's Military Intelligence Service – the division is Y," he quietly explains. Cynthia nods and turns her attention back to Brandon who seems to have located someone.

Brandon quickly runs through the events of the morning ending with, "so can you tell Mr. Michel that this information is declassified and it's OK for him to discuss it with me?" Then he waits for a response. "Thanks, I'll put him on." With that

Brandon hands the phone to Fred who cautiously raises it to his ear.

The voice on the other end has the crisp cadence of the military and is a little loud. Cynthia makes out the gist of the conversation. She can tell by the look on her dad's face everything Brandon said is being corroborated and his reluctance starts to soften.

Finally, after much resistance, Fred begins to give way and says, "Alright, alright. If the Department of Defense has declassified this information, then OK. Thank you. Goodbye."

With that, Fred turns to Brandon and says, "I took an oath when I got to Fort Hunt. We all did. We swore on our honor to our new country we would never speak of this...of our orders and how we fulfilled them."

"Yes, I understand," Brandon earnestly acknowledges. "To your credit, and to the credit of all the soldiers there, it looks like no one's ever said a word. That's why we're just now starting to learn that some kind of military intelligence was conducted at Fort Hunt. Since you were there, we'd love to hear from you, what it was all about."

"Basically, I did what my government asked me to do, we all did." Fred says rather pragmatically.

"I've located a few records and some pictures from that particular time – around 1942 to '46. We're trying to put it together, but the information is still... sparse." Brandon says.

"There are no records and few pictures because we burned everything," Fred explains. "Five days after the war ended, with victory over Japan, the order came to burn all documents, all records, everything. It took three days to do so but it was part of national security. However, I did keep some papers that were of interest to me. But everything else - we burned. Eventually, they removed or bulldozed many of the buildings to make the beautiful park that's there today." Brandon, Cynthia and Lucille glanced between each other, jarred by this revelation.

"During the war, there were many buildings, more than what you could see from the road. We couldn't get close," Lucille recalls. "After the war, I thought they took them down because they were old, not because of some national security issue." She looked at Fred for some explanation. "You never said anything about burning papers."

Fred looked at his wife and simply said, "I couldn't. But now, it looks like I can." Then he turns to Brandon, "What do you want to know?"

Brandon feels the tension from Fred dissipate and sets up his tape recorder. "I'd like to record our conversation." Fred gives the okay followed by Lucille then Cynthia. Brandon has a notepad with a list of questions.

"This is Brandon Bies of the National Park Service, Tuesday, May 30th, 2006, talking with Fred and Lucille Michel in Louisville, Kentucky about memories of Fort Hunt. First, Fred, how did you come to be stationed at Fort Hunt?"

Fred had a precise way of choosing his words and his diction was nearly perfect. The exactness, Brandon thought, was because he was an engineer. Brandon detects only a slight German accent on some words, so faint, you had to know what you were listening for to hear it.

Fred takes a breath and begins. "Well, we called it 1142 at the time, P.O. Box 1142, not Fort Hunt. I was chosen to be there because of my engineering degree and because I spoke fluent German and knew German customs. For what purpose would the army need this?" He waited for a rhetorical pause, "to interrogate Nazi prisoners."

Interrogating Nazis was not what Cynthia or Lucille expected, and they reacted with stunned expressions. Brandon takes the cue and asks, "I understand you were a German Jewish refugee who escaped the Nazis. How did you end up interrogating them?"

Fred begins with the retelling of his family's escape from Germany in 1936.

Mein Heimatland   Landau in der Pfalz, Germany September, 1936

Chapter 2

Mein Heimatland

Landau in der Pfalz, Germany
September 1936

There is tension and urgency in the air in the house at Mahlastrasse 12. The Michel family has received their visas to emigrate to the United States. What to pack? How much can they bring? Lilly Michel is paring down the list in her mind.

"What's important? What will I need? What can I do without?" She steps out of her bedroom door and calls down the hallway to her two young boys, "Fritz, Rudolph, remember to also pack your winter clothes – and hurry!" she adds. Then she turns back to her own suitcase and the impossible decisions scattered all around her.

Those boys, she thinks. *Boys! They are teenagers who will soon be young men. They will have to grow up quickly now.*

Fifteen-year-old Fred should be packing clothes, but he is standing gazing at his desk. He knows they are fleeing. They will be without their home. They will be in a new country. It's almost too much to think about. He looks to his desk. There are his drawing supplies and his stamp collection to consider.

He must decide. They will be leaving tomorrow. His open suitcase is on his bed half full. Can he fit everything in?

When fear freezes your mind, indecision becomes your enemy. He finds some socks and tosses them into his suitcase, then thinks about the weather turning cold and reaches for a sweater. He will miss walks with his favorite Uncle Otto who took him on hikes to the Trifels or the Rietburg in the verdant, wooded countryside of western Bavaria. Would he ever again explore the Edenberg, the Tiergarten or the Fort? He sits on the bed and realizes after all that's happened, they must now flee to survive. He's leaving everything he knows to escape to the unknown. Fear is welling up again. He needs to beat it down and keep packing.

As Jews, they felt the Nazi's target on their backs. Thank goodness his father, Richard, worked for Grandfather Brunner and Uncle Otto. They were distillers, wholesale wine dealers and bottlers. The fact that they still had work was a small miracle.

Fred was old enough to start noticing things. Little things at first, like a few years ago when one of his teachers who spoke out against the Nazi teachings just disappeared for a whole year. When he came back, he never spoke against any Nazi teachings again. Then other teachers were replaced. Then there were no more Jewish teachers or religious studies at school. Last year he had to switch to an all-Jewish school. Some of his gentile friends weren't talking to him anymore. Everything is changing.

There is a knock on the door to their apartment. Richard, who is in his vest with rolled up sleeves, doesn't bother grabbing his jacket and answers the door. It is a customs agent in a dark suit, and a bushy mustache, there to supervise the packing and approve transport of everyone and their belongings to the rail station.

As luck would have it, Richard knows this inspector who supervised distilling operations, a division under the jurisdiction of the customs office. The uniformed man recognizes Richard and gives him a pleasant but cordial greeting. The inspector slowly wanders from room to room, looking down beneath the brim of his hat, observing Lilly, who has moved to the kitchen and is purposefully selecting silverware and some pans from the cupboards. He then moves down the hall, stopping to watch what Rudy, Fred's younger brother is packing. As the inspector turns in the hallway to scrutinize Fred's room, Richard spots Fred's stamp collection. Richard is concerned about compliance with regulations and does not want to jeopardize their immigration in any way. Richard picks up the collection and asks the inspector if it is OK to take.

The inspector looks at Richard for a moment, then tells him, "Don't show me anything I haven't asked for." And with that Richard understands his long-standing relationship with the inspector gives them a break. "Here Fritz, go ahead and pack your stamp collection," Richard says as he quickly hands the binder back to Fred then returns to his own suitcase. The inspector looks over the rest of the room, which is now in complete disarray and slowly paces back down the hallway.

Fred doesn't realize he is holding his breath until he exhales. He watches as the inspector slowly posts himself at the front door waiting for the suitcases and trunks to be placed before him. Fred is distracted by thoughts of his friends, his school, his town – but he must focus. He tries to concentrate on what he will need. He picks up a folder with his schoolwork and opens it to some of his drawings. He is a good artist, especially his use of color and angular dimensions. He flips through his work and lands on a drawing from Elementary school, the book burning. He remembers that day well.

It was three years ago when all classes were ordered to march to the Paradeplatz and face the Indendantur on the Marktstrasse (parade or fairgrounds in an open shopping area). There were SA, the brown shirts, standing around the students. Somebody started a bonfire on the steps of the building. The SA on the balcony were grabbing books and tossing them over the railing, feeding the flames. Fred wanted to cover his nose, the smoke was curling and rising. Tiny flecks of ashes were dotting his coat. His teacher called out for attention which jolted him to shoot his eyes to the front of the crowd. Everyone had to look forward. Someone, an officer, was giving a speech. Then the ceremony concluded with all the children singing *Horst Wessellied*, the anthem song of the NAZI party. Finally, they were dismissed. It was the strangest thing Fred had ever experienced. Then it happened again and again.

Fred could feel his quiet, idyllic life slipping away. He loved his hometown. Landau was a picturesque hamlet made up of three and four-story cream-colored brick buildings. Some were adorned with wrought iron balconies like their neighbors, the Franks. Some had covered entryways but mostly he saw uniform dormers and wood supports that gave the whole town a unique Bavarian look. Landau was graced with a beautiful river walk and brick promenade along the Queich river which flowed through the center of town. He loved to walk downtown and see the people and all the shops. But like any young boy, he loved simply being outdoors, playing with the neighborhood kids or exploring the countryside. Now he was preparing to leave it all, his town, his friends, everything.

His parents enjoyed the respect of their community, which made Fred proud. His father served in the Bavarian Field Artillery Regiment during WWI. After the war, von Hindenburg made it clear his soldiers were not to be abused or harassed in any way. Fred's father became commander of the Reischbund Juedisher Frontsoldaten, a local veteran's chapter. It seemed he knew everyone in Landau.

Fred folds some trousers and tries to put more energy into packing, but his mind is full of distractions. He looks out the window at his street and tries to memorize all the bricks, the trees, and nuances of his neighborhood. He leans his head on the windowpane. At the end of his street is the Festehalle, one of the most beautiful art nouveau-style festival halls in all of Germany. His mother loved going there for concerts and plays. It pained him when his parents were no longer allowed to go inside.

"It was so much easier before Hitler," he thinks. His father had his routine and so did his mother. She stayed at home but was always busy. She had her clubs, her friends, her sewing, knitting and crocheting. She could do all of that because Fraenz was there. Oh, how he missed Fraenz. Would he ever get to see her again?

Fraenz Schreiner was only 17 when she came to work for the Michels. She became the maid and nanny. Fred and Rudy loved Fraenz and when he and his brother were old enough, she would take them to visit her family's farm in Edesheim.

Fred was lost in the happy memory of seeing Fraenz's goat in their kitchen. It would come in and eat the wool they used for knitting, then Fraenz would have to shoo the goat out of the house.

Was it only last year they lost her? It seemed like a lifetime ago. Yes, it was last year when the Nuremberg Laws were passed. Father was furious. The laws specifically targeted Jews, thoroughly crushing Jewish businesses and changing their legal standing.

But that law also made it illegal for Jews to have interactions with Aryans. He and Rudy could no longer swim in the public pool, and they couldn't fly the German flag. But what crushed him was the stipulation German women under the age of 45 could not be employed in Jewish households. Fraenz was a gentile. She had to go.

That changed everything in his life. Fraenz went back to her family in Edesheim. Would he ever get to see her again? Fred continued to grab clothing as his thoughts glazed over at the events of the past few years.

His father, Richard Michel, had always been loyal to the Weimar Republic. He had told Fred the Treaty of Versailles demanded harsh war reparations and put a lot of economic pressure on Germany, but that Germany was strong, and would come out of it. Richard worked hard and the Michels enjoyed a middle-class standard of living.

When a young upstart named Adolph Hitler started talking about doing away with democracy and advocating an autocratic government, Richard shrugged him off as another loud voice with no substance. But Hitler was constantly attacking the Weimar Republic and kept asserting they were influenced by German Jews and the Communist minorities. After all, Karl Marx was a Jew and a communist.

In 1922 Germany had missed a reparations payment which set off hyperinflation; and by 1923 the German mark was so devalued people literally needed a wheelbarrow to carry enough currency for a loaf of bread. Fred remembers his father describing what that looked like as people tried to buy basic necessities. But Richard had reassured his son the economy was now stable, since back in 1924 the Reichsbank separated from the government and issued a new Reichsmark backed by an international loan. The economy got better until of course, the crash of 1929, from which the world was now slowly healing.

The Michel wine distribution business weathered the ups and downs of the economy. Richard and Lilly were able to take their young sons on vacations and do some traveling in Europe.

"Hitler is a malcontent," he had told Fred, "A troublemaker looking to blame everyone else for Germany's problems." Richard had always instructed Fred that hard work and managing their money would get them through. He and most of his friends dismissed Hitler as extreme and went about their lives.

But Hitler would not be dismissed. After his disastrous Munich (Beer Hall) Putsch and incarceration, Hitler focused on taking over the Weimar Republic legally. Most Germans were unsuspecting of Hitler's intent. Richard, on the other hand, told Fred he was very suspicious of the new German Worker's Party. They were allowing this Hitler fellow too much control to recruit and alter the party platform. Since Hitler oversaw propaganda, he renamed this new, bigger group the National-Sozialistische Deutsche Arbeiterpartei (German National Socialist Workers Party) or NAZI party, growing Hitler's power. Richard simply didn't trust them or their rising star.

As Germany's economy improved, the Michels settled into middle class life. Fred enjoyed his family's routines of work and school, their social life with the veteran's group, his father's card club or nights his parents went dancing. Sometimes Fred was allowed to join them for plays and musical performances at the *Festhalle*. His father would discuss politics with friends, but it always ended with support of the Weimar Republic and President von Hindenberg.

Fred is daydreaming of the *Festhalle* when he realizes he is making little progress with his packing. He grabs winter shirts, woolen pants and tries to make them fit into his almost full suitcase. He remembers a harsh winter during the Great Depression when his mother gathered his old clothes and donated them to families who needed them. Many fathers were out of work. Luckily his father was employed in a family business. Somehow, they survived.

After the Depression, Fred slowly became more aware of things his father talked about. Richard commented on how newspapers began filling with right-wing anti- socialist columns spreading a consistent message of Aryan purity and the natural supremacy of the German people. The shift in this message was not lost on the Michels who saw German nationalism rise to their detriment.

As Hitler grew the Nazi Party, he also expanded its reach, enlisting strong-arm squads made up of local police and men who were out of work. He granted them broad discretion to use violence to harass without reprisal. Hitler gave this group a name and a uniform. They were Sturmabteilung, the Storm Troopers or Brown Shirts. Fred saw them on the streets of Landau and came to understand the Brown Shirts were all over Germany.

In 1930, Richard Michel took notice of the fact that the Nazi party got 20 percent of the vote and was now the second largest party in the country. They were winning seats in the German Reichstag or Parliament. By 1933, Richard felt Fred was old enough to understand politics and explained how Hitler was challenging von Hindenburg in the presidential election. At the time there was a deep fear of Social Democrats and Communism. Even though the Nazi party wasn't the majority, that fear coupled with a fragile government, was enough to convince von Hindenburg he should offer Hitler the Chancellorship rather than face political fallout or a Communist takeover. Since he and others in the government never took Hitler seriously, they felt they could placate him with the appointment and still control him.

Hitler accepted the Chancellorship, ousting Kurt von Schleicher, but what he really wanted was the presidency and complete control of the government. Richard understood much of what was happening and tried to explain it to his young son in terms he could understand without scaring him. But Hitler's rise worried Richard, who anticipated he would make some kind of power move.

Richard watched as Hitler, now Chancellor, built up the Storm Troopers to almost fifty thousand men. These Brown

Shirts seemed to be everywhere and harassed people, especially Jewish citizens, as they wished.

Fred was told about the Reichstag Building fire in 1933 which caused almost a million dollars in damage. Police arrested an unemployed Dutch construction worker who was on the scene, but Richard never believed he was to blame. The Dutch worker was a convenient scapegoat. Hitler blamed it on the Communist Party and vowed to crush them with an iron fist. That night around four thousand people were arrested, imprisoned and tortured by the SA. Richard saw through this event to the outcome, which was to oust the Communist party. Still, it hadn't gotten as bad as it would get.

After the fire, the political landscape changed quickly allowing Hitler to pass two important laws, The Reichstag Fire Decree and the Enabling Bill. Once Richard understood these laws, he could see the writing on the wall and braced his young family for what was coming.

The Reichstag Law suspended civil liberties of all German citizens, not just Jews. It controlled freedom of speech, freedom of assembly, it legalized phone tapping and made it legal to intercept and open mail. The Michels were acutely aware they had to be careful of what they said in public. Certain conversations needed to be kept private. Socializing outside the home became limited to the regular café or familiar places.

The second law, the Enabling Bill, gave Hitler full powers. His Cabinet could pass laws without the Reichstag so at that point, he could do whatever he wanted without oversight. Within three months, he issued a decree called *Gleichschaltung*, which meant all political parties, organizations and labor unions that weren't Nazi ceased to exist.

Fred knew his father was anxious concerning these new laws. How far would Hitler go? Was there anyone to stop him? Hitler still wanted the presidency and was maneuvering for the Army's support. The Army didn't like or trust Ernst Rohm who had helped Hitler build the Brown Shirts into what they had become, legal thugs. But Hitler suspected Rohm was plotting a coup, and he would need to sever ties with him to survive.

At this point, Fred remembers thinking his country was spinning out of control and he mostly was more afraid for his father than anything. But his father was a survivor and would make his move when he was ready. They were always careful, especially in public because of the Brown Shirts; but now there was a new threat, the Secret State Police or Gestapo. Herman Goering, a ruthless cabinet minister in charge of the Luftwaffe, wanted to use his new creation, the Gestapo, to reign in the Brown Shirts. He put Heinrich Himmler in charge and together they planned to use the Gestapo and Hitler's bodyguards, the SS to crush the Brown Shirts.

The Brown Shirts got wind of the action and took to the streets with thousands rioting. Hitler was enraged and in June of 1934, on what they called the *Night of the Long Knives*, he ordered Ernst Rohm and his lieutenant Edmund Heines executed without a trial. Goering took it upon himself to add eighty-five other political prisoners to the execution. They also executed Kurt von Schleicher, the last Chancellor of the Weimar Republic who Hitler had replaced. In one night, the Nazi's eliminated the rest of their political opposition.

On August 2nd of 1934, President von Hindenburg died. The Michels were bereaved at his passing and flew the German flag out of respect. However, on that day Hitler united the chancellorship and the presidency under the new title of Fuhrer, giving him complete control. There was now no legal way to remove him from office.

Richard Michel watched Hitler rise on the world stage. He withdrew Germany from the League of Nations and signed a nonaggression treaty with Poland. He drew up pacts with Italy and later with Japan. To the world he was trying to look like a peacemaker, but at home he was on a campaign to eliminate everyone he deemed "undesirable." Richard knew what this meant because he had barely escaped the violence one night in Landau.

Richard had gone out to a local café to play cards with his usual group. It was not uncommon for the Brown Shirts to randomly burst into an establishment, abuse and beat up the customers - Jewish customers. Richard was in the Café Central when they came in, roughing up people and pushing men against the walls. Richard was allowed to leave only because he had served as an officer in the German Army. He got out of there, but he knew things were getting worse.

Fred knew the final straw for his father came with the passage of the Reich Citizenship Law. This law stated that unless you were of German or related blood, you were not considered a citizen, only subjects of the state without full rights. Fred could see how deeply this hurt his father because his father fought for his country, loved his country, and served honorably. Now he was no longer considered a citizen.

Fred was remembering all those events that unfolded months ago, the new laws, the feeling of being unwanted, the harsh realities of discrimination, the fear of being targeted. As he packed his belongings, he thought back to the night his father sat the family down and told them he had made a hard decision, they needed to leave Germany. Too many Jewish businesses were attacked and closed or taken over. Too many Jewish citizens were being targeted, beaten and imprisoned. They were already on edge every time they ventured out in public. Richard had come to a decision which left them two choices. They could go to Palestine or try to get to the United States. Palestine was risky and they didn't know anyone or have contacts there. On the other hand, they had relatives in the United States. The choice was obvious.

Fred's mind flashes past that night, and he realizes he's trying to close his suitcase, but it is just too bulgy. *Maybe I can sit on it?* he thinks. He flops on the top and reaches for the clasps. Once he presses the metal and hears the "click" of each side, he sits back on the bed replaying the aftermath of that decision. They had decided to contact Aunt Tillie, Tillie Heller, his father's cousin who lived in New York City. Once she agreed to sponsor them and furnish an affidavit, the decision became real. They were fleeing to the United States and New York as quickly as possible.

It was September in Landau and still quite warm. It seemed funny to Fred to pull out his winter coat, but he realized he must take everything he would need. Soon they would leave Landau forever. His father was calling for him and Rudy to bring their suitcases into the hall and Fred snapped out of his reverie.

His mother was carefully tying up a box that held but a few cherished mementos and family heirlooms. Fred stops dragging his suitcase and places it in front of the inspector. He is drained and apprehensive about completing their escape and being ripped away from everything he has known. The inspector approves and tags all their luggage, the sum of their worldly belongings, then he leaves.

The next morning everyone is up early, nervous and anxious to get on their way. Because of the predawn hour, there is little traffic. They easily make it to the Landau train station and board the train to Koeln, then on to Hamburg to stay overnight. The port of Hamburg is large and confusing to Fred, but his father knows where he is going. Richard shepherds his family to the SS Washington which they board. It is not until they pass the three-mile zone that everyone allows themselves to feel some sense of relief. They have managed to escape with some of their personal belongings and

$98 dollars to their name. Fred knows starting over will be hard, but there is no looking back. He must look ahead.

When the Michels arrived in New York, Fred's eyesight almost derails his entry into this new world. An optician on board gives him a pair of glasses so he can pass the physical. They do not land at Ellis Island but rather at Pier 83 where their cousins pick them up. The group heads back to the family apartment in Harlem where they stay for a couple of weeks.

Taking stock of their new situation, Richard sits his family down and explains that now they are in America, they must speak English. "Not just at school or out in public," he decrees, "but also at home. In fact, I have been thinking," he goes on, "Instead of Fritz and Rudolph you should go by Fred and Rudy. It's more...American," he concludes. They all commit to immerse themselves in American language and culture.

The boys start high school, but it is a struggle to learn English, so they enroll in a first-grade English class. Richard encourages them to read comics and funny papers so they can pick up American dialect and fit in. Fred and Rudy are committed to picking up the elusive slang they hear on the streets of New York. Eventually, they get it.

Richard Michel proves to be a force of nature and immediately hits the pavement looking for work. He lands a position with Macy's selling wine in their liquor department. Because Lilly had been so skilled with needles and fabrics, she is able to get a job designing clothing for a high-end fashionable children's clothing line. In a few months they are able to afford their own place and move to Brooklyn to build their new lives.

As the Michel's situation improves in America, things are getting progressively worse back in Germany. In November of 1938, everyone in the Jewish community heard the frightening reports that Germany had unleashed a night of terror on Jews. They are calling it Kristallnacht, *Night of the Broken Glass*. Most of the synagogues in the country are burned down and many Jewish homes and stores have their windows broken and are vandalized. It is estimated that around seven thousand Jewish businesses are destroyed, and thirty thousand Jewish men arrested. They also hear there were few protests from the rest of Germany.

"Disgraceful," was all Richard could say. He was deeply ashamed and disturbed by the events in his homeland.

After Kristallnacht, thousands of German Jews apply for visas. At one point there are more applications filed for visas than there are Jews left in Germany, in part because many have applied to multiple countries trying to escape persecution. By 1938, few countries were accepting Jewish refugees.

That same year, the United Kingdom allowed a program called Kindertransport, an organized rescue effort for unaccompanied minors, to place almost 10,000 children from war-affected countries like Germany, Austria, Poland and Czechoslovakia into British homes. Private relief organizations in the United States did the same. If a family can get only one child out, they choose to send their first-born son to carry on the family name. Warner Michel, Fred's cousin is one of those children with a lapel tag and a ticket to St Louis, Missouri.

Even though the international community is outraged by the events in Germany, none want to interfere with another country's internal politics. The United States pulls its ambassador from Germany, but the general feeling of the country is to not get involved.

For Fred, his schooling and daily life carries on, while his family anxiously watches international developments. Fred graduates in 1939 from Brooklyn Tech, an engineering high school then promptly enrolls in City College not far from his home in Brooklyn. He is an engineering major.

That same year, news reports tracked Hitler's invasion of Poland, then Denmark, Norway, Belgium, the Netherlands and Luxembourg. While Fred is focused on his studies, the rest of the world is consumed with war. People are afraid that France might fall. Fred finishes his second year of college when the shocking answer is revealed to the world. On June 14th, 1940, the Nazis marched into Paris, but the United States has yet to get involved.

It was around this time that the Michels were desperately trying to get Uncle Otto out of Germany. They get word he has been arrested and taken to a camp called Buchenwald. A short while later they learn he has been transferred to Dachau.

While the family works diligently to keep track of Otto's whereabouts, the Michels are informed that camp guards can be bribed. The family pools their resources to pay for Otto's release. He is set free in December of 1941 and by the 26th, arrives in New York to join his family.

The timing of Otto's escape is fortuitous because the Japanese attack Pearl Harbor on December 7, 1941, and the United States enters the war. After that, the purpose of detaining Jews in Germany changes, and families can no longer exchange cash for freedom. Otto got out in the nick of time.

Once war is declared, Fred and Rudy can no longer sit back. Rudy is in his first years of college when he enlists. Fred is supposed to be drafted but is now deferred until he earns his Mechanical Engineering degree. The Army knows that with his degree, Fred will prove more useful to the defense of the United States.

MIS-X, MIS-Y Gathering Intel Louisville, Kentucky May 30th, 2006

Chapter 3

MIS-X & MIS-Y, Gathering Intelligence

Louisville, Kentucky
May 30, 2006

The room goes quiet as Fred finishes recounting his
family's escape from Germany. No one can imagine what life
would have been like had they stayed, or the courage it took to
face the uncertainty ahead of them. Though Cynthia has heard
this story before, the full extent of Nazi oppression on every
facet of her father's and grandparents' lives is brought into
sharp focus. Even though these events happened a lifetime
ago, hearing her father's vivid description makes it deeply
personal.

Cynthia has never been to Landau and has no desire to
visit Germany because of what her family went through. Still,
in her mind's eye she can see her father as an adolescent,
struggling with losing everything familiar to him. She
understands her dad's and uncle's reluctance to leave Landau,
their home, their schoolroom, the streets where they played,
their innocent lives. But she is also keenly aware of the threats,
violence, and the very real danger the Nazis posed to her

family because they were Jews. She suddenly takes a deep breath and lets it out slowly. Cynthia is filled with a sense of gratitude. She exists because of the sacrifices of her family.

Fred is reflective, yet realistic in the re-telling of his life events. After all, he lived through it, survived and thrived. The good fortune of his family was not lost on him. He knew he'd had it better than other Jewish refugees, some of whom were forced to leave Germany without their loved ones. Fred looked up and saw everyone riveted to his story. Cynthia decided they all needed a little break.

"Dad, let me get you some water," she offers. "Brandon?"

"Yes thanks, that would be great," Brandon said. He had been listening intently to the historical milestones through which Fred and his family had lived and appreciates being trusted with this personal information. The oral history of the Michel family's life leading up to their escape was both terrifying and fascinating.

"You were lucky to get your uncle Otto out alive. I didn't know prisoners could be bribed out of a place like Dachau."

"Yes, we were lucky. He lived near us in Brooklyn after he arrived in the U.S.," Fred added.

Cynthia returns with a tray, hands everyone a glass of water and takes her seat, sipping her own cool drink.

The intensity in the room seems to lift, and Brandon feels he can get back to why he is here. "That brings us to the beginning of the war and you being in college," Brandon summarizes. Just then a thought occurs to him, and he lets it sink in.

"Fred, you were just in college and around my age at the start of World War II."

"Yes, I was maybe twenty, twenty-one, something like that."

"It's an eye opener," Brandon realizes, then turns back to his notes. "I thought I'd take a minute to give you a little background on what was happening at the beginning of the intelligence program, the beginning of the war, and why the Army chose Fort Hunt."

Fred nods and Lucille agrees, "That would be most helpful."

Brandon flips over a page on the notepad and explains that since declassification in the 1990s, a broad collection of intelligence materials is now available to the public.

"I've been looking into the MIS-Y program and why they chose Fort Hunt for intelligence," Brandon begins. "I'm still uncovering a lot of information but let me give you a brief overview of what I've learned so far."

Fred again nods, and Brandon continues. "In 1941, maybe six months before Pearl Harbor, we knew we'd need an intelligence hub for east coast intelligence and perhaps surveillance or Signal Intelligence Service. Whatever the country needed. The Office of Naval Intelligence sent Lieutenant Harry Gherardi to London to study the British POW interrogation set-up. The U.S. intelligence experts concluded Fort Hunt would be the perfect east coast location and they would emulate the Brit's program.

"Then of course on December 7th, 1941, Pearl Harbor was attacked, and we were at war. That's when we got serious. Until that strike, the U.S. did not have a formal intelligence division in place. In January of 1942, Secretary of War Henry Stimson obtained permits to take over Fort Hunt on the east coast for the duration of the war, plus one year. He needs to set up a similar intelligence facility on the west coast.

"Fort Hunt is an obscure piece of land hugging the Potomac River, which oddly enough, had been given to the United States by George Washington himself. It was valuable because of its proximity to Washington, D.C."

What better use for our founding father's land, Cynthia thinks.

"During the 1930's, Fort Hunt was used by the WPA and CPA, two Roosevelt New Deal agencies. Workers housed there were working to extend the George Washington Memorial Parkway all the way to Great Falls Park. A group of Civilian Conservation Corps, the CCC, had men working on landscaping and improving state parks. All that stopped after Pearl Harbor." Lucille lived in Alexandria at the time and remembers the CCC workers along the parkway.

"In February of 1942, Major General Carl Spaatz traveled to England to set up the U.S. 8th Army Air Force headquarters and was briefed on the British intelligence section, MI-9, headed by Colonel Norman Crocket. Spaatz is duly impressed with how effective they are and immediately wants a similar program in the U.S. Colonel Crockett is enthusiastic and supportive of developing a U.S. version of their program, offering to help with training. By the time the War Department secured Fort Hunt and designated it as East Coast Intelligence Headquarters, it then became the location of two proposed branches of U.S. military intelligence; MIS-X, which was counterintelligence including *Escape & Evade*, and MIS-Y, interrogations.

"The Secretary of War approves construction of barracks, interrogation rooms and anything else the new programs will need for interrogators and prisoners alike."

Brandon looks up, "Fred this last part was your area – interrogation. It was the biggest program and the first."

"How many prisoners did they process?" Cynthia asks.

"There were just over thirty-four hundred prisoners interrogated at Fort Hunt between 1942 and July of 1945."

"That's a lot of Nazi prisoners," Lucille comments, not wanting to believe so many enemy soldiers were within a few miles of where she was living.

"A lot of soldiers, but a testament nonetheless to how successful the program was," Brandon says.

"I didn't know the number of prisoners." Fred is surprised at the quantity. Brandon nods then goes on to explain, "We patterned our interrogation after the British version where they would take prisoners, especially high-ranking ones, and place them in isolated estates deep in the

English countryside with no chance of escape. The whole estate and grounds were bugged for surveillance. The Brits listened in on every conversation in bedrooms, barracks, dining areas or on the grounds. Prisoners were treated well, almost lavishly. Over time, their defenses came down."

"The tactic was to convince captives that even though each are on opposite sides, one day after the conflict is over, they will all be friends. Since the captives are going to lose anyway, the message was, why not cooperate now and make it easier on yourself? The Brits found this approach very successful."

Now Brandon switches gears to talk about challenges unique to the U.S. program.

"However, here in America, the military didn't have access to large estates or countryside manors to impress captives and conduct this type of interrogation. The best the Army came up with were parks and forts which could be modified to hold prisoners. Fort Hunt would just have to do, and they had to find other ways to persuade captives to talk."

"By July of 1942, Fort Hunt was operational and ready to conduct interrogations. The first prisoners were from North Africa, then later in the war it looks like prisoners came from captured or sunk U-boats."

"The Army did have another issue to contend with," Fred offers. "The Geneva Convention rules."

"Why is that?" Brandon looks up from his notes.

"Bringing German captives directly to Fort Hunt before being processed through neutral arbiters in Switzerland or through the Red Cross was a violation. The solution was to call 1142 a "processing center" rather than a PW camp. We bent the rules a little." Fred gives a little nod to the indiscretion.

"How long were prisoners with you?"

"PWs were with us anywhere from a couple days to a couple of months, but I would say the average stay was a week to 10 days. The other thing I suspect was against the norm was the listening devices. It was considered bad form to listen in on prisoners, but the Army quickly decided that the only thing more repulsive than surveillance was Nazis, so they went ahead."

"That many prisoners would generate a lot of interrogations." Cynthia is visualizing the typewriters and stack of papers like the ones in Brandon's lap. "Who did all the typing and what did you do with all the transcripts?" She looked at her father.

"The soldiers in the listening area typed up what they heard. Sometimes we would type up our own interviews. But all the paperwork had to be filed and cross-referenced. We had a fellow who had a good filing system and kept everything organized, especially if you needed to recall something like a past interview for specific information."

"Do you remember who that was?" Brandon asks.

Fred thinks a minute. "A fellow from Georgia."

"By the time you get there, it's closer to the end of the war and you are out of school, with a degree. Did other interrogators also have degrees or some college?"

"The soldiers I was with, for the most part, were well educated, some with degrees. But first, we were trained at Camp Ritchie."

"Yes, I saw the transfer document. There was a list of soldiers sent from Camp Ritchie to Fort Hunt, but I wasn't sure what Camp Ritchie was for? You were being trained on interrogation techniques?"

"Yes, and other aspects of intelligence gathering. Since it was towards the end of the war, we focused a lot on U-boats and what was happening in the Atlantic. By listening to U-boat chatter we might identify specific U-boats and the grid patterns they used in the Atlantic, thereby allowing us to track submarine movements."

"That would have been incredibly useful," Brandon realizes.

Cynthia is marveling at the intelligence programs and then asks Brandon, "What about that other part you mentioned? What did they do?"

"MIS-X? Fred, did you know about the other divisions and what they did?"

"No, I didn't know of any other divisions besides interrogation. That was my area."

"I think you'll find this part interesting. I'm still uncovering a lot of information." Brandon grabs for a different notepad and starts to flip through pages.

"The MIS-X division was called *Escape and Evade*. Again, we fashioned it after the Brits."

"Common theme," Cynthia muses.

Brandon smiles then launches into his understanding of the program. "The British developed Escape & Evade because after WWI it became embarrassingly apparent how ill-prepared they were at helping servicemen evade capture or escape. In fact, there were no protocols in place for debriefing servicemen once they returned. In 1939, the British Government conducted a serious assessment of what they needed to do and developed E&E, which became the British Military Intelligence section, MI-9."

"This is actually a more proactive approach, to train soldiers before they are shot down or captured," Fred surmises out loud.

"Exactly. Here's an example that might help explain it. If servicemen, especially pilots or soldiers are flying over or parachuting into enemy territory and are shot down, they need to know how to evade capture, and if they were taken, how to successfully escape and not get re-captured. They would need, at the very least, a reliable compass and map of the area where they went down or where they were caught. These items would have to be small or inconspicuous enough to be easily concealed either in their uniforms or personal belongings."

"The program leaders tried to think of every scenario or outcome before pilots left the ground. To provide the necessary items, the E&E program created silk maps of bombing mission areas. Silk was used because it didn't shred when it got wet, like paper, and the ink wouldn't run. If the pilot's plane went down, they could easily conceal a piece of silk or retrieve it if sewn into the lining of their jacket. A silk map would be invaluable in helping them find their way back. E&E also meant providing survival boxes of water and a couple days rations, currency, and even items like hacksaw blades." Brandon paused and looked up.

"Yes, these would all be necessary and very useful," Fred reflects as he processes the reasoning behind the initiative.

"I think that's why there were so many extra buildings. At its busiest, Fort Hunt had something like eighty-five permanent and temporary structures on its grounds," Brandon tells them.

"There were buildings I didn't know the purpose of, but there were plenty of soldiers using them. So yes, that could be right." Fred is stretching to remember the grounds and numerous different buildings.

"Going forward, by October of 1942, the Military Intelligence Service X is formed, and the U.S. E&E program is up and running," Brandon continues.

"Originally MIS-X had five sections." Here he ticked them off on his fingers: "Interrogation, correspondence, prisoner of war locations, training & briefing and technical. At some point interrogation simply became MIS-Y, but the rest of the MIS programs continued under the X division."

"From what I gather, only small sections of the grounds were taken up with the MIS-X program in comparison to the interrogation facilities. The groundskeeper building housed correspondence, and I think it was called the *Warehouse*. It had a mechanical area, printing press and parcel room. The warehouse was set up to make silk maps and assemble the survival supply boxes. The program also created five million uniform buttons that contained hidden compasses that were sewn onto the pilots' uniforms."

"Ok, now we're getting creative." Cynthia can't help but chime in. To her, the undercover covert activities are the most intriguing part of how to fight a war.

"If you liked that, then you'll be interested in the rest of what the program did." Brandon smiles. "The intelligence team understood that when soldiers are captured and sent to camps, the only way to communicate with them would be through letters and packages. The E&E team also knew what items soldiers needed to escape. The challenge was how to conceal those items in objects that could somehow be delivered into the camps without arousing suspicion."

"Quite a challenge," Lucille remarks.

"Yes, it was," Brandon admits. "To do this, they again took a lesson from the British MI-9 program, then went even further. In my opinion their solutions were nothing short of ingenious," he says with a small shake of his head. "For example, they enlisted the help of certain American companies, like the Goldsmith baseball company in Cincinnati, and privately brought them into the war effort. An electronics manufacturer made a special miniature radio transmitter housed in separate capsules. These capsules were then sent to Goldsmith who hid the capsules in specially color-stitched baseballs."

"And who would suspect a baseball?" Cynthia asks.

"At that time, not the Nazis!" Lucille chimes in.

"Exactly." Brandon is going deeper into the process. "To send other radio parts they hollowed out the handles of hairbrush and shaving brushes, smoking pipes and ping pong paddles, inserted the contraband and reassembled each one. Razor blades were magnetized to act as a compass and included with shaving items. They figured out how to hide compasses in watches.

"To send paper items like maps, IDs or currency, they would steam the paper off a Checkers or Cribbage board or split playing cards, with varying degrees of success. Different glues and adhesives react differently to the steam so certain brands of playing cards were more dependable than others. Then they would carefully place the paper items, whole or in pieces, between the cardboard layers of the playing board or cards. Once retrieved, the pieces could then be re-assembled and used. These doctored items were then packed in designated boxes they called *loaded* packages and were sent like care packages to POW camps."

"Ah, those were the packages – the *loaded* packages." Fred jumps in. "There were lots of mail runs. This is one thing I noticed, but continue," and he waved Brandon to go on.

Brandon changes course for a moment. "Have you ever read *The Escape Factory*?" It was a book about all of this, by Lloyd Shoemaker. He was also at Fort Hunt." He glanced around the room.

"Yes, I heard of it, but I never read it." Lucille finally offers. "Everyone was talking about it back in Alexandria because it mentioned Fort Hunt. There was talk of a prisoner being shot but if I remember correctly, the prisoner didn't want to be sent to Britain to stand trial on charges, so he rushed the fence knowing he'd be shot, and he was. Didn't the book come out in the '90s?"

"Yes, in fact my boss, Matt, had Shoemaker, the author, come to Fort Hunt to speak in the early '90s. During the war, Shoemaker was a corporal and handled the packages," he explains. "At that time, he was one of only four people alive who could give a first-hand account. Then he passed away in 1995. After that everyone thought there were no surviving veterans."

"So you were surprised to find me," Fred quips.

"Exactly." Brandon admits.

"If I understand this, some care packages have socks and books and clothing – regular stuff, and some packages have that stuff, plus a baseball with a transistor radio." Cynthia concludes.

Brandon affirms, "Right. They'd bring everything to the Warehouse and stuff certain boxes with both items. Then all the packages, loaded and straight, were sent as humanitarian parcels to POW camps. Sending so many packages, sometimes on short notice, presented another problem. They didn't want to use the Red Cross and risk putting that organization in jeopardy. So, they created two fake organizations, the War Prisoners Benefit Fund and the Servicemen's Relief as covers.

"You know I heard of those organizations, and I just assumed they were legit!" Lucille realizes. "I had no idea."

"The fake organizations were especially useful," Brandon goes on, "especially if there was an urgent need for large or time-sensitive packages. Developing and controlling the conduit was vital. At its peak operation there could be as many as a hundred parcels a day. I think the average was around seventy. All items were mailed out of Baltimore."

"Baltimore?" Lucile is surprised. "You mean someone had to drive up to Baltimore to mail everything every day?"

"Yes," Brandon continues. "Apparently the postmaster in Baltimore added canceled destinations to the stamped package, which helped further disguise their true origin."

"That's a lot of driving, about sixty miles one way. Back then, the roads weren't as good either!" Lucille knows what she is talking about.

"So, this really was Hogan's Heroes kind of stuff," Cynthia observes without making it a joke. "I mean the radio in the coffee pot, the razorblade compass, all of that wasn't too far off."

"No actually it wasn't," Brandon grins. "And it was very effective too. The technology division became so efficient at sending covert items that near the end of the war, prisoners asked them to stop sending packages. They had no more room to hide all the contraband."

Brandon flips over his notepad and jumps back in. "Back at Fort Hunt, across the street from 'The Warehouse,' was the old hospital building and was called the 'Creamery.'

"Yes, I remember the Creamery," Fred remarks.

"This building housed correspondence and coding or coded messaging. Did you know a soldier, Silvio Bedini?" Brandon looks up. Fred shakes his head. "He's a cryptologist, quite accomplished, in fact, he is a Historian Emeritus at the Smithsonian. His was the first name I found. I called him, but he wouldn't talk to me either." Brandon glances at Fred and continues. "I think he was part of this coding division. They sent letters back and forth to POWs, or as you called them PWs. Even though the correspondents were captives, the military was able to collect useful intelligence they nicknamed *barbed wire intel.*" He looks up for emphasis then back at his notes.

"Certain airmen called CUs, or code users, were taught how to communicate through coded letters. If captured, the CU would send a letter to a fictitious address which the Post Office knew to route to P.O. Box 1142. The cryptologists at Fort

Hunt would then decode these messages. If, for example, a letter came in with a date written in all numbers, it was identified, decoded, and sent through the chain of command. The decoders would then set up correspondence with that CU. The coders also gave American POWs a heads up if a package was coming."

"So, they could do what? Be on the lookout for it?" Cynthia ventures.

"Exactly. Knowing the package was coming would put POWs on their toes to make sure it wasn't intercepted. Doing this under the noses of their camp guards had to give them quite a boost." Brandon confirms.

"There was also a program called MIRS, Military Intelligence Research Section. In this division, translators combed through German newspapers, captured documents, scientific journals, anything that might have useful information for the war effort. Then they would bullet the information and distribute it." Branon looks up from his notes. "As an interrogator you'd probably see those sheets."

"Yes, we got bulletin-type information to stay up to date with what was happening," Fred says.

"You had no idea there was another, separate program going on?" Brandon asked.

"I knew there was a separate program which was very hush, hush. Nobody was supposed to inquire about it, nobody *did* inquire about it. I just heard it existed, but I had no idea all of this was going on," Fred resolutely stated.

"That brings us to your area." Brandon smiles, focusing again on Fred.

"You had to have gotten a lot of information from your interrogations." It was a leading statement Brandon hoped would give Fred an opening to respond.

"We did get information I think was helpful," Fred remembers. "The interrogation area produced a "Red Book," which was the order of battle for the German military operation and a "Green Book," which was an order of battle for the Japanese military. The Red Book was distributed and proved useful for the D-Day invasion."

"That brings us up to your arrival at Fort Hunt." Brandon says. "After you enlisted, how did you become an interrogator?"

P.O. Box 1142   Wichita Falls, Texas Summer, 1944

81

Chapter 4

P.O. Box 1142, Fort Hunt, Virginia

Wichita Falls, Texas

Summer 1944

Fred is sitting in a hot tent in the desolate rolling plains, somewhere between Dallas and Oklahoma City. It is, at best, dry grassland with a generous helping of dust. Only the hardy bluestems manage to offer some color alongside a stand of oak trees. Fred has never seen a cactus, but someone points out a Texas prickly pear, along with a warning to watch out for scorpions. This isn't the wild west, but it's wild enough for Fred.

This is no man's land, he thinks as a trickle of sweat finds its way down the middle of his back and lands at his belt. *Nothing but heat and nothing but waiting.*

He has no orders and is confused. He thought he was headed to Europe like his brother. Instead, he is just waiting, anxious to get orders, to contribute something to this war.

It was only a few months ago he graduated from college and immediately enlisted. He is now a young man of twenty-three, educated, physically fit and ready to serve his new country. He wanted to go into the Navy but there was a shortage of Army personnel, so he was assigned accordingly. That was July. Rudy, his brother, has already been sent back to Germany with his unit. He is an interpreter helping to find Nazis. He is doing something.

Fred was placed in infantry and sent to Florida for Boot Camp. While there, he was rounded up with a handful of guys, who like himself, were immigrants, classified as enemy aliens. They were bussed over to the U.S. District Court in Jacksonville and sworn in as U.S. citizens. The Army knew if these soldiers were shipped out to Germany as enemy aliens and got captured, they could be shot.

Before Fred finished basic training, he was diverted to Texas. This is where he's been sitting for a week already with no activity. He gets up to stretch his legs. Fred cuts a trim figure in his uniform. The round face of his adolescence has transformed into a square jaw. The sandy blonde hair of his youth is darker brown and shorn to regulation length. He grabs some water and turns to see a welcome sight - soldiers arriving.

Young men in Army uniforms wander into the tent, sweating, throwing down their duffels, looking around with the same expectant looks on their faces Fred had. He is grateful for the company but can offer no answers to why they are all here.

One by one the soldiers move inside and find places to sit on benches and wooden folding chairs. There is a metal water dispenser on a side table that looks like a large thermos which

Fred has been singularly enjoying. Now the soldiers form a line to quench their thirst.

As the men settle in, Fred sits at the end of the row and strikes up a conversation with a young soldier named Werner Gans. To his surprise, Fred learns Gans is from Mannheim, Germany, which is in the Rhine Palatinate, only a few hours from Landau. They immediately bond over their regional heritage.

Soon Fred meets other soldiers and quickly realizes many of them speak German, are Jewish and escaped Nazi Germany before the war. They talk freely, eager to know each other's backgrounds, their hometowns and how they came to be American soldiers. Fred discovers some were lucky enough to escape with their families while others were sent to the United States alone as young kids.

Werner Gans escaped Germany before Kristallnacht in 1938 by using his student visa to get to Cuba. From there he made his way to Boston and enrolled in school with a music scholarship. He was only 15. Luckily his parents made it out two years later.

Henry Kolm is from Vienna, the son of a physician. He looks like a sensitive and intelligent young man with dark hair and sad eyes but as he tells his story, Fred notes the breadth of his vocabulary. Henry explains that after the Nazis annexed Austria, his father wisely decided his life wasn't worth his property and signed it all away. Henry's grandfather had just died, so his father took them to Czechoslovakia to try and convince Henry's grandmother to escape with them. She refused, not seeing the danger. Henry's father then took his family to Prague and eventually out of Europe.

Later he found out his grandmother was sent to the Theresienstadt Ghetto, a waystation to the extermination camps. One of his uncles ended up in Auschwitz. There is little bitterness in Henry's voice as he states the facts of how his family members died. Fred hears the resolve in his voice, to remember his family members' names and say them out loud so as not to forget how they died. As they chat, Henry is struck by bizarre events of his past. "By 1938, I had seen Hitler march twice: Once down the Ringstrasse in Vienna and then tanks blazing down the main street in Prague."

It was still incredulous to Henry that he had lived through these events, but he seemed defiant in the moment and paused before finishing his family's story. "An uncle of mine fled to Prague and was promptly arrested by the Gestapo. He was in a kind of holding area and had not properly been searched. I'm proud to say he ended up shooting eight Gestapo before he shot himself." Fred was trying not to look stunned, but he marveled at this family's resistance and bravado.

Henry went on to tell Fred how his parents had to alter their visas for the family to make it out of Europe. They got as far as Achen, Germany before they were all pulled off the train.

"We were going to be sent to a camp, but my father paid to have us smuggled out to Luxembourg," he recounts. "We slipped out at night and went on to Brussels, finally reaching

Paris. Luckily, I speak French as well as English and German."
He finishes by telling Fred how they applied for visas which
came in the nick of time.

"In 1939, Germany invaded Poland and my family was on
the last passenger ship that crossed the Atlantic."

One by one other soldiers start sharing their harrowing
experiences escaping Nazi Germany. A shorter soldier with
dark, alert eyes, a pointed chin and prominent eyebrows that
accentuated his expressive face spoke up next. Peter Weiss was
also born in Vienna. His family escaped to France in 1939, but
his mother had gotten Portuguese visas to emigrate to the
United States, so they had to leave from Portugal.

"It was 1941 when we made it to the Portuguese docks,
but we couldn't find passage. My mother, however, was
determined. She ended up paying someone $100 to forge our
visas, extending the dates because Portugal was sending
everybody back to where they came from if they found an
expired visa." Peter explains. "We got out by the skin of our
teeth."

As shocking as Fred finds some of these stories, he
realizes how much each family risked and how much they had
sacrificed to immigrate. These men were grateful to call
America home and now America could use their talents. The
United States Army needed their language skills, their
knowledge of German customs and geography, their
education, and their intellect. Even though none of these

soldiers had orders, they would all end up at the same intelligence training facility.

After about 3 weeks of watching soldiers come and go, those who remained were shipped to St. Louis, again with no explanation, and transported by rail to a place in Maryland called Camp Ritchie.

Camp Ritchie is the designated east coast military intelligence and counterintelligence training camp turning out interpreters and interrogators. Soldiers who graduate from here will be referred to as *Ritchie Boys* and will be either embedded with American troops returning to Europe to act as scouts, interpreters and translators, or sent to another facility to interrogate high-level Nazi prisoners.

Fred and his group arrive at Camp Ritchie in mid-April 1945, the same week President Roosevelt dies. Fred and the others gather around the radio and listen to the report. Roosevelt died of a stroke compounded by very high blood pressure and congestive heart failure which had been contributing to the decline of his overall health.

Stunned men in uniform let the rest of the information wash over them. FDR had taken office in 1933 at the height of the Great Depression. He endured a decade of stress and put forth unparalleled determination pulling the U.S. and the world economy out of the depths of the Depression. Just as things were improving, Pearl Harbor was attacked, and the United States was thrust into the world-wide conflict.

Everyone knew FDR had been stricken with polio at a young age. In 1921, he discovered the soothing, spring-fed pools of Warm Springs, Georgia which allowed him pain free movement. The temperate weather and buoyant waters always rejuvenated him; so much so that he made an annual pilgrimage to Warm Springs, establishing a polio treatment center and setting up a "Little White House." Warm Springs is where he died.

As the men of Camp Ritchie work through their grief, they are more determined than ever. The campaign against Rommel's Africa Corp was nearing a victorious end and the Allies were now focused on invading and liberating Europe. The U.S. was bombing Germany by day and Great Britain was bombing them at night. Training focused on learning to assess daily aerial photos and understanding bombing strategies and execution. Most of the men were Army, but there were some Navy men as well. The war in the Atlantic was not going well for the Allies. *Wolfpacks* of German U-boat submarines were wreaking havoc on merchant ships and warships alike. Understanding your enemy was the first order of business.

Fred has been taking advantage of the resources at Camp Ritchie, regularly using the library. One day he is called in by the librarian who starts to give him a tongue-lashing for an overdue book. Standing there sheepishly, he realizes he never checked out the missing book. When he asks for the library card, he sees the name Werner Michel. Overjoyed, he realizes his cousin is at the same facility and starts checking rosters to find him. He reunites with Werner, who is in officers' training, and is soon to be commissioned. They haven't seen each other since they were kids, and now they have only a few short weeks to reconnect. Werner is eventually sent to Washington while Fred continues in intelligence training and can only guess where he will land up.

A few weeks later, on April 30th, they get the news, Hitler has committed suicide. There is contained excitement throughout Camp Ritchie. Do they dare hope the end of the war is in sight? The camp commander and instructors calm the optimism of their charges, reminding them Germany has not yet officially surrendered. They commit themselves to staying in the present because they still have a job to do.

Exactly a week later, May 7th, 1945, Germany officially surrendered, and specialized groups of American translators and interpreters were sent to Germany to look for Nazis. There is much speculation as to what will happen to high-level German officials who have committed atrocities and talk swirls of a war crimes trial in Nuremberg. The soldiers at Camp Ritchie are again reminded they still must defeat the Japanese.

Fred immerses himself in interrogation techniques which include how to ask pointed questions; what to listen for; how to corroborate information; and how to document answers. They do a lot of role-playing and goad each other with resistance. But their directive is always to stay calm, remain in control and get the prisoner to trust you. There were no threats or use of force or violence of any kind. It is never even a question.

The soldiers are taught how to understand the Nazi mind-set and use it to their advantage. They are given a manual listing various ways to approach PWs. One area Fred finds fascinating is Nazi vanity. It started with Hitler and ran down the Generals all the way through the party. Ardent Nazi supporters like to boast and talk about their great accomplishments. The directive is to let them.

Soldiers are instructed in courses on Order of Battle, photo interpretation and counterintelligence. Fred is aware of different languages being spoken at Camp Ritchie ranging from German to Japanese, French to Italian with a couple of Russian speakers thrown in the mix. Fred is excited to be learning something he feels is important to the war effort. He makes friends with more of his fellow soldier students like George Mandel who took the same photo interpretation class. George is a soft-spoken but very likable and intelligent young man. He and Fred amuse each other, quietly joking around their dry wits.

George was born in Berlin to a family very much like Fred's. His father had been a decorated World War I veteran and worked in banking. Like Fred, George's family was told they had nothing to worry about from the Nazis because of his father's military record. But they also saw the warning signs and emigrated to New York in 1937, just after Fred arrived.

Sitting on their bunks across from each other one evening, George slowly opens up. He's always been a little shy and relates quickly to Fred's low-key demeanor. As they talk about their first impressions of America, they laugh remembering their initiation to New York City and the challenges of learning English. George tells Fred that after he finished high school, he enrolled in Yale to study chemistry.

"When war broke out, I wanted to enlist," he explains, "But they told me I would be more valuable with a degree. So, they put me in an accelerated program that had summer classes and I ended up graduating in August of '44 at nineteen!"

Fred had not been much older, but still it seemed young to graduate from college and head off to war. George went on, "Some of the fellows I graduated with went to Oak Ridge, Tennessee. But I was considered an enemy alien, so they sent me to Georgia for basic training where I had the opportunity to become a citizen."

"Same as me, but I was in Florida," Fred says, remembering the process.

"When they found out I spoke fluent German, I was diverted here," George finishes. Fred acknowledges having traveled the same path.

The first weeks at Camp Ritchie are both stimulating and challenging. Fred is learning a lot and feels more confident in his skills. Interrogators are not supposed to discuss specifics of their intelligence conversations in a common space, only in designated areas with personnel involved with the PW. Fred, George, and their fellow interrogators abide by this rule but find ways to advise and help each other. Late evenings and nights are the only times they have to socialize.

By the end of the first month, Fred and George have the lay of the land. They head inside the warm mess hall for dinner, filled with overlapping conversations and intermittent bursts of laughter. The line is short, and they grab a tray which the cook quickly fills with the evening's offerings. The men pick up their waters and turn to their regular table now filled with familiar faces and easy conversations.

The food seems to be improving, Fred thinks. Although not as good as home, the chicken and vegetables were not bad. Since his induction, he has become suspicious of stew, but tonight he can easily identify everything on his plate, which he finds reassuring.

The mess hall has become a comfortable place to relax and enjoy affable conversation. Eric Kramer has joined their group. Eric is about the same age as Fred and came from Munich, which is also in the Bavarian Palatinate region. He made his way to the United States by himself in 1937 at age seventeen. Eric and Fred have much to talk about.

"When I came to this country," Eric says, "I was living with the sister of my grandmother, sleeping on her couch in the living room. They were quite poor. I got a job that paid me $8 a week and I had to give them $5!"

Eric's parents were still in Germany, but as he told Fred, "Things got worse, and I had to get them out. I ended up booking them passage on an Italian steamship. They got here in January of '40."

Fred listens to the accounts of how his friends and their families escaped, thankful his family got out when they did, together. It didn't take long to move beyond the harrowing tales of the past and look ahead to Saturday night. The discussion quickly turns to finding the closest USO and getting to the next dance.

The USO will have to wait because the next day Fred, George, and about twenty men in his class are told to pack up, they are being assigned and relocated. One by one they climb aboard the bus, clueless to where they are headed. There are no orders, and no one has told them of their assignment. Everyone thinks they are headed to Europe to hunt Nazis.

The Camp Ritchie bus, however, ends up at the newly built Pentagon. All the men get out and the driver goes inside to talk to someone. The driver soon returns with orders to take them to an undisclosed location. First however, everyone must transfer to a bus with all the windows painted over with dark paint. As Fred and the others file onto the bus they realize they can't see out and have no idea where they are going.

After about an hour of traveling paved roads, then dirt roads, the bus pulls onto a gravel drive and lurches to a stop. It's hot and Fred can't wait to get off the claustrophobic vehicle. He steps onto the gritty parking lot and takes a deep breath. It's warm outside, they are in some kind of wooded area, and he wishes they were under the shade of the nearby tree canopy. Each man grabs their duffle and waits for instructions.

Fred looks around on either side and sees a wooden fence edged on top with barbed wire. There are a few buildings that might be barracks and a guard tower in the distance.

Suddenly a crackle from a loudspeaker on the pole behind them in the parking area makes everyone jump, and a voice booms out; 'Orientation in Command Center, attendance is mandatory!' The men look at each other, grab their gear and follow whoever looks like they know where to go.

They walk down the gravel road to one of the larger plain wooden buildings. Once inside they drop their bags and stand inside a large room with a small dais at one end. Everyone is expectantly facing that end of the room when the camp commander briskly comes in. He is just over six feet tall with dark trimmed hair and a no-nonsense look about him. Everyone snaps to attention and the commander delivers his welcome, followed with, "At ease."

He begins, "Because of the secretive nature of what we are about to do, all of you will take an oath. I will pass this paper around," which he holds up briefly, "for you to read before you sign it, but basically it says," and here he adjusts the paper and starts to scan the contents.

"Let's see...safeguarding information of prisoners... that after the Great war of 1914-18, sources of information and how we secured that information was revealed by our Intelligence and Secret Service people who, after the war wrote books and articles, disclosing sensitive information."

The commander looks up. "We will not make that mistake again." Then he reads more. "The lesson from that experience is obvious. Nothing concerning methods or sources should be revealed during or after this war for the benefit of present or future enemies of the United States."

"Then it goes on... Each officer, enlisted man and civil employee must realize his personal responsibility for preserving the most rigid secrecy and for avoiding any discussion or reference to the source of the information or the methods by which it was acquired. The much larger number of officers who utilize the information need only know the degree of its reliability."

"The same rules and the same responsibility apply with equal force *after* the war!" he finishes with emphasis on the word *after*.

"You may read this in full, but right now, raise your right hands." All the soldiers stand at attention and raise their hands.

The commander continues, "I certify that I have read the foregoing statement on safeguarding PW information and I also fully understand that I shall be bound by these orders and this certificate *after* the war, and I undertake to maintain complete secrecy and to refrain from publishing any article or book violating these orders, nor will I give to others any information which might be useful by them for such purpose. You will answer in the affirmative." Every soldier responds with various "I wills" and "I dos." It sounds like sloppy wedding vows to Fred, but the point is made.

Then each man lines up to read the document and sign next to his typed name.

Once everyone signs, the group is dismissed and directed to their quarters. George and Fred are assigned to a small bunkhouse of about eight beds. It is a simple framed building without insulation, but it does have a large pot belly stove in the middle. Lavatories are positioned at either end, with a row of standard issue military cots, thin mattresses, small pillows, and a single Army blanket on each one. Nothing fancy but comfortable enough. While the men are stowing their belongings, new orders boom from the loudspeaker, "Everyone is required back in the Command Center.

Immediately they head back to the building they just left, somewhat confused. Once again, the commander reminds them of the oath they just took, only this time he spells it out.

"This means do not talk about what you will do here to your family, your friends, your future wives, your future employers – no one. Understood?" And with a little spittle expelled on the last word the commander yells, "Dismissed!" Fred and the others are a little irritated as they head back to their barracks. Of course, they understand the oath they just agreed to and signed.

The next morning at breakfast as they sit drinking coffee, one of the more sociable guys named Arno Mayer leans into Fred and George. "You know, all that stuff about the oath yesterday?" Both men nod. "Well, it turns out this guy left the first meeting and went right to the payphone to call his parents. He told them he was OK, where he was and what he was gonna do. What a dummkopf!" Arno shook his head in disbelief. Then he leans over again, "That soldier is no longer on the premises." And with a short bob for emphasis, he gets up to refill his coffee.

The first day at 1142 the soldiers are given assignments and taken under the wings of seasoned interrogators. Fred and George are assigned to Captain William Hershberger, the resident expert on advanced technology. They meet him at the Command Center and head outside to walk towards other structures which house interrogation rooms.

As they walk, Fred looks around taking in the pastoral setting and is glad to be stationed here. The woods beyond the fence are thick, which he finds both strangely comforting and familiar. The fort itself feels like a big campground, the only security presence being the guard houses at intervals of the fence. One would never know there was a war going on from the look of the place. That is, except for the jeeps and military vehicles parked along the gravel paths outside certain buildings, and the uniformed soldiers hurrying between them.

All the structures they walked past are quite plain and uniformly built, the only distinction is their size. Fred notices that some buildings are bigger, probably barracks, and some smaller, most likely officers' quarters. There are three stand-alone huts down a side road and Fred wonders what they are used for. He figures he will find out as he gets acclimated. The place feels relaxing, even though it is quite isolated. Then he sees some courts, tennis courts down the hill. Yes, this was going to be OK.

Hershberger has been talking the whole time, telling them that he arrived at Fort Hunt in early 1943. "I've seen lots since I've been here. Staunch Nazis, belligerence, fear, complicity. After a while you get a sixth sense of how to tap that one chord inside a prisoner to get the information you need. Eventually you can tell pretty quickly – in one or two questions whether or not the prisoner has any useful information." He stops and turns to Fred and George, "You'll get there. Right now, our focus is gathering good intel. We're going to talk to everyone from mission pilots to critical prisoners to professional spies. Our intel has to be solid. We will help plan and guide the strategic destruction of the German war machine."

As they reach another plain wooden structure, Hershberger stops under a tree to answer one of George's questions about his background. "I grew up in Ohio and learned German mostly in high school, and some college. I studied electronics and went to work for Sears and Roebuck fixing radios. Later on, I worked as an engineer for a couple of radio stations."

"Did you enlist when the war started?" George asked.

"No, I was drafted a few months before Pearl Harbor and went right to the Signal Corps. I was stationed at Camp Shelby in Mississippi. Eisenhower was the chief down there."

"Did you get to meet him?" Fred can't help himself.

"Oh sure," Hershberger went on. "I was a radio operator. The Signal Corp had great training and one guy from our class ran the radar unit in Oahu and spotted the Japanese coming to Hawaii." Fred and George are duly impressed.

"We were gonna ship out to the Solomon Islands, but they came in and picked people for officer training."

That seems to be all Hershberger wants to share because what he tells Fred and George next, is immediate and pressing. "Listen, I've been given a special assignment to find out as much as possible about Germany's nuclear weapons, anything to do with uranium or any related issues. I want you to listen out for this. We'll be interrogating together until you get the hang of it. We usually start out in pairs."

Hershberger tells them he specializes in advanced technologies and reports everything to Vannevar Bush. Bush is the head of the National Defense Research Committee which initiated a program called the Manhattan Project. All pertinent information will be sent to General Leslie Groves who runs Oak Ridge in Tennessee.

"And just so you know, all interrogations are recorded."

"They're what?" Fred asks.

"This whole place is bugged." Hershberger explains." So, when you interrogate someone, no need to take notes - just listen - everything is being recorded. If you hear something relevant or important, we'll type the interview and send the important information up the chain of command. They'll determine what to do with it."

He motions behind him and says, "This is one of the interrogation buildings – it's got rooms inside where we talk to prisoners. Microphones were installed in the ceilings with listeners on the other end." Then he turns and heads towards the road that intersects where they are standing. "Come with me."

He starts walking away while the two new soldiers quickly follow. Hershberger points out the Infirmary and Officer's Quarters.

"There is an officer's club, which is pretty nice," he comments. "There's a pool, tennis courts and a golf course too. Everyone can use them, especially if you need to soften up a prisoner or reward them for good information. We can talk about that on a case-by-case basis."

He takes Fred and George to a field just past the stockade. They don't see another building or structure and wonder where they are headed. Hershberger leads them around the fence down what looks like a natural berm facing away towards the river. The small hill turns out to be an underground bunker camouflaged with shrubbery. Inside the berm is the listening hub Captain Herberger just mentioned.

They round the edge of the embankment; Fred sees a door between the greenery.

"This is the listening post," Hershberger motions as Fred and George move in closer. "We have soldiers assigned here to listen. Wanna take a look?" He leans over, grabs the handle, and swings the door open as wide as he can, given the narrow opening.

Inside Fred and George see a row of booths set up with listening devices and equipment they do not recognize. They do however identify the typewriters. At one table two soldiers sit with their backs to them, hunched over, apparently concentrating. Then George recognizes Peter Weiss. It looks like he is in training.

Hershberger lowers his voice as to not disturb the soldiers, "This is a state-of-the-art Memovox recorder," and he motions to one of the large square boxes that could be mistaken for a record player with some kind of red disc spinning in the middle.

"It's O.K., captain," the other soldier turns around. "I'm doing training and it's pretty quiet right now.

Introductions are made and of course Fred, George and Peter all know each other. Hershberger continues to explain how the listening system works. "There are microphones and receptor devices hidden in all the buildings including the barracks, the mess hall, even the latrines."

Corporal Stern, the other soldier who is training Peter pipes in, "We actually have some microphones hidden in the trees along one of the paths."

Hershberger smiles and continues. "We have about 14 locations set up. All the wires from each of those locations are run underground here to the hub. If there's something interesting happening, we turn on the Memovox to record the conversation which is played back through these speakers. Once important pieces of the conversation are identified, they're typed up and the transcript is sent to HQ."

"This," he points to a panel on the wall with *in* and *out* plugs resembling a small switchboard, "is a kind of routing system. We can plug in any of the devices we choose."

That was it in a nutshell, except for waiting for something important to be said.

"Do you find listening to their conversation to be useful?" Fred asks. "Do you learn much?"

Hershberger sums it up. "Yes, especially if we have something specific to identify. We hope the prisoner lets his guard down or discusses something we know he's hiding. We can then use that information in the next interrogation. We like to surprise the prisoners with what we know," he says with a smile. "See how that works?"

There are slow nods as the soldiers grasp how they will work together with the listeners. *Quite the system*, Fred thinks. Then he reasons aloud, "So, by hiding the listening hub, we don't advertise to prisoners they are being monitored," he reasons aloud.

"Exactly," Hershberger confirms. *This is going to be a good team*, he admits to himself, impressed that these new soldiers were thinking. "You should also know there's a secret underground center with offices, a conference room and another listening area too."

"Once the interviews are typed up, we have a filing system to keep all the transcripts and excerpts organized," Herberger goes on to explain. "We've got a guy, Spivey, who has a system, and it works." Then Hershberger pauses with a little chuckle.

"Spivey was almost too good at his job. We were buried in paperwork, transcripts, extracts, pictures, maps, drawings – all kinds of materials. Major Szlapka directed Spivey to come up with a better library system to organize everything and be able to recall materials when we need them – and have it ready by Monday. He tells him on a Saturday!" Hershberger gives into a laugh.

"Damn if Spivey didn't come up with a great system. Szlapka was so thrilled he made Spivey Chief Clerk. Now Spivey gets to manage all of it!" He winks. "You guys'll get to know Spivey."

"C'mon," Herberger said to Fred and George. "We actually have to get to work now." With that the small group heads back to the interrogation building.

As they walk, Hershberger wants to explain something. "The listening devices were never something the U.S. condoned. But the Brits have a system like this, and it works, so we adopted it." He glances over to make his point. "The other thing you should be aware of are Geneva Convention rules. Bringing German captives directly to Fort Hunt for a few days might be considered a violation so we are a 'processing center' rather than a PW camp. Got it?"

"Got it," Fred and George affirm in unison.

When they arrive back at the main building, Hershberger goes over to a desk where folders are stacked and grabs the top two, handing one to Fred and one to George.

"Your first assignments," he says.

Fred opens his folder. He sees the name Dr. Carl Helmuth Hertz and immediately recognizes the name of the renowned family of physicists which includes a Nobel prize winner. *How in the world did we get him?* Fred thinks.

He keeps his outward reaction in check, but inside, he is extremely pleased. *This is going to be very interesting*, he thinks.

In their first week, 1142 interrogators Fred and George are blessed, baptism by fire. They jump in, do the research, learn on the fly, and trust their guts. Captain Hershberger is a knowledgeable and capable teacher, which Fred appreciates.

By the time they get their first furlough everyone is ready to go into town, any town, and see someone besides fellow soldiers or prisoners. The interrogators set their sights on one place, the USO in Alexandria. The United Service Organizations offers a lifeline to soldiers who desperately need a mental break and conversation with a person of the opposite sex.

Arno's friend Leslie Wilson talks Fred into joining them. Fred found out Leslie had a girl he was sweet on, so the weekend couldn't come soon enough. Saturday night they head out of Fort Hunt's fences to the main road and stick out their thumbs. Alexandria is only about five or six miles, but no one wants to waste valuable time walking when they can be dancing.

The USO is an empty storefront that has been turned into a dancehall with a small live band on the weekends serving punch and Coca Cola. Even though the military did not restrict beer consumption, the USO didn't serve it, only snacks and cigarettes. Fred didn't smoke and he preferred German beers, so for him this was purely social.

Earlier that afternoon, a nineteen-year-old USO volunteer rushed to get from her job to the USO to decorate the venue. Lucille Berryman is a slender, vivacious brunette with a fun, outgoing personality, and seemingly boundless energy. The soldiers love her because she's never met a stranger. She is, if nothing else, easy to talk to.

Lucille was born in Washington, D.C. and grew up in Alexandria, which makes Fort Hunt her home turf. She knows the surrounding areas up and down the Potomac very well.

After high school graduation in 1943, the draft left her hometown devoid of all eligible young men. Lucille decided to take a job with the claims division of the Civil Service Commission and started volunteering her time at the USO. Thanks to her brother who offered her services, she struck up and maintains correspondence with some 54 different servicemen while still helping to organize, decorate and attend dances three times a week. Lucille likes to stay busy.

After running from work to the USO, she quickly finished decorating the stage and putting tiny candles on each bistro table around the edge of the room. Now all Lucille wants is a shower and a change of clothes before the doors open. But tonight, she cut it too close. It is already seven and the band is tuning up. She ducks into the girl's bathroom to try and do something with her hair as soldiers start trickling in.

By the time Leslie Wilson pushes Fred though the front door, the place is hopping with a good rendition of Glenn Miller's *Tuxedo Junction*. Soldiers are pairing up with girls who are there to dance. One couple glides by in perfect swing time, underarm turn, backstep and twirl back together as they bring the music to life.

Leslie navigates to the bar and glances around the perimeter tables for his girl. Lucille has just come out of the bathroom and meets up with her friend Janet who insists she get on the dance floor. She is still a little frazzled but bucks up and puts on her best smile.

As they round the corner of the bar, Leslie turns and catches sight of Janet, his girl. He gives her a big hug then catches Lucille by the arm.

"Here, you dance with my friend," and he gives Lucille a gentle, but firm thrust straight into Fred's arms. Then he and Janet sync to the music and dance off.

Fred awkwardly looks at this young girl with a broad if not confused smile on her face and introduces himself. "Hi, I'm Fred." When it came to girls, Fred was not quick on his feet and was immediately out of his depth.

"I'm Lucille. I'm one of the volunteers," she says, a little breathless. Something about this guy's kind, intelligent eyes throws her off balance, so she waits.

"I guess, we should – dance?" Fred half smiles, half asks as he offers his hand. It was his fumbling, sweet unpretentious response Lucille immediately finds attractive and in the next minute she is gliding around the dance floor wrapped in his arms. Neither of them knows that this dance will determine the rest of their lives.

P.O. Box 1142 interrogators

Breaking the Silence   Louisville, Kentucky May 30th, 2006

Chapter 5

Breaking the Silence

Louisville, Kentucky
May 30, 2006

Fred is telling Brandon about enlisting and his journey to
Fort Hunt. Brandon remembers the transfer list he'd copied at
the National Archives.

"I have a list of soldiers who completed Camp Ritchie
training and were transferred to Fort Hunt." He digs through a
folder of papers and pulls out a copy of those graduates. "Eric
Kramer, Peter Weiss, Henry Kolm, Arno Mayer ... and your
name is here." He hands Fred the transfer order. Fred seems
to remember more than a few names. He tells Brandon about
getting off the bus and taking the oath. It occurs to Cynthia
how unusual it was to take an oath when they had no idea
what exactly they would be doing.

Brandon still wants to ask about the grounds, the
buildings, and the layout of the fort. This is information he can
use for his wayside exhibits if all else fails. "So, you had
barracks for the prisoners and I'm guessing interrogation
rooms?" Fred nods and describes what he remembers.

"Next to the barracks was an open area where we played baseball, along with tennis courts and a pool." At the mention of the pool Lucille can't help but wink at Cynthia.

Lucille decides to fill in the story. "Fred showed me a picture of his buddies at a pool, and I knew it was Fort Hunt. He thought no one knew – but everyone around Alexandria knew where all the pools were!" she laughs.

"Of course, after he realized I knew where he was stationed, he was either going to have to kill me or marry me," she jokes. "Obviously, he made the right decision."

Brandon can't help but laugh along and thinks the interplay between these two is endearing, just like his grandparents. Cynthia is mulling something over and speaks up.

"A lot of the soldiers were German Jews. How did all of you feel about talking to Nazis?"

Fred smiles and explains, "It was our job, our orders, to interrogate any prisoner they brought to us."

"How did you get information out of these guys?" Cynthia is trying to cut to the chase. "Was it...physical?" Her voice trails off. She has seen images of Abu Graib prison, waterboarding, torture, and prisoner abuse that has recently been in the news.

"No, no." Fred shakes his head. "No force, no physical violence of any kind. No, that was not our way of doing things. We just didn't see the purpose in it. We knew that approach wouldn't work. Besides, you would never be able to trust the information you got. We never thought using force made any sense."

Fred goes on to explain, "I was assigned to 1142 because of my engineering degree and because I spoke fluent German. That way I could interrogate specific prisoners and scientists." Almost as an afterthought he goes on, "As we discussed, all the barracks, the interrogation rooms, even the latrines were bugged." Brandon remembers a picture he found of a large bell-shaped listening device.

"All of the audio fed into a command center in an underground bunker, heavily camouflaged. Soldiers recorded and listened to everything."

"But you also conducted regular interrogations, right?" Brandon asks. "What was the normal process of interrogation? What kind of prisoners did you talk to?"

"We got many U-boat personnel, captains, and some sailors. The scientists came later. Sometimes we got basic information, like name and rank, maybe what function they performed, either German Army or Kreigsmarine, or where they were captured. That gave us some guidance as to the nature of the questions and who would conduct the interview. I did a lot of interrogations with Berger."

"Who was *Berger*?" Brandon catches the name again.

"That was Major Hershberger, William Hershberger. He was my CO. Back then he was a captain. I was assigned to him from day one and we worked on interrogations together."

"Was he there at the start of the program?"

"No, I don't think so." Fred gives a slight shake of his head. "But he had experience before he came to 1142. Berger was an American, from Ohio, but he was fluent in German."

"Really?" Brandon is intrigued.

"Yes, he learned it in high school. And he was good enough to become an interrogator with us." Fred muses. "He was also an engineer and radio specialist before he came to 1142. So, to answer your question, no he wasn't there at the start. But his experience qualified him to interrogate German U-boat PWs about their radar system, which was quite advanced from ours. George Mandel, my bunkmate, and Berger, Major Hershberger, were two interrogators I worked with the most." Fred lists his closest compatriots but doesn't feel the need to explain they were gathering nuclear information for Vannevar Bush and General Leslie Groves.

"Was Berger the one who assigned you different interrogations?"

"Yes, as I said he was my superior and we did some together."

"Let's walk through an interrogation, how did it work?"

"We would match the PW with the right person or team. Berger knew sonar and radio systems, George was a chemist, and I am a mechanical engineer. We would interview people who had information related to our fields."

"Did you do this separately or together?"

"Sometimes two or three people with different disciplines would interrogate one PW together. We'd take turns with questioning on different topics, depending on the kind of information we needed."

"If you did it separately, would you then share information?"

"Yes, we shared information. If a PW mentioned something about uranium, then the interrogator would flag that as important. By the way, the first time George heard of someone purifying uranium, he couldn't imagine why anyone would want to do that," Fred added with a laugh. "But we typed it up and sent the information through.

"I should point out that during interrogations you don't always get information all at once," Fred clarifies. "We had to listen. We had to tuck little pieces away and not look surprised or react if we heard something important. We might discuss it afterwards, but it was typed up and sent on."

Brandon casually jots down the name of George Mandel under William Hershberger, then asks, "Did you research information on each prisoner?"

"Usually, but sometimes we played it by ear depending on the response of the PW," Fred explains. "We'd start out with easy questions in relaxed conversation. What's your name? How old are you? Maybe I could detect an accent and comment on where they might be from; perhaps offer them a cigarette, anything to put them at ease. Each question would get more personal until we got to the heart of what they did or identified specific information we were after." This was exactly the flow of the interview transcript Brandon had with him. It confirmed to Brandon that Fred knew what he was talking about.

"We wanted to relax them and bring down their defenses. We would try to get as much information as we could in one to two hours, that was the average length of an interrogation."

"After we got going and could sense the PW was letting down his guard, it was fairly easy to tell with only a few questions if this person knew anything of importance. If not, the prisoner might be moved to a different facility."

"You said an interview was usually a couple of hours, but how long did a prisoner stay at Fort Hunt?"

"Sometimes we only had a few hours, sometimes the PW would be there for a week. Only a few valuable prisoners stayed longer," Fred answered.

"Did you ever try other tactics beyond the standard interview practices?" Brandon asks.

"We'd try any number of approaches. If the PW was with us for a little while, we could take time getting them to let down their guard. Playing chess or cards – we even taught them how to play horseshoes, which they really liked; oh, and baseball." Fred smiles remembering the various sports tactics they employed. "We also used informants, stool pigeons," Fred adds.

"Really? How did that work?"

"An enlisted man, possibly a make-believe officer or even a PW who was sympathetic to our side, was quartered with the PWs in their barracks. They would pose as another PW and try to get them talking or just listen to conversations. Of course, that would take place over days. I did that a couple of times myself, only because having a German in with Germans was more believable and ultimately more productive."

"How effective was it? Did they ever suspect people were planted in the barracks?" Brandon is enjoying the covert nature of this ruse.

"It was fairly effective," Fred explains, "because the people we put in there, whether it was me or someone else, were very well trained. No one ever gave themselves away," he smiles.

"But you had transcripts of all conversations," Brandon clarifies, "and you could refer back to any conversations if you needed to."

"Yes," Fred nods. "For example, if a PW was reluctant during questioning, we'd send him back to the barracks. Typically, his bunkmate would ask how it went? Did he say anything? The PW might say it was easy or that he told us meaningless things. He might tell his fellow prisoners he was careful not to talk about the anti-sonar skin on their U-boats. Well, the next day we would ask his bunkmate about those anti-sonar skins."

"Brilliant," Cynthia says, totally engrossed.

Brandon follows up, "Did you ever think they figured out there were microphones and played into that?"

"Sometimes. If a prisoner tried to alter the truth, make things up or steer us in the wrong direction, we'd share

117

information and let them know what we already knew. Oftentimes they were surprised by the depth of our intelligence and stopped playing games.

"The attitude shifted towards the end of the war. I remember one afternoon listening in on the prisoner barracks. This one German officer wanted each person to resist giving up any information. But the other prisoners pushed back, arguing with him. They were saying, 'Why should we resist? They're nice to us! Besides, we may lose the war anyway, so what does it matter?" Fred smiles. "The prisoners were telling their own officer to comply with us!"

Fred was amused by the mini-insurrection, adding, "There was a lot of peer pressure among the PWs to conform and help us out. That's something you don't get with physical harm."

"Right, right," Brandon agrees. "By the way, what was your rank at this time?"

"Corporal."

"Was everyone in your group corporals or were there a variety of ranks?"

"Most of us were corporals. However, we wore officer's insignias during interrogations. Think about it; we were all 22, 23 and 24-year-old soldiers at the time. The Germans respected rank. As interrogation officers, if someone did not present at the prisoner's rank, or maybe one step below, we wouldn't expect good results."

"Did you have a variety of uniforms?" Brandon ventures. "How did you get the uniform you needed for the interrogation that day? Was there a supply closet?" Brandon half-jokes.

"Yes, there was," Fred confirms. "We had all different insignias, some uniforms, and before you interrogated someone you would become the appropriate rank. One time I even got to dress as a Lieutenant Colonel."

"It sounds like, with only a couple of exceptions, that most of the prisoners were compliant."

"Yes, for the most part. Before I got to 1142, I was told that there were a lot of uncooperative and disagreeable prisoners coming in. But once Rommel was driven out of North Africa and the U.S. went into Italy, the attitude of the Germans changed. They were more cooperative. They knew the war was winding down and they didn't want to be handed over to the Russians. They were scared to death of the Russians."

"Really?"

"Yes, it was common knowledge and a common fear." Fred assures Brandon. "Most PWs were not fervent Nazis or supporters of Hitler and if they were, they denied it. A lot of the PWs reasoned that if they cooperated, it might get them back home sooner.

About that time, we were getting a lot of scientists. Most of them had surrendered. They wanted to be in America and continue doing their work. Once we got them talking, they were eager to share their inventions, their discoveries. Many were really good teachers," Fred admits.

"It sounds like it went smoothly if a prisoner cooperated, but how did it work with someone who was resistant?"

"If a prisoner was stubborn, we took another direction. For example: We had one U-boat captain who just wouldn't talk, he refused to tell us anything. Our response was to inform him he would be handed over to the Russians. Usually this got a reaction. But not this guy. He didn't budge. No reaction at all. I mentioned before that we had a closet of uniforms and a couple of our guys spoke Russian." Fred's demeanor lightens as he continues.

"We told this stubborn U-boat captain he'd be handed over to a Russian General if he didn't cooperate. Still, he said nothing." Everyone is riveted by the story. "We blindfolded him, put him in a car and drove him around the grounds for about an hour, landing at some bunkers. "

"Yes, I'm familiar with the bunkers, on the other side of the park," Brandon admits. "They were built for the Revolutionary War. But go on."

"The bunker was dark, empty and as you pointed out, far away from the living quarters. They brought the prisoner inside to wait. Shortly after, in walks one of our guys dressed in a Russian officer's uniform, speaking Russian, telling him he was going to take custody of him. At this point, PWs typically would *reconsider* and opt to stay with us." Fred uses an air quote gesture. "We didn't have to do this often, maybe a couple times, but it usually worked.

"But this time," Brandon is chuckling, "I'm guessing it didn't?"

"You're right. After all this, he still wouldn't cooperate. Once we realized we'd get nothing out of him, he was passed on to another PW camp."

Brandon asks, "If a prisoner *did* cooperate, was he rewarded?"

"Yes, if a prisoner cooperated there were things we could do, incentives that would keep them talking. We might show a movie in the main building; or in some cases take them into town for a nice dinner. It depended on the prisoner and the information we got. This proved useful because it showed other prisoners it was in their best interest to help us."

"How was the food in camp, by the way?" Brandon asks, expecting the usual negative response.

"We had a German cook, or someone to cook authentic German food for the prisoners, and it was pretty good. We had Army food for the enlisted men."

Brandon isn't expecting that.

"The American cooks, not as good." Fred gives a "so-so" sign.

There it is, Brandon chuckles to himself, then says out loud, "I bet the prisoners appreciated that."

"Yes, it helped with morale. Speaking of which, I should explain most prisoners had a morale officer assigned to them as well as the interrogators. The morale officer made sure the PWs' needs were met. I did that for some of the prisoners: made sure they had basic supplies, like toiletries and such. Or, if they asked, writing paper and pencils, things of that nature."

"But you still reported all conversations?"

"Oh yes, we still listened to conversations and reported anything important we heard."

"I see. Let's shift gears now to the people you interrogated. Who was the first one and what was that conversation like?"

"The first prisoner I talked to was a physicist named Hertz, Dr. Carl Helmuth Hertz."

"Hertz? Like *megahertz* - Hertz?" Cynthia can't help but put the name and science together.

"Yes, that was Carl Hertz's family. His great uncle, Heinrich Rudolf Hertz proved the existence of electromagnetism," Fred explains. "His father, Gustav Hertz, was a Nobel Prize winner in physics. Carl was also a physicist and very important to Nazi Germany."

"How did he end up in our custody?" Brandon wonders out loud.

"He was captured in North Africa by Americans and sent to a camp in Oklahoma. I think in some way he planned on getting captured because he had carefully written down the names of all the physicists he knew who had left Germany to come to the United States. That was his fallback plan. He was able to communicate with some of those scientists who were working at the Pentagon. Once they reported his presence to headquarters, he was pulled out of the PW camp in Oklahoma and assigned to Fort Hunt. He was completely cooperative and with his pedigree and scientific credentials, treated not only with respect, but also given certain privileges."

"What were some of his privileges?"

"He was free to move around the camp, take occasional outings like a boat ride on the Potomac and so on. He was very smart, always two or three steps ahead. He was insistent we needed to watch the Russians and predicted the Cold War."

"What kind of information did you get from him?"

"He had been a student at the time of the war. He was aware of the weaponry Germany was developing but he wasn't part of it. He was captured and held for a couple years in Oklahoma, so this rendered his information obsolete. He was out of touch. However, he was still valuable because of his status and reputation. Hertz knew every physicist in Germany and all over the world, scientists like Fermi. He knew their areas of expertise and identified who would work with the United States after the war. This was useful to us."

"How long was he at Fort Hunt?"

Fred thinks for a minute. "He was there for about nine months, which was actually longer than most PWs, but he was a desired guest. We had some huts on the property that housed three important guests. Hertz was number one, Heinz Schlicke was two and General Ulrich Kessler was three.

"I was Carl Hertz's morale officer, and we became good friends. In fact, after the war, he came back to Washington for a conference, in the 60's."

Fred nods at Lucille. "We took him back to see Fort Hunt, but the little hut was gone, so were most of the buildings."

Lucille adds, "We went on to Charlottesville to show him Monticello and the University of Virginia. He was very nice and so smart. He was a professor at Lund University in Uppsala, Sweden, as I remember. He went there after the war."

"Yes, he was released directly to Sweden so he could complete his Ph.D." Fred confirms. "He met his wife there as well. She was a doctoral student, a medical doctor. He ended up staying there and teaching. So, it worked out for them."

"Carl went on to develop the inkjet and echocardiograph. And as I recall he received the Lasker Award from the United States for Ultrasound technology used for medical diagnosis."

"It sounds like you developed a close friendship with Hertz," Brandon observes. "Did you have the same sort of easy-going relationship with most of the prisoners? Or was it unusual to be friendly with your captives?"

To Brandon it seems these scientists and educated men were connecting on a completely different professional level. Because of that, Fred could successfully balance the dynamics of calm interrogation while maintaining control.

"Our relationships with prisoners depended upon the prisoners and their attitudes. Most of the scientists I interrogated were men of science first, not fervent Nazis; and yes, sometimes friendships developed. When it came to Hertz, we did develop a friendship and then corresponded for years after the war. Later his wife wrote and told us when he passed, a victim of cancer. I think that was the late 70's."

Cynthia is taking this in. Of course, the connection her father had made with a fellow scientist was on a different level, which endured after the war. She is proud of how her dad treated his prisoner and the respect they shared as life-long friends even after the war.

"Let's move on to the next person," Brandon suggests. "Who else did you talk to?"

"Yes, the next prisoner I interrogated was, at the time, very important. This was after Germany surrendered in the summer of 1945."

Fred remembered the men he interrogated next came from one of the more remarkable incidents that occurred towards the end of the war, the capture of the Nazi super submarine, U-234.

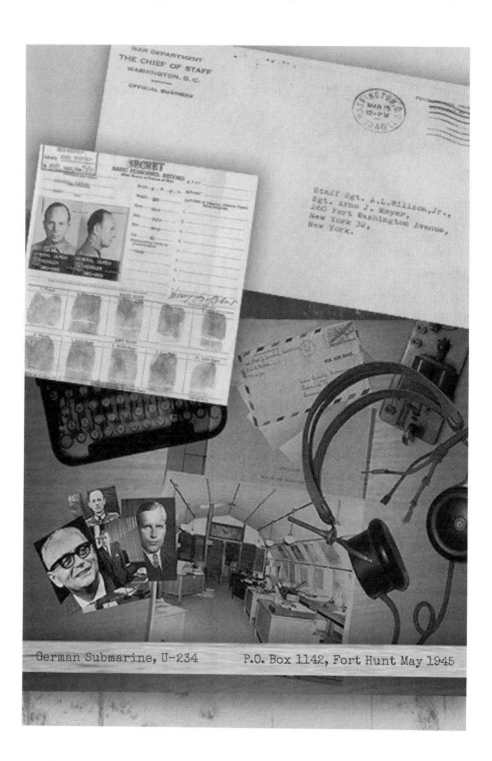

German Submarine, U-234   P.O. Box 1142, Fort Hunt May 1945

Chapter 6

German Submarine, U-234

P.O. Box 1142, Fort Hunt, Virginia
Late May 1945

In May of 1945, war developments were happening quickly. After Hitler's death and Germany's surrender, Fort Hunt is busier than ever interrogating and processing captured military personnel, U-boat personnel, Nazi generals, and hundreds of German scientists who are surrendering. Fred is coming into his own as an interrogator, especially extracting technical content. He has learned a lot from Captain Hershberger and picks up more useful techniques from other interrogators, like Rudy Pins.

Rudy is one of the seasoned soldiers, having arrived at Fort Hunt in 1942 in the same covert manner as Fred. Rudy trained in the Corps of Engineers, then transferred to Fort Belvoir in Virginia for concentrated instruction in camouflage specialties. When an Army major realized he spoke fluent German, he found himself transferred on super-secret orders and bussed to Alexandria, Virginia, where he was told to meet someone at the post office. A sergeant came up in a jeep and brought him to 1142.

Fred was amused at his clandestine arrival and he and Rudy became fast friends. He was sympathetic to Rudy's background, which was similar to many of his fellow German-Jewish soldiers.

Rudy's parents sent him alone, at 14 years old, to live with foster parents in Ohio. His brother was sent to Palestine. While both brothers escaped, his parents weren't so lucky. The Jews in their hometown of Hoexter were rounded up by force after the war began. He got the sad news last year that his parents died in the ghetto of Riga, Latvia.

"And your brother?" Fred asked. "What became of him?"

"He was struggling on a kibbutz, but now he seems to be establishing himself as an artist." Rudy had told him. "Who knows, maybe after the war..." and he let his voice trail.

Fred wondered aloud if their interrogation efforts were doing any good. Rudy assured him that what they were doing mattered. Even though Rudy missed formal training at Camp Ritchie, he nonetheless jumped in and became an adept interrogator. He told Fred since he'd been there, he knew for certain one bit of information they ascertained proved quite valuable. They discovered where the Germans docked their submarines.

"This all happened months before Germany surrendered," Rudy began. "We found out the Germans built fake platforms over submarine pens, so the Allied bombing was always a couple hundred yards off. Once the intel came through, adjustments were made, and they successfully hit their targets." This reassured Fred that 1142 information was making a difference during the war.

Rudy went on to tell Fred that Henry Kolm learned of a ball-bearing plant in Southern Germany, which was taken out. Henry also used intel and research to locate power plants along the Rhine and Ruhr Rivers, important energy sources. Allied bombs destroyed the dams. All these incidents helped destabilize the German war infrastructure, and ultimately contributed to her defeat.

Fred is gaining confidence and has become adept at processing prisoners, which is good because of the recent uptick in activity. After Carl Hertz, most of the PWs Fred talks to are U-boat personnel. He and George tag team with Captain Hershberger, but after one interview George hears something he admits is a little confusing.

"This guy is talking about enriching uranium. Why would someone do that?"

"Not sure, but it could be important." Fred says. "They may be working on a bomb."

"Type it up and send it along." Berger also suspects it's part of Germany's atomic bomb efforts. "And see if you can find out anything else."

George learns that Germany was in fact working on an atomic bomb, though the program seemed to have stalled. He also gets information about proximity fuses and different types of detonation devices, information that will prove useful.

Shortly after Germany's surrender in May, a massive U-boat, U- 234, is captured by the USS Sutton and brought to Portsmouth, New Hampshire. A group of Army personnel will pick up the crew and bring them back to 1142. Henry Kolm is chosen as the group's interpreter. Henry is a good choice because he can translate German into English as fast as he can read or speak it. Interpreting on the fly is his forte.

Henry and the group return to 1142 with a couple busloads of the crew and officers. Once the PWs are processed into barracks, Captain Hershberger asks Henry to brief his group on all intel related to U-234. Hershberger gathers his team of interrogators in one of the meeting rooms where they are all seated, facing the captain who turns the meeting over to Henry.

"First off, U-234 is the largest type of U-boat ever constructed. I'd say it was twice as big as an average U-boat. The Nazis reconfigured the entire boat, loaded it with prototypes of their newest technology and weaponry, all of it going to Japan." Henry wishes he had a schematic or some kind of illustration but verbal description will have to do. At least he has a clipboard and pages of notes for reference.

"To get everything into the U-boat, they altered the lower torpedo tubes, cargo holds, keel and upper-deck torpedo compartments. The sub was loaded with prototypes including a new jet engine and a disassembled Messerschmidt. Along with the weapons, there were forty-one crewmembers, six officers and nine passengers from the Third Reich onboard.

"The passenger list includes people 1142 will interrogate. Johann-Heinrich Fehler, the captain, whom I have met; Lieutenant Karl-Ernst Pfaff, Second Officer; General Ulrich Kessler, Luftwaffe; a Messerschmitt pilot, scientists, including Dr. Heinz Schlicke, and Kay Nieschling, the Naval Fleet Judge Advocate who was designated the liaison officer between Germany and Japan for the entire Pacific arena." There is a low rumble of reaction among the attending soldiers. Hershberger glances around the room for quiet and okays Henry to continue.

"Captain Fehler had two Japanese passengers, an Imperial Japanese Navy Lieutenant Commander Hideo Tomonaga, a leading Japanese submarine designer, and Lieutenant Commander Genzo Shoji, an aircraft expert. When faced with surrender both Japanese officers opted instead for a more honorable death. They retired to their cabins, took luminol, which you may or may not know is a powerful barbiturate, and died 36 hours later. Fehler buried them at sea." The men hearing this for the first time, take it in stride, then wonder aloud if this was the first submarine to carry Nazi secrets to Japan?

"Was this the only U-boat taking weapons to Japan? Were there others?"

"How much technology does Japan have?"

"How advanced are their weapons?"

"Are they capable of building an atomic bomb?"

The fact that Germany was handing over some of their most highly advanced technology to Japan rattled the soldiers.

"Did you see the submarine?" Fred asks.

"Yes. I went down the sail, the hatch, and I got to look through the periscope." Even this trained soldier was excited about the periscope. "I got quite friendly with Captain Fehler." Everyone was impressed with Henry boarding the submarine, and truth be told, they were a little envious.

"It was up alongside the dock and the hatch was open, so I went down. Captain Fehler was very proud of his sub and showed off all the things it could do. I found him very apolitical. He's a regular Navy guy, a career guy who was more interested in new technology than warfare. While we talked, they were unloading cargo, cases of documents, and other stuff - a lot of stuff."

Henry flips a page on his clipboard. "They had a swinging boom crane on the dock and hoisted out ten canisters containing over twelve hundred pounds of uranium oxide, among other things. I saw a Henschel glide-bomb Junkers jet engine, three disassembled Messerschmitt airplanes, and two complete V-1 rockets. I was told they had fuel formulas, complete drawings for destroyers, aircraft factories, and some diplomatic mail."

Henry continues. "That H-293 glider bomb is basically a radio-controlled glide bomb with a rocket slung underneath. Fehler mentioned in conversation they were working on a new V-4 rocket which he heard could reach the U.S. but it was still in development. They had prototypes of this new electric torpedo and of various fuses and detonation devices. I think they're using the infrared and microwave technology we've heard about here at 1142." He looks up at the interrogators who validate Henry's comments. This is an impressive list of weapons the soldiers understand could have had grave impact on the balance of power. They are concerned at how advanced the Germans are in certain areas.

Hershberger picks up on the recovered uranium oxide and knows immediately this is going to be a big deal. It signals like a beacon to the Manhattan Project leaders.

Henry continues and identifies Second Officer Karl Pfaff as the officer who was overseeing the initial loading of the U-boat, the person who knew the manifest well. Pfaff was detained while the rest of the crew was bussed to 1142. He would be coming later.

The interrogators of 1142 know vaguely about the Manhattan Project and the development of an atomic bomb. Hershberger is more in the loop than most and is careful about what he can share. In the summer of 1945, he knew the teams at Oakridge in Tennessee and Los Alamos, were struggling, each with different issues. They are working on two bombs with different cores, one using uranium and one using plutonium. Each bomb has its own method of construction and presents unique challenges regarding detonation.

Although Hershberger has no way of knowing how much time or money is being spent, he knows it's a slow, complicated, and expensive process to enrich uranium. He is also aware the U.S. simply does not have enough of this resource and could use more. The amount of uranium oxide from U-234 could only help. Granted, he has heard very little about any problems with plutonium, so he surmises this is not an issue. But he is keenly aware a key topic of the forthcoming interrogations must center around the detonation devices themselves.

He mentions this to Fred and George who admit they have little knowledge on the subject. However, both men now know to prioritize this topic in their interviews.

Hershberger receives background information on the crew and passengers which he uses to make assignments. Henry Kolm and Rudy Pins are a good match for General Ulrich Kessler, commander of the Luftwaffe. Henry already has a friendly and comfortable relationship with Captain Fehler, so he will continue interrogating him, as well as the Second officer Pfaff, when he arrives.

One of the U-boat passengers, Heinz Schlicke, is a German scientist Hershberger understands is very important. Schlicke was not only the director of the Naval Test Fields in Keil but also a specialist in radar, infrared and countermeasures. Immediately after U-234 is captured, Schlicke is taken into custody and given a handler from the Navy, Lieutenant Commander Louis Alvarez. Hershberger doubts this is his real name because it's common for high-level *interrogators* to use pseudonyms. Still, within days of capture,

Schlicke is quickly transported to Anacostia, a base outside Washington, D.C.

Alvarez arranges for Schlicke to give a series of nine presentations, briefing a select group of military brass, scientists, and intelligence personnel, including Captain Hershberger. These highly controlled talks cover infrared and microwave technology, submarine advancements in sonar and radar, homing devices and torpedo detonation and accuracy. Hershberger wants Fred at these lectures since he will be Schlicke's interrogator.

Military personnel are advised before each of these presentations that questions from the crowd would only be taken *afterwards* and must be approved by Alvarez. Hershberger notes that right after the first talk, Schlicke is taken back to U-234 in Portsmouth to retrieve the prototypes of his fuses. Besides proximity fuses, Schlicke has prototypes of infra-red detonators. Scientists at the Manhattan Project, including Louis Alvarez who was in fact, a real scientist working on detonation devices for both bombs, are still trying to work out bugs on the plutonium bomb. There is less than two months until the scheduled test called *Trinity*.

Alvarez has been grilling Schlicke on detonation. The procedure they have been theorizing is that detonating uranium is likened to a shotgun being fired. The Manhattan team plans to shoot uranium through a shaft slamming into a plug of more uranium. By colliding the pieces, critical mass should be reached, and a nuclear fission chain reaction would then occur using the isotope U-235 to sustain it. Hopefully, that's what the July test will prove. Alvarez knows any information that would help confirm this theory to be true, would be valuable. Detonating plutonium is another challenge.

Heinz Schlicke was also at the forefront of various marine technologies that have put Kriegsmarine warfare ahead of the Allies. Everyone is interested in his explanations, diagrams and real examples of this new technology and how it was efficiently used.

By the time Schlicke makes his final presentation, Alvarez is done with him. Schlicke and Captain Fehler are transferred to 1142.

Schlicke arrives at Fort Hunt with another handler, Jack Alberti, also a Navy guy and a specialist. Alberti drives over from Washington daily, always dressed in civilian clothes. Fred, as Schlicke's "1142 handler" becomes friendly with Alberti as well.

Schlicke has become quite cooperative and agrees to write a textbook about microwave technology, its transmission and device designs. Alberti is overseeing the project and monitors the progress. The textbook is taking up a lot of Schlicke's time, but he is nearly finished. Fred will get him after the book is complete.

Much of Schlicke's information centers around naval warfare technologies. Fred can see why this PW is so important. The man is brilliant, and Fred realizes just how advanced German technologies have become in this field. He quickly gets up to speed on how to interrogate Schlicke, reading and re-reading transcripts from his presentations.

The transcripts include detailed information on different aspects of submarine warfare. Schlicke presented material on infrared homing devices, heat detection, cloaking against radar, amplification of hi-speed messages to submarines, and improvements in radar locating apparatus. There are even illustrations and schematics on how to build some of these devices, the systems they would affect and references to the theories behind the science.

The Germans had been working on active warning systems which would alert their submarines of oncoming airplanes before the vessels surfaced. This system was named Flamingo I, II and III. It is an omnidirectional infrared warning system for detecting heat radiation from infrared searchlights used by aircraft looking for enemy submarines and has a range of ten kilometers.

Fred scans the rest of the transcription and immerses himself. Schlicke describes how the German submarine fleet changed to diesel oil which, unlike gasoline, left no traces of oil on the water when they surfaced. Enemy planes were already using ultra-violet lights which easily detected the oil slicks and pinpointed a sub's whereabouts. Schlicke also described the German's new "cone" design for their U-boats which meant they could more easily deflect sonar.

Fred has a list of topics on which to interrogate Schlicke, the first being their advanced cloaking device for submarines.

It is a four-millimeter-thick rubber coating, painted on the hull like a skin and contains small air bubbles which absorb sonar impulses. This would greatly help Allied submarines and Fred's engineering mind is quickly assessing the technology, its application and benefits.

Then there is the *schnorchel*, which basically allowed German U-boats to connect with the atmosphere via tubes, one for air intake, the other for exhaust. The result was that German subs could travel longer distances underwater. The schnorchel was a game changer.

Added to Fred's interrogation topics is heat camouflage. It turns out the Americans had a heat deflecting device called the Fitzgerald. Fred wasn't immediately aware of it, but learned the Germans used infrared camouflage paint to deflect it.

During his presentations, Schlicke covered how the Germans were improving long distance navigation, reception, and amplification of receivers as well as the use of infrared decoy transmitters. Along with the transcripts, Fred found a drawing of an explosive boat with self-steering capabilities using radiation heat from ships as a guide, and more information on the use of VHF frequencies. That was an area of expertise for Captain Hershberger. It's a lot of information to take in and Fred understands the best protocol is to allow Schlicke to lead him through it. Luckily Schlicke would prove to be an excellent and willing teacher, which ultimately benefited both.

Fred's first interview with Heinz Schlicke is conducted in one of the standard interrogation rooms with Captain Hershberger. When Schlicke comes in, Fred recognizes the difference in the outward appearance from the scientist who had given the highly technical lectures under duress, to the person he was now going to engage in conversation. In person, Schlicke is about his height, five feet, ten, with a broad forehead and slightly receding hairline; but gone is the stress and fatigue from his dark eyes. Over the past few weeks, he and Schlicke have had amicable and friendly conversations while he wrote his microwave manual. Now the dynamic is slightly different, and Fred wants to ease into things.

As he takes his seat across the table, Schlicke is relaxed, even congenial. Sitting face to face is certainly more intimate and less intimidating.

Fred and Hershberger are also easy going. Since Fred has had more interactions with Schlicke, he uses the excuse of bringing Captain Hershberger up to speed to maintain a cordial if not professional demeanor. Hershberger mentions attending Schlicke's last presentation and Schlicke acknowledges seeing him. Fred knows Schlicke has decided he would like to stay in the United States, now that the war is over, and continue his work. He is fully cooperative.

Hershberger begins by asking him about U-234. He already knows much about the sub, but it is easy, familiar territory for Schlicke and a way for him to get comfortable with Hershberger. Fred prompts him by asking what led to its capture. Schlicke explains that when they left Keil, Germany in March they were performing maneuvers to test the performance and capabilities of the *schnorchel.*

"We collided with another U-boat during the exercise."

"Were you damaged?"

"Yes, so we put into Norway for repairs. By mid-April we were out and could run at schnorchel depth. Fehler," he says in reference to the captain, "decided to spend a couple hours at night running on the surface. But then, he thought we were having radio trouble because the Goliath transmitter seemed to stop working. What we didn't know is that Allied forces had captured Kriegsmarine Headquarters."

"Ah," Fred acknowledges. "What happened then?"

"This was early May and we picked up part of a British and American broadcast that said Admiral Karl Donitz had become Germany's head of state after the death of Adolph Hitler. Fehler didn't believe it and surfaced to get better radio reception. Then we heard the command from Donitz for all U-boats to surrender. Fehler still thought it was a trick, so he contacted U-873 and that captain convinced him the message was authentic."

"So that's when you decided to surrender?"

"Yes," Schlicke paused but wanted to explain. "At this point there was a dispute between General Kessler and Fehler. Kessler wanted to redirect the boat to Argentina. I think Kessler planned to go there and wait out the war."

Fred and Rudy Pins had already learned from Henry how self-centered Kessler was, and that he would do anything to save his own skin.

Schlicke continued, "I think he had planned from the beginning how he, alone, was going to survive."

Henry also confirmed that Kessler had valuables stashed in his compartment on the U-boat. Once the Americans thoroughly unloaded everything, they found furs, jewelry, cameras and gold ingots, everything to ensure Kessler could bargain for a comfortable life. On the other hand, as Henry had told them, Fehler was a good captain who just wanted to surrender and get back to sea.

"If Kessler had gotten his way, the ship would be in Argentina. Who knows what would've happened to us and the crew?" Schlicke confides.

Upon hearing this, Fred knows that if the Germans had made it to Japan with the jet engines and paired them with Japan's kamikaze pilots, the Allies would have been devastated.

"Fehler reasoned that if the British or Canadians got us, we'd be put in prison, and it might be years before we got back to Germany. He said the Americans would let us go home, so we set a course for the U.S. First Halifax, Nova Scotia, then Newport News, Virginia."

Schlicke failed to mention that after the decision was made to change course, Fehler dumped all their Enigma machine documents and classified papers, along with their

Tunis radar detector and a radio communication system. Even though the war was ending, he did not want that technology falling into enemy hands.

Hershberger and Fred have accomplished what they set out to do - get Schlicke to completely relax. The interrogation goes on smoothly from there. Schlicke is an accomplished scientist, with expertise in radio location techniques, jamming protocols, camouflage, remote-control devices, and various metals used in electronic components; all subjects that greatly interest Hershberger. Schlicke also explains his work with microwave and infrared electronics and radar-based wartime technology. He tells Fred about the fuses on which he had been working, explaining the differences between a proximity fuse and the challenges of a timing fuse.

"A proximity fuse will detonate when the bomb reaches a certain altitude or proximity to the Earth. I was working on the infrared and microwave components, using both light and timing to achieve detonation."

Fred realizes this is something the U.S. knows little about and takes the opportunity to instruct Schlicke to sketch it out. He rises to get paper and a pencil.

While Fred steps away Hershberger asks him, "What was your role going to be in Japan?"

Schlicke tells him he and General Kessler were being sent to Japan to set up low frequency transmitting capabilities so the Japanese could talk directly to the Germans without interference by the U.S. Fred returns with paper and pencil and hands it to Schlicke who proceeds to sketch a diagram.

Fred whispers to Hershberger, "You may want to step out, you have a call. Something about Kessler." With that Hershberger excuses himself.

Schlicke looks up from his rudimentary sketch and starts to explain the theory behind his drawing. "Proximity fuses are good for traditional bombs. Detonating an atomic bomb of either uranium or plutonium is different."

Fred nods, recalling what he heard about uranium and the U.S. efforts at Los Alamos after Alvarez. He is piecing it all together as Schlicke continues.

"Plutonium is more complicated to detonate than uranium. In order to achieve critical mass, an atom of plutonium has to be hit by a neutron that splits it, releasing energy and producing two neutrons." Here he uses the pencil to point at the paper where he has drawn a nucleus that now has two neutrons next to it. "Those two neutrons then slam into two more plutonium atoms, splitting them, releasing energy and creating four neutrons which release energy and create eight neutrons and so on until the chain reaction builds into an explosion."

"Ah," Fred understands. "So, the problem is sustaining the reaction?" he asks.

"Yes, that's one problem. Another challenge is simply having enough plutonium in the chamber, so that when the split atom releases neutrons, they will hit other plutonium atoms – and that will keep the reaction going."

"Then, of course, there is the larger problem I think our guys are grappling with," Fred says as he looks up from Schlicke's drawing. "How to start the process in the first place. Detonation."

"Precisely." Schlicke confirms. "There is a design I have been working on which uses multiple detonator shafts configured in a circle on the bomb. "

"Ventilation shafts?" Fred asks. "To vent radiation?"

"It might seem that way at first, but in fact, they are designed to allow light waves or infrared rays to enter the shaft. That is my theory, my prototype. A device using infrared light that could trigger multiple detonations simultaneously, basically at the speed of light."

Ingenious, Fred thinks as he concentrates on Schlicke's explanation and then encourages him to sketch out a diagram of what he just described.

In the next interrogation room, Henry Kolm is sitting down with Second Officer Karl Pfaff. He was released and sent to 1142. Pfaff is a young, good-looking officer who is tall, just over six feet, with a full head of dark hair. Henry can't help but rib him about his height on a submarine. Pfaff smiles and relaxes; just what Henry wants.

Henry casually asks, "Why were you detained in Portsmouth?"

"They suspected we were carrying uranium oxide in the metal containers on board, and in fact we were. When they unloaded the boat, they took the containers and stored them in a building near the wharf. Of course, they were concerned the containers were booby trapped," Pfaff reveals.

"Were they?"

Pfaff just smiles because there was booby-trapped cargo, just not this cargo.

"I didn't think so. At any rate, they sent me in to supervise the welder who was going to open the containers while your top officers stayed in a separate room." Pfaff didn't need to elaborate because Henry understood exactly what was happening.

"After it didn't explode, the top guys came out and inspected what was inside. They confirmed it was uranium and immediately made plans to take it elsewhere." Then he remembers something.

"There was one civilian in the group, a skinny man wearing a fedora. I asked who he was, the guy in the hat, and someone said it was Oppenheimer." Henry had heard his name in association with the Manhattan Project. He nods and Pfaff ends with, "There was about five hundred and forty kilograms of uranium oxide on board."

Henry acknowledges. "That's about twelve hundred pounds." He doesn't comment further and can only guess where that uranium is headed.

After talking with Karl Pfaff, Henry joins Rudy Pins because they are both assigned to General Ulrich Kessler. As soon as they lay eyes on him, they know they have their hands full. Kessler is a proud, stuffy Prussian and looks like every German general character in the movies, complete with Nazi swagger. He is very brusque and disagreeable, clinging to Nazism. Henry and Rudy start to work their magic and slowly the General softens up.

But Kessler is trying to be cagey and feels confident he can play these interrogators to get better treatment and a quick transfer back to Germany. They have him pegged and are having none of it. They know he is an opportunist and would say or do anything to manipulate them and his situation.

Kessler knows it is in his best interest to cooperate, but he is jockeying to position himself for the best outcome, denying he wanted to go to Argentina and insisting he lobbied to surrender off the coast of Florida. Rudy and Henry glance at each other, taking this with a grain of salt.

Henry is struggling with a bigger issue. Hershberger was given the directive to have the interrogation team find out specific information. They needed to determine which German general ordered the bombing of Amsterdam after the Netherlands surrendered. This was a war crime and if they can identify the responsible officer, they will be shipped to Nuremberg. When asked, Kessler said it wasn't him, he had nothing to do with it. It was a subordinate general named Heinrich Aschenbrenner.

"OK," Henry says, "We'll see about that." After the interview he and Rudy stand outside the building under a tree.

"Did you buy that stuff about Aschenbrenner?" he asks Rudy.

"Not for a minute."

"We have Aschenbrenner in custody. I'm going to get him transferred down here. We'll see what Kessler has to say then." He and Rudy smile at the impending fireworks.

It takes a couple of days, but Aschenbrenner is transferred to 1142. Henry interrogates him separately. Aschenbrenner is as easy-going and amiable as Kessler is difficult and arrogant. Of course, he blames Kessler for the bombing.

After a couple of weeks, Henry tells Kessler another officer of common rank will be sharing his cabin, and the interrogators all listen. Aschenbrenner will not be intimidated by his former commander, and they immediately start fighting about rank and seniority.

In the listening bunker, about twenty men huddled near the speakers, monitoring the rising voices, shaking their heads in disbelief at the ensuing argument. The Memovox turntable is whirring, etching the red vinyl while the listeners take notes.

Kessler: "Make no mistake, I am *your* superior."

Aschenbrenner: "Then tell them you ordered the bombing."

Kessler: "You will say and do what I tell you!"

This goes back and forth for a while with no real point, no resolution. The listeners begin to realize this is ridiculous and maybe the Generals suspect they are being monitored.

After forty-five minutes he's heard enough. "Get those guys out of there. They can plead their case in Nuremberg." With that, they are transferred out of 1142.

Henry is struck with the sheer stupidity of the pointless conversation. It would be proven at Nuremberg that Kessler did in fact order the bombing of Rotterdam after the Dutch surrendered and because of other atrocities both he and Aschenbrenner are sentenced to life in prison.

Fred is now interviewing several different PWs on numerous topics within his area of expertise. He speaks to the Luftwaffe pilot from U-234 who was supposed to reassemble the jet engines and train the Japanese pilots. He talks to radio technicians and radio navigation fellows about radar, sonar, and remote control. These advancements, added to what he and Heinz Schlicke talked about, have created a constant flow of new vocabulary. Everyone is trying to keep up and stay ahead of the new terms, new sciences, and new innovations.

That night at dinner, Fred and George sit with Henry discussing what they heard. "They rattle this stuff off and it feels like a whole new language, all new sciences are emerging. We need to keep up. All of us." Fred was honest about the learning curve.

"I know," Henry chimes in. "And their attitude! It's something. Just let them think you already know everything they're saying," he says with a wink. "I interviewed Rudolf Hess, Hitler's military advisor. He loves to play chess, so I indulge him every time we talk. He could tell I had an Austrian accent and mentioned vacationing in a small village in Austria named Turach Plateau. You could only reach this place by going up a 50-mile dirt road and when you get there, there are only 2 cabins for mountaineers. I asked him if he stayed at the Sieglerhof Hotel or the Seehotel Turach? You see, my father had taken us there for a couple of weeks one summer. Well, Hess's jaw dropped! He thought I had a dossier on every detail of his life and knew everything about him." He gives Fred a playful jab to the arm. "It's all perception."

Just then another solder, Leslie Wilson, slides into a chair with his dinner tray skimming to a stop and promptly challenges everyone. "Guess who gave us a ride this weekend?" Apparently, he had gone to New York for the weekend and was recounting the trip. When no one responds he answers his own question.

"Arno and me was thumbin' a ride into town, and we get picked up by Mrs. Eisenhower!" He wasn't sure what reaction he expected but he was met with a torrent of abuse.

"Get outta here!"

"You're crazy."

"Sure, sure, was Betty Grable with her?"

"Tell me another one!" The insults are flying.

151

"No, no, it was her I tell ya!' Leslie was embarrassed. "No, I'm tellin' ya it was Mrs. Eisenhower," then he turns, "Arno get over here."

Arno Mayer had been at the next table and pulls his chair over to join the conversation. "Tell 'em!" Leslie urged.

Arno leans in, almost in a conspiratorial tone and starts, "You know we aren't supposed to hitchhike." They all nod. "But if you remember last weekend, it was raining cats and dogs, the bus was late, and we have to catch the train out of Washington to New York."

"We think, who's going to pay any attention? So, we put our thumbs out and this very elegant car drives up with three ladies in it. We tell them we're going to Union Station and the driver says she can get us to Washington, not to Union Station but close. We told her we'd be infinitely grateful. The lady in the back squeezes into the front seat and we take the back."

"Yeah we were soaked by then, so of course the gals didn't want to sit next to us," Leslie admits.

Arno continues, "We start driving and they're talking and it's a nice conversation, then they decide they'll take us all the way to Union Station after all."

"Can you believe it!" Leslie shakes his head.

"Yeah, but how do you know it was Mrs. Eisenhower?" Henry asks.

"They called her Mamie." Leslie explained. Another round of insults laced with doubt and humor flew around the table; but Leslie feels the need to prove his story before the

152

brass hears about their hitchhiking adventure. He reasons that if it was Mamie Eisenhower and they weren't supposed to be hitchhiking, making a pre-emptive strike with a thank you note might kill two birds with one stone and head off any trouble.

After dinner Leslie writes a letter thanking Mrs. Eisenhower for her kind gesture and asks her to please confirm she had, indeed, picked up the two men on the side of the road during a rainstorm. Wilson sends it addressed to General Eisenhower, Chief of Staff, Pentagon.

Before the week is out, Sergeant Leslie Wilson and Private Arno Mayer are summoned to the Fort's CO's headquarters. Both men are afraid it is a reprimand, however, they are handed an envelope delivered by courier from General Eisenhower. The letter says that '*although Mamie is very busy, she was happy to verify that indeed she did pick up the two servicemen.*' The letter went on to explain they always like to pick up servicemen going to town and appreciated him taking the time to thank her. And that was that. Without a reprimand, Arno and Leslie determined it was OK for their hitchhiking to continue.

The next day Captain Hershberger calls Fred and George into the main building and tells them they were right about all the new terminology everyone is hearing. For no other reason than accurate interrogation, the powers that be requested his team put together a dictionary with descriptions and translations. He thinks Fred and George can handle it because of their backgrounds. The two agree and immediately start collaborating on a complete list of German terms. They not only get the dictionary done quickly but Fred takes it upon himself to compile a list of German slang to further help his co-interrogators.

Hershberger is very pleased with the speed and thoroughness of the collection, comprised of more than a thousand terms. He quickly routes it through the proper channels, gets it printed and distributed to all Fort Hunt interrogators. The Army also releases it for use in other interrogation facilities.

Fred's interviews with Heinz Schlicke continue through July, with more diagrams, more in-depth explanations of various technological advances and other useful information. Fred learns a great deal about detonation, the use of specific metals and infrared light.

Hershberger decides the information Fred is collecting might be helpful to the Manhattan Project. He carefully gathers what Fred has learned and quietly delivers this information to Vannevar Bush.

Operation Paperclip   Fort Strong, Boston June, 1945

Chapter 7

Operation Paperclip

Fort Strong, Boston Harbor, Massachusetts
June 1945

A group of seventeen soldiers from 1142 are heading to Boston. Among the team are Henry Kolm, Eric Kramer, Werner Gans, Peter Weiss, Leslie Wilson and Arno Mayer, along with two officers. Then an additional nine enlisted men are added to the contingent. They realize they will have their work cut out for them in Boston.

When Germany surrendered in May, an overwhelming number of German troops were forced to lay down their arms and give themselves up. There were German scientists and engineers scattered all over Germany who the Allies wanted, most notably the Peenemunde rocket scientists led by Werner von Braun.

Henry Kolm reports to General Clayton Bissel who is assistant Chief of Staff for Intelligence in the War Department and is known to "bend the rules" when necessary. Bissel knows there are hundreds of German scientists who will most likely be grabbed by Russia or England, thereby robbing the United States of the opportunity to acquire that intellectual advantage. General Bissel decides he wants those scientists in this country.

Had Roosevelt been alive, Bissel probably would've gotten the order; but as things stood, the State Department would not commit to bringing these Germans into the country.

Ultimately, Bissel decides to take matters into his own hands, illegally grabbing wanted scientists and holding them until they can gain legal entry. He talks to each soldier who will be involved in this operation individually to assess their level of commitment. He tells Henry he was willing to risk his own life on the battlefield and would now risk going to jail if it served the best interest of the country. Henry agrees and is now part of the mission.

The 1142 soldiers are on their way to Long Island in Boston Harbor, which is home to Fort Strong. General Bissel instructs them to create a secure, temporary holding facility for at least a couple hundred incoming German rocket scientists and engineers, a challenge well-suited for these men.

Germany is in chaos after its defeat, so Bissell sends a second detachment to Schweinfurt, Germany, to prepare a holding base with housing and even a school, where the families of these scientists would be safely held under the protection of the United States. Bissel's plan was to bring scientists through Fort Strong through Boston Harbor or through Squantum Naval Base. No customs or immigration officer was to know anything about this operation.

When the 1142 contingent arrives in Boston, they make their way to Long Island. They survey the land and immediately realize how much work needs to be done and that a sizable workforce will have to be assembled to complete the job. The island has a lighthouse on a hill, overgrown with shoulder-high weeds. There are two Civil War era barracks, a partially collapsed dock and a well that needs a new pump. Three sailors are protecting the entire island using sonar to secure Boston Harbor.

After a few days of surveying the island, they have a "to-do" list to accomplish their mission. They will need to renovate the old barracks into individual rooms, restore the kitchen and mess hall to usable condition, repair the dock, and mow the weeds, all under a shroud of secrecy to keep from exposing the operation.

They quickly realize any soldier who guards these prisoners will know who is here. The identity of these prisoners must not be compromised. U.S. soldiers will eventually go on leave and could talk or let something slip. Henry reasons the only workforce they can trust are prisoners. The team selects a dozen reliable guards from 1142 and forty to fifty German PWs from a nearby camp.

Henry has a list of the skilled laborers they need and makes his choices from the prisoners: two professional hotel cooks, two bakers, two tailors, a barber, several tough construction workers, a handful of carpenters, a plumber, an electrician, a locksmith, a physician, and a few office personnel fluent in English, *just like Noah's Ark*, he chuckles to himself. But there is one crucial position missing, a typist.

Henry considers himself a good typist, but he tips his hat to the skills of one prisoner, Hans Gass. This man is a professional typist and had been a personal aide to a German general. Not only that, but come to find out Hans Gass was the European typing champion. Henry is delighted at his good fortune. Gass would prove invaluable to the mission: plus, he gets along right away with Leslie Wilson - always a good sign.

The team gets to work renovating the island, and per usual, things start moving quickly. After Hitler's suicide in May, reports come in that Werner von Braun, his brother Magnus and about 100 scientists left Peenemunde, traveling south to Mittelwerk, another rocket plant in Bavaria. The British had bombed the Peenemunde facility, forcing the Germans to move the rocket program underground. Von Braun's scientists were holed up in a place called Haus Ingeburg, a ski resort located near the Bavarian plant.

Von Braun had broken his arm in a car crash and was still in a cast when he sent his brother, Magnus, to find some Americans. They wanted to surrender to America, not Russia. Magnus got on his bicycle, found an American infantry unit and von Braun's whole team surrendered. Over the next months, the group is shuttled around Europe, ending up in Nordhausen where they wait. They are offered a deal. Come to the United States voluntarily as contract workers for a designated period of time, and their families will be housed and protected until they can be reunited. The scientists agree and by August, they are bound for the United States.

In early August the United States successfully dropped two bombs on Japan. The Trinity test in July was successful and the Manhattan Project team figured out, almost at the eleventh hour, how to detonate the plutonium bomb. President Truman struggled mightily with the decision whether or not to use it. Ultimately, he reasons that unleashing this terrible weapon would, in the end, save lives. Once the decision was made, the targets were chosen.

"Little Boy" is the uranium bomb with the shotgun-style detonation and is designated for the first target, Hiroshima. The bomb was dropped from the Enola Gay at 8:15 am on August 6th, 1945. The second bomb, "Fat Man," is the round plutonium bomb that was dropped on Nagasaki from the Bockscar at 11:02 am on August 9th. Had Emperor Hirohito not encouraged his country to continue fighting after the first bomb, the second may never have been dropped. However, to end the war, the second bomb was released.

First estimates set casualties in Hiroshima at 80,000, the number of people who would have died instantly from the blast. In the second attack on Nagasaki, instantaneous casualties were estimated at 40,000. The death toll from the aftermath of radiation and widespread destruction is estimated to climb to a final count of over 200,000.

On August 15,1945, Japan surrendered, and on September 2, the formal surrender agreement was signed aboard the U.S. battleship Missouri, anchored in Tokyo Bay. The war is indeed over, but the 1142 soldiers still have work to do.

Once Japan surrenders, Von Braun and his group are transported to the U.S. on a troop ship. The boat arrives at Boston Harbor during a terrible storm; in fact, there has been five straight days of rain. Their transport stops at Nixes Mate, which is nothing more than an outcropping of rock sticking out of the ocean. It was famous for prisoner or pirate executions where their lifeless bodies would be left. The U.S. Government eventually bought the island, built a retaining wall, and added a beacon. If nothing else, Nixes Mate is completely isolated.

As the scientists wait onboard the ship, pitching mercilessly back and forth, the storm barely lets up and most are seasick. The pilot boat is unable to get to them, so Henry and his team commandeer a whaling boat. Captain Corky's old but still seaworthy vessel stinks of cod. As the storm rages, the German scientists carefully disembark the boat using a boatswain's ladder and climb aboard the smelly whaler. The transfer is inauspicious to say the least. They make it to Fort Strong despite the unrelenting storm and land on the rickety and somewhat unstable dock. All the men make it off the fishing boat, through the rain to the main building. Once inside, they dry off and immediately feel better. The mood lightens and they enjoy cold beer and hot cider. This truly was a most unusual method of relocating Nazi scientists into the United States of America.

The 1142 team has done an amazing job setting up the facility. They have typewriters, cabinets, a teletype machine, mimeograph machines, desks, first aid equipment, kitchen equipment, a barber chair, record player, linens, government-issued fatigues and uniforms, mess tables, a panel truck and even a 16 mm motion picture projector and screen. Their carpenters turned the barracks into a hotel, which the first guests nicknamed "Haus der Deutschen Wissenschaft," *The House of German Science.*

Other prominent German scientists are approached and convinced to take America's offer. One famous naval architect, Professor Ernst Schneider, was reluctant; he didn't want to leave his life's work. He was the co-inventor of the Voith-Schneider cycloidal ship propeller, an omni-directional thruster. The Americans had intelligence that the Russians planned to pick him up in the middle of the night. Once he realized the danger he was in, Schneider reluctantly agreed to come to America and an engineering battalion gathered his technical records, his library and key equipment, removing him in the nick of time. The Russians arrived to find an empty house and Schneider ended up at Fort Strong.

More groups of scientists arrive at the Boston facility. There was the Mercedes-Benz engineering team who designed the huge V-12 engines that powered the assault boat fleet which invaded Norway. They'd modified their engine designs, worked out bugs in the bearings they used and ended up with a large, dependable diesel engine the United States Army was anxious to install in military vehicles, tanks and ships.

By the time the Peenemunde scientists arrive, there are nearly three hundred scientists on site. The locals think it is a field hospital.

Each scientist, now considered an enemy alien or illegal immigrant, is interviewed at great length by Arno, Leslie, or Henry to determine their backgrounds and areas of expertise. Later, George Mandel is sent up to Fort Strong to lend a hand.

Back in Washington, D.C., there is a new program in development, and Werner von Braun is considered the first candidate. The program is called Operation Overcast, and it provides a vehicle for the government, the Joint Intelligence Objectives Agency, and the OSS, (which will become the CIA) to fast-track the citizenship process of people who are deemed desirable. Operation Overcast also allows for the families of the desirables to be included in the process.

The program is set up for temporary, limited military custody and contract work. Truman is briefed on the idea sometime in August. He eventually signs off, allowing applications for permanent residency and employment; but with one stipulation. No active Nazis or Nazi supporters will be allowed to stay in America.

The President's directive means that some of the most important German scientists wanted by the JIOA and OSS, would not be eligible. Nevertheless, officials within these agencies decide to independently bypass the Presidential directive by basically whitewashing incriminating information like Nazi involvement from the backgrounds of each of the people they want.

There is a ranking system in place for immigrants, numbered from one to five - five being a strict Nazi who would most likely be headed to Nuremberg if released. Henry and the team interview each scientist and type up their dossiers, including a ranking number. Most of the Germans score one or two, low level party members, not die-hard Nazis. However, the 1142 men did classify some scientists as threes and fours. This proved challenging because if the higher ups still wanted these men, their grades would have to be lowered, their dossiers and backgrounds changed to meet the requirements.

Washington reviews each resume and deletes or alters questionable background information thereby dropping higher rankings, from perhaps a four, to an acceptable grade, like a two. The changes to that scientist's background are then typed up as an addendum to their dossiers and sent back attached with a paperclip. This dossier and attachment will accompany the scientist wherever they are placed.

Henry 's first encounter with von Braun sets the tone for his interrogation. Werner von Braun was a very proud man. With a "von" in his name, Henry knows he either came from nobility or his family owned land. At any rate, Henry finds him very well-educated with an aura of aristocracy about him.

Henry starts by asking about his work with rockets and missiles. Von Braun is especially proud that he developed the V-1 and V-2 rockets and was most unapologetic for what these rockets cost in human life. He tells Henry that he began developing this weaponry back in 1930 because it was a line of defense not forbidden by the Treaty of Versailles. As he developed more sophisticated weapons, they had to move the testing site outside the city, and eventually built the facility at Peenemunde, the tip of an island that juts into the Baltic Sea. He explains how the V-2 missile was more of a rocket, a long-distance weapon, powered by a jet engine and could travel at the speed of sound. It went up, almost to the edge of space, then fell back to earth at supersonic speed.

Von Braun continued, "I must admit, the V-2 wasn't necessarily the most accurate, but sometimes the damage can be more, shall I say, psychological, causing greater fear. I was working on a longer-range rocket, one that could possibly reach the United States. I just ran out of time." He said this with a smile as a verbal nudge to what he could have done. "I think there is a great future in what we can accomplish with rockets and going to space," he concludes.

Henry listens, trying to be impassive. Werner von Braun, the scientist of deadly rockets, was now talking about going to space and doing it for the same country, on the same side as Henry. It was now Henry's job to make that happen.

Henry knew von Braun was a card-carrying Nazi party member who was also SS and had been identified in uniform

166

standing with Hitler. Henry had heard rumors von Braun used prisoner laborers in his factories at Peenemunde and Nordhousen. He typed up all the background information in von Braun's dossier himself, ranking him a five knowing he was closer to a six, and sent it off to Washington. It doesn't take long before the von Braun dossier is back in his hands, complete with a paperclip of "updated" information which no longer contains certain details about his past activities and allegiances. His grade on his official record is within the acceptable range and now he can be admitted into the United States.

Protocol at 1142 determined that a morale officer be assigned to each person or group, and Arno Mayer was assigned to the Peenemunde scientists. A group of lower ranked PWs are sent back to Fort Hunt and Arno accompanies them by bus.

At the same time, George is sent up to Boston to help with the interviews. It is December and George misses his friend. He writes to Fred asking when he might join them. Unfortunately, Fred was not assigned to Fort Strong which was too bad because the interrogators could have used his expertise. Fred did share some good news; he made sergeant and Hershberger was now a major.

Arno arrives back at 1142 with the scientists and is glad to be back in familiar surroundings. It is getting close to Christmas and some of the men want to go into town to buy gifts to send back to their wives. Arno arranges a shopping trip to Lansburgh's, a large department store in the Washington, D.C. area.

December weather in Washington can be quite cold and the only coats the PWs have are the ones they wore when they surrendered - dark leather, Nazi style kidskin overcoats. Arno is mortified when he stops to look at the group he is about to take into town. If that isn't bad enough, the Germans pull out Tyrolean, Alpine hats and stick them on their heads.

What can he do? Arno is suddenly paralyzed with fear. Does he dare take these men out in public dressed like this? He quickly offers them U.S. Army coats and hats, but they refuse. They are quite comfortable and want to wear their own clothes. But like a good morale officer, Arno dutifully yields, loads his German charges onto a bus and heads downtown for an afternoon of shopping.

They return after nightfall and Arno looks like he's been through the mill and back. He slumps into an open chair and proceeds to recount the ordeal to his appalled and at the same time, amused fellow soldiers.

"They stuck out like sore thumbs!" was his opening line. "Those stupid hats! And those coats!" He shudders at the reactions they got from downtown shoppers.

"We went to a nice department store," Arno begins. "In fact, it was a Jewish department store," he points out for irony.

"You know I don't think they realize; *we* are Jewish!" Arno says in exasperation referring to his German charges.

"They almost blew our cover! Of all things, they wanted to buy underwear for their wives back in Germany. I had to interpret this request for them." By now, Arno is red-faced and embarrassed, prompting his audience to snicker more.

"The lady behind the counter holds up silk panties, and these guys ask if there were any with long legs, made of wool – because of the harsh winters. Of course, the department store didn't have that!" The men can no longer stifle their laughter.

"The poor woman behind the counter was very confused, but still she asked what sizes they needed? At this point the Germans pulled out their slide rules, trying to convert centimeters to inches to figure this out!" Now there is unabashed laughter.

One of the other soldiers regains his composure long enough to ask, "How do you measure for ladies' underwear with a slide rule? Did they end up buying anything?"

Arno is young and unmarried, so the embarrassment of this whole ordeal turns him bright crimson. "Yes, yes, but we paid and got out of there. By then, the clerk got suspicious, and I saw her call the department store guard, so I shoved them out the front door to the bus as fast as I could!" Arno rubs his head, wishing his cheeks would cool down as he endured the good-natured ribbing. "To add insult to injury, now it's my job to get these things back to Germany!" he lamented. In the end, Arno uses a military pouch for the delicate unmentionables.

The war has officially been over for several months and many of the dossiers from Washington arrive at Fort Strong with revisions attached using a paperclip. It is determined the scientists can now be moved inside the country to designated facilities and programs. Some are assigned to the Aberdeen Proving Ground, north of Baltimore and some go to the Signal Corps while others go to Huntsville, Alabama. Any of the Germans with rocket experience are sent directly to Fort Bliss, Texas, including von Braun and seven of his fellow scientists.

There is much talk of new candidates for Operation Overcast, and Heinz Schlicke lands near the top of the list. The vernacular is changing, and the soldiers start referring to the program as Operation Paperclip, because of the attachments. Since Fred is handling Schlicke, he begins the paperwork. Another interrogator, John Gunther Dean, is Schlicke's morale officer. He too has become friends with the scientist and is charged with retrieving Schlicke's family from Germany.

Dean has orders to take prisoners back to Europe, then travel to the city of Keil in the British Zone. Once there he collects Schlicke's wife and two children. Dean is traveling in civilian clothes which allows for more flexibility during this tenuous trip; but it's risky. An American serviceman caught out of uniform could be considered a spy.

Dean has experience and easily manages to navigate Schlicke's family out of the country without incident. The Navy specifically wants Schlicke for his microwave and infrared expertise so they arrange for him and his family to be sent to Canada so they can legally immigrate to the United States. In return, Schlicke is contracted to work for the Navy for the next four years and is assigned to the radar division at the Naval center at Sands Point on Long Island.

The day Schlicke is being transferred out, he and Fred wait outside on the same gravel drive where Fred arrived over a year ago. Fred has spent nine months interrogating one of the most important German engineering minds to come to Fort Hunt. As they stand under towering oaks speckled with golden hues of fall, they face each other with mutual respect. The transport is rounding the drive and it's time to say goodbye.

"It has been very, how shall I say, enlightening, talking to you these past few months," Fred tells Schlicke with a smile. Schlicke knows his knowledge of cutting-edge sciences was over the heads of many of his captors.

"But you paid attention," he ribbed Fred with a grin, "and you seemed to catch on to my lectures very quickly."

Both men are now smiling and grasp each other's hands. There are no hard feelings. "Good luck in Sands Point. You will like Long Island." Fred tells him.

"Thank you. Good luck to you too." Schlicke replies, grateful and optimistic. Then he digs into his duffle bag, "I want to give you something," he hands a hardcover to Fred. "This is a book I had on the boat, on U-234. It's not much, but I want you to have it. I thought you might remember me with this."

Fred is genuinely moved and takes the book, noticing the charred edges. "Thank you, Heinz." He says looking directly at his charge. Schlicke turns and gets on the transport with other men who are about to start new lives in America.

A few weeks go by without much activity. Some of the soldiers not yet discharged are sitting around the mess hall after dinner, enjoying a second cup of coffee. One of the guys happens to comment on how effortlessly the PWs and their families are folding into American society. It seems rocket scientists have a straight ticket through immigration. That's when von Braun's name came up.

One of the men involved in his transfer to Texas comments on his current situation. "Yeah, von Braun is constantly making a stink about wanting to get his family over here. Thing is, he's not married. It's his parents he wants; they're being held in southern Germany, Bavaria." The soldier adds, "von Braun is always comparing his situation to the men who are married, with wives and kids. Of course, he wants special permission to go back to Germany and get his parents."

"Seems fair," another soldier pipes in.

The first soldier continues, "Well, that's what the brass says, and they give him permission. And get this, when he gets back to Germany, von Braun up and marries his cousin; and then the four of them, the new wife, him and his parents, all head back to Texas. It's an entourage!"

The men are chuckling at this turn of events and Arnold Kohn decides to jump in. "During this whole process, one of von Braun's scientists sent for his mistress instead of his wife. Once his wife learned she was left behind, well, she had something to say about that." This time the men enjoyed a genuine laugh.

The 1142 soldiers had interrogated close to six hundred scientists on the island, and were enjoying a respite, after months of intense work. Their efforts proved immensely useful, but they are still missing valuable documents like certain drawings of the V1 and V2 rockets, additional plans for more advanced rockets and rocket fuel formulas. Henry Kolm has been asking about this list and finally has an update.

"You guys know we've been after the rocket intel for some time, right?" Everyone mumbles agreement. "Our ground team went to Peenemunde and found a couple of guys who said they saw soldiers take all the documents to a salt mine and bury them." Several of the men stopped talking and turned around, now interested in Henry's new information.

"The ground team finds this old salt miner who knows exactly what they'd done." Henry is relishing the story. "We sent a couple of engineer battalions to the salt mine to see what they could do. They dug out the opening to the mine and found these meter-cubed armor plates that had been welded together. Inside the cubes were all the documents. They got 'em out just as the Russians pulled up cause the Russians had the same tip!"

A collective sigh of relief streams through the group and the men return to their other conversations and coffee.

Things at Fort Hunt slow down considerably over the next few months, and personnel start to clear out. More PWs are given the opportunity to work for the government and thereby be absorbed into American citizenry. U.S. soldiers are transferred or discharged and another smaller, select group of Germans comes in.

Reinhard Gehlen is the notorious spymaster of German military intelligence, the security service of Himmler's SS and senior intelligence officer on the Eastern Front. He is a diminutive, thin man with dark piercing eyes and a history of utilizing Nazi strong-armed tactics to gain information. In April, just as Allied troops were closing in on Berlin, Gehlen decided to cut his losses and make a deal with the Americans. He is cunning and ruthless and uses his position and resume to negotiate what he wants. When he arrives at Fort Hunt, his reputation precedes him. He may prove useful to the United States, but he is an unsavory character, to put mildly.

This was someone Fred knew nothing about; but if anyone could manage this prisoner, it would be Rudy Pins. Pins is assigned as Gehlen's morale officer.

"What's up with this guy?" he asks Rudy as they walk to the mess hall.

"Gehlen? He's a survivor." Rudy summarizes. "He started planning his surrender to the Americans back in 1944. He had microfilm files on the Soviets buried in steel drums in the Alpine Redoubt, Bavaria. When he surrendered, he used the steel drums as a bargaining chip. The information he had on the Red Army, along with strategic, political intel on the Soviet Union proved to be quite extensive; something we could use. And now he's here."

"War makes strange bedfellows," was all Fred could say.

"Well, he must have something we want because Eisenhower never wanted to deal with German Officers, but Gehlen is different. He's meeting with Admiral Leahy, Bill Donovan, and Allan Dulles, the OSS, and a handful of War Department people. They're supposedly striking some kind of agreement; then, I think he'll go back to Germany."

Many of the soldiers stationed at 1142 are reaching the end of their enlistment and are being moved to Fort Meade for discharge, to other assignments or on to help with the trials at Nuremberg. Very few remain.

A new service is being formed inside the U.S. government called the Central Intelligence Agency, or CIA. The 1142 interrogators get word that the higher ups are looking for recruits. Who better to staff this new department than seasoned intelligence personnel from the MIS-Y program. Rudy Pins, Fred Michel, George Mandel and Angus Thurmer are approached, one at a time. George wants to continue his schooling in higher education, and Fred wants to get a job in the private sector so he can marry his girl, Lucille. Rudy and Angus, however, give it serious consideration and decide to join the new department.

Uncovering the Past   Louisville, Kentucky May 30, 2006

Chapter 8

Uncovering the Past

Louisville, Kentucky
May 30, 2006

Cynthia and Lucille are riveted to Fred's admissions and explanations. In his career with the military, they knew he was involved with initiatives he could never talk about. Finding out that during World War II he was involved with this branch of military intelligence, welled Cynthia with a pride she had never before felt. Brandon was still talking as Lucille glanced at her daughter and they shared a knowing look. Fred was their hero.

Brandon thinks he has a broad knowledge of WWII and is somewhat familiar with the capture and importance of U-234, but Fred's detail brings the incident and the importance of it to life.

Brandon envies Henry Kolm who was able to board the legendary submarine and talk candidly with its captain. After Fred introduced Brandon to his first assigned interrogation, Heinz Schlicke, a name completely unfamiliar, Brandon can only imagine what it was like to be on the cutting edge of world changing technologies and weaponry. One thing became apparent, there were more moving parts to the Manhattan Project than Brandon realized.

"I had the name of Jack Alberti, but I didn't realize in what capacity he was involved. Did he speak German?" Brandon asked.

"No, I don't think so, I really can't remember. But Schlicke spoke English quite well."

"Did you work on the book with him?" Brandon asked.

"No, no he worked on it with the Navy people, but Hershberger and I did interrogate him from maybe June to September. After I was discharged, I went to work for a small company called Melpar. As a supervisor, one of my responsibilities was to help get Navy contract work. One day I found myself in Sands Point and decided to look up Schlicke." Fred smiles. "He was sitting at his desk, and I came up and tapped him on the shoulder," Fred makes a motion of tapping with his hand. "He turned around and was quite surprised! He sure didn't expect to see me but recognized me right away." Fred laughs remembering the look on Heinz's face.

"He had this beard, not a full beard but a small beard apparently to blend in with the Navy environment, but he looked like a typical German submarine commander." Then Fred chuckles, "You know he was working on what we now call stealth technology."

"Really? What year did this reunion happen?"

"It had to be....let's see, 1950," Fred says. "Shortly after that he completed his service for the Navy and went to work

180

for a company in Milwaukee, the Allen-Bradley Company. His specialty was contact materials for electrical contacts, and he developed ferrite-based electronic components. He ended up writing another book called Electromagnetic Compossibility. After that I lost track of him." Fred finishes.

Then, as an afterthought he says, "You know I still have the book he gave me from the sub, from U-234. It was a little charred from a fire. I'll have to show it to you."

"Yes, I'd like to see that," Brandon can't help but be impressed. "And who else did you speak with from U-234?"

Fred finishes the list of PWs he and Hershberger interrogated: the Luftwaffe pilot, the radio technicians, and radio navigation fellows who were to set up communications between Berlin and Tokyo.

"Let's talk about other prisoners. Weren't we also interested in German aircraft and rocketry?"

"Yes, very much so."

"Did you interrogate anyone from that area?"

Fred describes how 1142 soldiers interrogated scientists at Fort Strong in Boston harbor and processed many rocket scientists, including Werner von Braun and his group.

At the mention of his name, Cynthia perks up, "Von Braun? He was at 1142?"

"No, no, he was at Fort Strong in Boston Harbor. George went up but I didn't." Fred clears things up explaining that when some of the scientists were transferred to Fort Hunt, his job became processing Operation Paperclip scientists.

"Operation Paperclip. What is that?" Brandon asks. Fred is surprised he isn't familiar with the program. Fred went on to explain how each scientist had a dossier and revised information attached with a paperclip.

"So, if the person was valuable enough, we grabbed them first, to keep them out of the hands of the Russians or Japanese, and made them citizens regardless of what they had done?" Cynthia summarizes. "Even being a Nazi?"

"Yes, that's correct." Fred acknowledges.

"Well, what d'ya know." Cynthia slumps back in her chair and crosses her arms.

"Is that the way von Braun was brought into this country?" Lucille asks. She remembers a striking German scientist at the forefront of NASA's space program and all the praises showered on him. She is trying to reconcile that image with what she was just told of how he had gotten citizenship.

"You know he lived in the same area of Alexandria as Werner and us." Lucille realized with a jolt.

Fred knew von Braun had also been an SS officer but chose not to disclose that detail, then remembers, "After the war we found he had a state-of-the-art wind tunnel which the Allies managed to dismantle and bring here. It was used for years afterwards in our space program."

"And you mentioned you worked on a dictionary of some kind?"

"Yes, George Mandel and I worked together. It was published by the intelligence division of the War Department.

I may have a copy here," and he turns to Lucille who takes the cue.

"I think it's with your other papers, I'll find it," She got up and headed to the closet in the second bedroom to retrieve the document.

"Our work was unique at the time because it not only included the translation of each word, but also a detailed explanation of its meaning." Fred says of the dictionary.

"This was towards the end of the war. Did you then finish out your time at Fort Hunt?"

"No, I was transferred to Fort Meade before being discharged."

"What happened to Captain Hershberger?"

"I think he returned to civilian life."

"I'd like to find other vets if they are still living. I've jotted down the names you've mentioned." Brandon looks over his notes.

Fred is ready to help, but also knows Brandon is facing obstacles. "You may or may not know that a lot of military papers and personnel records were lost in a fire in St Louis," Fred cautions. "That was quite a while back."

"Yes, yes, I did know about that. Eighty percent of the U.S. Army records from WWII were destroyed in that fire."

"Yes, including a lot of the records of people I mentioned so you may have a hard time tracking them down."

Just then Lucille returns not only with a copy of the Dictionary, but also with Fred's list of German slang words.

"This is great!" Brandon says as he takes the pages.

"What did I miss?" Lucille asks.

"The St. Louis fire in '73," Fred answers. "A lot of Army records were lost. No sprinkler system or smoke detectors. Much of what was destroyed were original documents with no copies or backups. It's inexcusable, inexcusable," he says as he shakes his head. Fred is thinking about all the men with whom he served at 1142.

"Do you think you might be able to find any of them?" Fred asks, referring to the veterans.

As a twenty-something, Brandon had assumed his octogenarian host was the only Fort Hunt vet still alive; but now, he is beginning to rethink this. "We can certainly try. Do you have someone in mind?"

"How about George Mandel? We kept in touch for a little while after the war. Maybe we can find him?" Fred suggests.

"Sure, I will do a search tonight. If you have any other names, besides those you've already mentioned, I'll see who I can find."

With that Fred remembers a list of promotions he'd kept. He asks Lucille to get the binder with his war papers and Cynthia jumps up to help her mom. Cynthia admires her mom's organizational abilities and considers her the curator of the Michel family history; but she also didn't like her mother jumping every time her father needed something. *A different generation*, she thinks.

Lucille has all memorabilia filed in boxes by year. Each box has binders, also labeled by year. The binders contain plastic sleeves with precious papers, photos, letters, and other keepsakes safely protected, and of course, dated.

Basically, Lucille knows where everything is. "I'd rather get it than have Fred dig through one box," she tells Cynthia as they reach the doorway.

The 1940's box was already out of the closet and Lucille knows exactly where she is going. She opens the lid and points to the four-inch thick "war" binder, which Cynthia grabs.

"God, what's in this thing?" she groans as she lifts the overstuffed organizer. Once she picks it up, it's definitely bulkier and heavier than she realized.

"I catalogued everything your father gave me, especially anything from the war. You know him. If nothing else, he's thorough," she said, leading Cynthia back to the living room.

"Yes, I know my father all too well," Cynthia complains as she trails behind. She reaches her father and places the 1942-1946 folder in his lap.

Brandon can't help but notice the tiny dates written neatly on small white labels placed near the corner. "Impressive," Brandon tells Lucille with a smile.

"I like to keep things organized," she admits.

The National Archives lost a good one in her," Cynthia thinks as she takes her seat.

Fred balances the binder as he carefully flips through the yellowed pages. There are old letters from his parents,

185

correspondence from his mother and other relatives. Everything has been methodically saved. Then Fred turns another page and Brandon sees a certificate of some kind dated March 1946.

"Is that from Camp Ritchie?" he asks.

"No, this is a list of promotions, from Master Sergeant to Technical Sergeant and the grades, one through four." Fred hands the page to Brandon. "These were soldiers I served with. You can see the date, 4 March 1946. This was after the war but before I was discharged."

"Mind if I make a copy? There's a Kinkos near the motel." he remembers. Fred nods permission as he flips another page to find a couple of old photos, including the famous, or now infamous poolside shot, which he passes to Brandon. There are various letters and some military correspondence with a marker indicating the exact spot to return the Dictionary.

"Fred, do you remember who came with you from Camp Ritchie to Fort Hunt?"

Fred turns over more pages until he finds a discolored document with a list of names. The aging paper has Army letterhead, and the typed names are missing tails on the T's and half formed bellies of some S's, a tell-tale sign of Army issued Royal typewriters.

"This is a roster I kept of the guys who came to 1142 at the same time I did. I think this is the list from Camp Ritchie." Fred scans the list, reading it half to himself, half out loud.

"... Werner Gans, Peter Weiss, Henry Kolm, Eric Kramer, George Mandel, Arno Mayer. They all arrived with me in 1945." Fred looks up and offers the paper to Brandon who takes it and scans the names.

"If you don't mind, I'd like to copy both lists."

Fred nods permission as the clock starts to chime. Lucille glances at her husband, aware the hour is getting late and reliving these memories has taken up the whole afternoon.

"We've covered a lot of ground today," she says as much to Brandon as to Fred. "Let's take a break for now and pick this up tomorrow." They can tell by her tone it wasn't a suggestion.

"Yes, I think that would be good." Fred admits. "I am getting tired."

Brandon looks up, "Sure, sure, we can start again in the morning."

Fred hands the binder back to Lucille who places it on the table. Cynthia eyes it, thinking she will have a closer look later, on her own.

Brandon packs up the recorder and his papers and realizes he feels a kinship growing. Talking to Fred has been like talking to his own grandfather. What started as a mission to gather information about Fort Hunt, is turning into friendship, wanting to get to know Fred better.

Brandon shakes hands with Fred and Lucille as Cynthia rises to walk him out. She pauses at the door watching Lucille lead Fred down the hall for a short nap before dinner. She catches Brandon at the threshold and tells him, "I had no idea!

I had no idea what he did during the war, who he interrogated – that he even was an interrogator! *We* had no idea," she motions towards her mom.

Brandon appreciates the candor and the impact of uncovering such deeply private experiences concerning their family. "I know, it's overwhelming. It's a lot to take in and a lot to understand in one day."

"I'm still trying to wrap my head around most of it. I knew, literally, bits and pieces of what dad went through fleeing Germany as a kid, settling here, his career, but this is so much more than I ever could've imagined. Do you think we can find anyone else?" Cynthia was starting to grasp how big this could be if other soldiers were still alive.

"We'll find out, I guess," Brandon admits. "Your dad is the only person we've found and thank goodness he finally agreed to meet with me." Brandon is now feeling indebted.

"He's been incredible, really. I'll go over these lists tonight and search for George." Then he pauses and admits to Cynthia what he's been thinking. "I knew he was uncomfortable breaking his oath, but I think he's slowly realizing the importance of talking about the war. His story, the story of Fort Hunt or 1142, well, it's never been told - and it needs to be."

"The operative word here is slowly." Cynthia wryly adds, which brings a small laugh. "If you do end up finding other soldiers, I would really love to talk to their families. I think we'd have a lot in common."

"First I have to locate them *then* convince them to talk to me," Brandon is still doubtful he'll find anyone. "I'll start with George and see."

Cynthia gives approval with a smile, and they agree to resume tomorrow morning around ten o'clock.

As Brandon walks to his car, he is tired yet excited. He has just interviewed one of the guys who lived it. He remembers the stories his own grandfather told and how he could bring his military experiences to life. What started out as a project to gather information for roadside signs has turned into a hunt for veterans who were secret heroes. He wants to learn their story. He feels he owes it to them and to the country.

Lucille comes out of the bedroom knowing her daughter will be a firehose of questions directed at her. But she has questions of her own. Each collapse into their favorite spots, Cynthia on the couch grabbing a pillow to hug and her mom settles into her cushioned blue barrel chair that seems to wrap around her.

Cynthia gathers herself then begins. "I'm still processing the fact that dad never told us any of this. I mean, I know, he was military, and he couldn't, but this is big. What he did was," here she searches for a word, "important! This is important information and dad was part of it! Have you ever heard some of these names before? Like his bunkmate, George Mandel?"

"Well George, yes. And the letter from Nuremberg," Lucille motions to the binder, "from Rudy Pins. But the other men he mentioned today, no. Even Carl Hertz when he came to visit - I knew the basics, that he was a scientist your father knew, but I never got the whole story – this story," Lucille admits.

"And what about this Operation Paperclip stuff? What's that all about?" Cynthia is trying to come to terms with giving Nazis a pass into this country when so many today struggle to gain citizenship. "I guess 60 years later after living through the Cold War, I get it, but wow, I'm not sure how I would've felt at the time."

"Me neither." Lucille agrees. "I'm glad I didn't know about a lot of this."

Lucille's thoughts are drifting to her husband and how very tired he looked by the end of the interview. "Listen, let your father sleep and don't hound him after dinner tonight," she cautions."

"And what about this oath he took?" Cynthia could see this was the crux of their ignorance. "I have to give it to dad for never breaking it." She looked at her mom with a smile, "but then again, that's dad."

"If he took an oath, his lips were sealed. That's why he never told me about it or the fact that he interrogated Nazis." She looks at Cynthia, "When Brandon called, I can see now why he was so conflicted."

Cynthia sees for the first time in a long time the number of years etched on her mother's face. She sees the worry her mother has for her husband. Lucille has weathered many challenges with Fred. The war, their families, his career, their moves and now this. Cynthia realizes that what she is seeing in her mother's eyes and in her furrowed brow is just how much she loves her husband.

"It looks like no one else said anything either. I mean if it weren't for declassified documents, and Brandon being so persistent, we may never have known."

"We'll let this rest until morning," Lucille resigns herself. "I know your father will always do the honorable thing, the right thing. I love him for that, and I do understand," she is processing. "It's just a lot to find out about after all these years. And he had to keep this to himself. That's a lot to ask, but if anyone could keep that secret, it's your father!"

This brings a knowing smile to both women. Then Cynthia says, "I told Brandon to come back around ten tomorrow morning."

"That's fine," Lucille takes a deep breath and glances at the clock. "I'd best start dinner," she says as she rises. Cynthia pops up to follow, "I'll help. Pork chops?"

"Of course, just the way your father likes them," Lucille says half joking.

"I'll start the potatoes."

Brandon arrives back at his motel room after a brief stop at Kinko's. He carefully copied all the delicate pages and photographs Lucille entrusted him, placing the new copies in a folder on top of the originals, and sliding everything back into his briefcase.

He orders a pizza and decides to change out of his uniform before it arrives. Once he's comfortable, he walks out to grab a coke from the vending machine and intercepts the pizza guy.

Back inside his room, he pops open the Coke and relaxes with a warm slice. Leaning back, he thinks about everything he's heard today. Could Fred be right? Could one of his old friends still be around? More importantly, if he does find this George Mandel, would he be reluctant to talk, just like Fred? Brandon reasons that using Fred's name might give him an edge that could convince George to open up. Then again, if he does find George, maybe he won't be as stubborn as Fred.

Brandon starts a second slice but can't resist the urge to get on his computer. He wipes his hands and does a quick Google search for George Mandel. He almost chokes on his Coke when Dr. H. George Mandel, professor at George Washington University, Department of Pharmacology and Physiology immediately pops up. He is the right age and in the right field of study, plus he immigrated from Berlin in 1937. *This has got to be him,* Brandon thinks. Brandon finishes his second slice while he reads about George's accomplishments, then contemplates a third slice before realizing he should check in with Vince. He cleans his hands and grabs his phone.

"Hey Brandon, how'd it go today?" Vince is excited to hear what the reluctant Fred Michel finally ended up telling him.

"Great. It went great, that is after I got the DIA on the phone and convinced him this information was declassified."

"What?" Vince is surprised, laughing at Fred's determination. He didn't think Brandon would need his contact, but he was glad the DIA was enough to convince Fred this is legit.

Brandon recounts the call he got from Fred *in* the airport, just as he was about to board, Fred's reluctance when he arrived and how he ultimately resorted to calling the Pentagon. Brandon explains that once Fred got a verbal OK, he was more relaxed, even helpful. Brandon feels Fred is, in a way, relieved to finally talk about his Army experience.

"Did you meet his wife, Lucille? Vince asks.

"Yes, she is very nice and supportive. His daughter Cynthia was there too." Brandon takes another swig of Coke. "But get this, Fred never told Lucille or his daughter what he did during the war. Neither of them knew Fort Hunt was an intelligence hub. And Fred told me he interviewed German scientists, U-boat captains, and other U-boat personnel. The interrogation side was more extensive than we thought."

"And his wife and daughter didn't know about it?" Vince is surprised.

"No, he never said anything about German prisoners or interrogations or any intelligence work. Neither Lucille nor Cynthia knew what he did during the war."

"That's pretty incredible. Not saying anything for sixty years, hard to believe."

"Yeah, I was surprised too, but he kept telling me he had taken an oath. All the soldiers did."

"We should try to find that oath or get a release of some kind in writing. Let me work on that. Did you talk about Fort Hunt? How was his memory?"

"Listen, for 85 - this guy is incredible. I don't know whether it's long-term memory or the fact that he's kept this bottled up for so long, but he was very detailed about what he did and who he talked to. It was amazing." Brandon pauses then recounts some of the highlights of their conversation about the super submarine U-234.

"He was insistent, even adamant that they never used force, torture or any kind of violence while interrogating. This was old school for sure. He told me that's how they were trained. Talk to the prisoner, be nice until the prisoner lets their guard down. Other guys on my list may have more to add or corroborate what he told me."

"Other guys?"

"Yeah, Fred gave me a list of soldiers he served with. I did a search for his bunkmate, George Mandel."

"Any luck?"

"I think I found him. He's a professor at GWU and lives in Bethesda. Can you believe it? Right there." Brandon realizes.

"Are you going to call him?"

"I think I'll call when I'm at Fred's tomorrow. Using him as an introduction may help. I have no idea if this guy will be willing to talk to me, but it couldn't hurt having Fred open the door, you know?"

"Good idea. Keep me posted. You fly back Thursday, right?"

"Yeah."

"OK I'll see you in the office on Friday. Call me if anything else comes up. I'll let Matt know how it's going." With that Vince hangs up.

Brandon is feeling good and reaches for a third slice of now only lukewarm pizza, then settles back. Finding Fred and hearing his story is one thing. Locating George would be something else. He has no idea the enormity of the story he is about to chronicle.

More Revelations   Fort Mead, Maryland July 25, 1946

Chapter 9

More Revelations

Louisville, Kentucky

May 31, 2006

The next morning Cynthia's eyes pop open early from sheer adrenaline. She lays in bed remembering all the conversations from the day before. Last night after dinner, she tried to obey her mom's directive and cautiously badgered her father with only the most pressing questions.

She realizes her father is still getting used to the idea of being able to discuss what he thought he'd locked away years ago. He had a front row seat to some of the most pivotal events of WWII and she could only imagine what else would be revealed. As she lay there listening, a mourning dove cooed, and a few birds started to welcome the breaking glints of sunrise. She is still bothered by her father's overall mental state, although talking with Brandon seems to have helped.

Last night after her parents retired for the evening, she opened her computer to begin her own research. She typed in Fort Hunt that brought up a pastoral landscape with links to the National Park Service, and a description of the Virginia respite just south of where she had grown up. Fort Hunt was originally land donated by George Washington and was used as a defense post in the War of 1812 and in subsequent wars up to the First World War. This she knew. But Brandon was right, there was nothing about WWII. No mention of Nazis. No mention of a secret government intelligence center. That history had not been chronicled, or at least hadn't become mainstream. Going further, she typed in Military Intelligence, MIS, finding links to articles about Japanese speaking interpreters during WWII, their service and even a language school. Still nothing about her father or what he and his fellow soldiers had done.

She tried Escape & Evade, which led to a link on a British training program and a book published later called, The Escape Factory. That's the book Brandon mentioned earlier today. She made a mental note to swing by the library. She clicked on the British training and her screen filled with intelligence and counterintelligence activities. She was beginning to get an idea of what her father was involved with and goings-on at Fort Hunt. She had read into the early morning hours.

Now lying in bed, awake at the crack of dawn, her mind is running though some of the most impactful information. Before she goes too far afield, she decides to get up and get the day started. She wants to bake something for breakfast and have everything ready by the time Brandon arrives. First, however, she thinks...coffee.

At ten o'clock Brandon finds himself standing once again at Fred's door with a raised hand. He taps firmly and this time the door opens to a warm welcome and he is ushered to his spot in the living room. Friendly banter about his accommodations keeps things light as Brandon sets up his recorder and carefully hands the original papers and photos back to Lucille. Cynthia offers Brandon coffee, and everyone settles in.

"I searched for George Mandel last night and guess what?" he paused, "I think I found him." Fred's eyebrows raise as he leans forward. Cynthia glances at her mom who was also surprised.

"I thought we could call him today, together," Brandon suggests.

"I don't want to just call him out of the blue," Fred is immediately conscious of how long it has been since they'd spoken. Then he reconsiders, "Sure, sure we should call." Fred knows he should reach out to his old friend. "Where is he now?"

"I was very excited to find him," *alive*, Brandon thinks but goes on to give Fred the particulars.

"My search turned up a professor of pharmacology at George Washington University. This professor's age and background fits the George Mandel we're looking for. He lives in Bethesda, and I got a number for him at the university. Looks like he's still teaching and chairs his department. His bio said he's also involved in cancer research and several other specialties. I think this is the right George Mandel. Shall we give him a call?"

"Right now?" This was moving a little fast for Fred.

"Sure, why not?" Brandon's youthful enthusiasm is both off-putting and contagious at the same time. "If he's not there, we'll leave a message," Brandon finishes.

"O.K. Yes, you're right. We should call," Fred agrees. Brandon pulls out his phone and hits the speaker button.

The line rings and a standard voice message confirms they have reached Doctor George Mandel, pharmacology department, please leave a message. Brandon plunges ahead first identifying himself and saying he is with his friend Fred Michel, to which Fred adds, "Hi George, this is Fred. It's been a while. We should talk." Then Brandon wraps up with his number and a request for George to return the call. Just making the call seemed to brighten Fred and it plainly showed on his face.

"Maybe he's teaching – a summer session?" Fred suggests. "He'll call back I think." And Fred sits back in his chair, relieved and satisfied at this first step of reconnecting with his past. The memory of his fellow soldier and friend is comforting.

Brandon starts his recorder and slugs the head of the tape with the new date, May 31st, 2006, then thinks about where to begin.

"Today, Fred, let's talk a little more about the kind of information you collected through your interrogations.

202

Anything that would've helped in the war effort," Brandon pauses then decides to prime the pump.

"Let me first say that according to documents at the National Archives, your interrogations generated something like 5,000 reports through the end of the war. That's a lot of material."

"Yes, all the reports, our interrogations and any drawings or diagrams were filed so we could refer to them, recall the paperwork from the files for interrogation or as we needed it."

Brandon points out, "Some of the reports and interrogation transcripts still exist. They cover topics from enemy intelligence to weaponry design and troop movements, even some diagrams."

"Yes, we were able to find out many things." Fred recalls some of the details. "One thing I do remember which you might find interesting…there was an issue with train depots and supplies. We were bombing German railroad depots and yards, but then the trains were still getting their supplies through. We learned the Germans were loading and unloading everything where certain roads crossed the tracks – and they used a different crossing each time. Once we had that information and figured out where the supplies were being transferred, our bombings were more successful. "

"That would have been important," Brandon realizes.

"The information on train supply transfers was – useful," Fred is carefull to acknowledge this accomplishment because he was never one to boast, he let his actions speak for themselves. No need to make it a big deal. The 1142 interrogators had managed to pull off something. Fred wasn't sure if that something was exceptional; but, for the first time in many years he felt that maybe what he contributed made a difference.

"I think the efforts of 1142 were extremely important." Brandon is starting to grasp the full scope of what these soldiers had done. They produced intelligence that led to the accurate bombing of munitions plants and U-boat facilities; the revelation of new technologies that would shape modern warfare, the Space Race and impact our everyday lives. Brandon appreciates all that Fred is telling him, but he also realizes that intelligence at Fort Hunt was compartmentalized and Fred was not aware of the other programs. If Brandon can find other veterans, he might get different stories or more information. The thought skids through Brandon's mind, then refocuses on Fred.

"I guess this brings us to the end of the war. What happened to the prisoners and to your fellow interrogators?"

"The prisoners we had were mostly designated for Paperclip and the U.S. rocket programs and were relocated. Some of our guys stayed to collect, translate and process captured German documents. Some soldiers, like my brother Rudy and cousin Werner, and my friend Rudy Pins, went to Nuremberg to help with the trials. Other soldiers went back to Germany to debrief prisoners, but most of us from 1142 finished up and were discharged."

"You never kept up with any of your fellow soldiers?" Brandon was still surprised at how quiet this group had kept all these years.

"Rudy Pins and I corresponded when he went to Nuremberg. Mandel and I corresponded for a while, until he enrolled for his doctorate. Then we just lost touch." Fred says matter-of-factly."

"So that was the end of the interrogations?"

"It was the end of that phase, yes; but then other Germans were brought in, the Gehlen group. These were hardened spies. I didn't have anything to do with them. I think Rudy Pins did. Reinhard Gehlen was a kind of spymaster we set up back in Germany before the Cold War. He was an expert on Russia and the Russian military. The people that handled Gehlen ended up being the first people recruited for the CIA. I was not one of them."

Then Fred thinks to ask, "How did you find George, by searching on the computer?"

"Yes, I used a White Pages search and George came up." Brandon explains. "I got lucky."

"Well, let me help you look." Fred offers. "Let's go to the kitchen table where we have some room."

With that, Brandon grabs his computer and follows.

Fred and Brandon begin looking for some of the other names on their list. Brandon types in Eric Kramer. A few Kramers came up, but only one was about the right age and lives in Sleepy Hollow, New York. Brandon is amused at the name.

"Sleepy Hollow – like the story? Where is that?" Brandon asks.

"Just outside New York on the Hudson, I think." Fred tells him. Brandon notes the information, "I'll try to get in touch with him."

"Eric had a similar background to mine. We were both at Camp Ritchie and transferred together to 1142," Fred remembers.

This goes on for a few more names: Peter Weiss, Rudy Pins, William Hershberger, Henry Kolm and Bill Hess. Brandon has other names which Fred doesn't recognize, again reminding Brandon one intelligence branch didn't know what the other was doing. The compartmentalization explains why Fred knew only the interrogators with whom he worked.

Cynthia is sitting in the living room, thumbing through the "war binder," looking at black and white snapshots with white wavy edges, including an ID picture of her then very young and handsome father in his Army uniform. She pulls out a slightly damaged picture of her mom sitting on her dad's lap, or sitting on a railing on a boat, it was hard to tell. It looks like they had gone to Coney Island because she notices that destination emblazoned on the life ring hanging behind them. Cynthia notes her mom's plain black jacket offset by a white blouse and her arm casually slung over her father's shoulder. Lucille of course wore a skirt which showed off her trim legs and black, clunky heeled shoes. Cynthia smiles at the sheer joy on her parents' faces and thinks her mom might have been labeled a loose girl back in the forties, but today would be considered just a girl having fun. She pulls out the Army ID shot and the black and white of her dad and Uncle Rudy in uniform thinking Brandon might want to get a copy of both.

She walks into the kitchen with the photos and finds Brandon and her dad at a good stopping point. They have made progress in their search for 1142 vets with several possible leads for Brandon to run down. Lucille hands Brandon the number and address of Werner Michel, Fred's cousin who was also at Camp Ritchie.

"Here you go, Brandon," she says as he takes the paper. "We'll give Werner a call, introduce you and let him know you may be contacting him."

"Thanks, thanks so much." Brandon has much to do now and feels like he's on the clock. If these vets are still alive, he wants to find them.

Cynthia reaches over and lays the small stack of pictures on the table, "Look what I found! Pretty handsome soldier don't you think?" she winks at her dad. "And a cute couple," she adds to her mom.

Fred blushes, Brandon smiles and picks up the decade's old photos, studying the uniforms and the lightheartedness of the boat deck photo. "You two look like you were having a good time," Brandon can't pass up the opportunity to rib Fred.

Lucille leans in, "Oh I remember that picture. We went all the way to Coney Island. We were getting serious at that point," she mischievously tells Brandon.

"You both look pretty un-serious if you ask me," Cynthia teases.

"Well, I would never go to Coney Island with just any soldier," her mom jokes. "Remember those shoes?" she says half to Fred and half reminiscing out loud.

"No," Fred responded, a little flustered at all the relationship talk. "I didn't care about your shoes."

"Well, I think you look very stylish," Cynthia props up her mom.

The playful banter keeps up for a while and Brandon watches the dynamic. He can see Fred's straight as an arrow perspective being worn down over time with familial repartee. *You have to laugh at yourself sometimes*, he thinks, *and who better to teach you than your family.*

It was getting late, and time for Brandon to go. Looking for his old Army buddies has given Fred fresh hope, but the activities are again wearing on him. Lucille, ever protective, can see Fred is tiring and suggests they continue over the phone and by email.

Brandon takes his cue, packs his case with his notes, papers, and recorder. He moves toward the door, but this doesn't feel like a goodbye. It feels like they are just getting started. He again thanks Fred, Lucille and Cynthia for letting him come and for all their help with his project. He has learned more in these two days than the last months of research.

Once phone numbers are exchanged Fred stops. "I have some rosters in my old papers. I'll find them and we can send you copies," he glances at Lucille who nods in agreement. "We'll also scan the pictures if you want them," he adds.

"Thanks again, I appreciate all your help and yes, I would like a copy of the photos, if you don't mind." The men shake hands. "Let's keep in touch on anything else you may remember or any other information you find, and I'll let you know if I hear back from George."

"Sounds good," Fred confirms. "I am very interested to see if he responds."

"Me too." Brandon is genuinely hopeful.

Lucille gives Brandon a hug and then he turns to Cynthia, "Let's keep talking as this develops." She knows he is thinking the same thing about reuniting her father and George. She agrees to stay in contact. With that, Brandon is gone, and Cynthia turns to her parents. They have a lot to talk about.

Brandon heads to the car assessing his situation. By sheer luck, he found Fred and thanks to modern technology, he may have found George. Beyond that, he isn't sure where this is going. It is still too new.

As he heads to the airport, he thinks of George Mandel, amazed he is still teaching. *Would George's recollections of the war be as good as Fred's? More importantly, would he agree to talk?*

He returns the car, checks in at the airport and settles at his gate, then calls Vince. He runs down the high points of Fred's interview and the call to George.

"Fred was actually nervous to call him," Brandon recounts. "I guess after 60 years it would be a bit of a shock."

"The whole story is a bit of a shock," Vince quips. "And you found his friend too, that's remarkable. What's your take on finding more of these vets?"

"I have no idea what the odds are." Brandon is searching for words. "I could maybe find another person besides George, or this could be it. I honestly don't know. But I want to try. Fred says he may have a list of some names of soldiers he served with. I was thinking I could use the Social Security Gap Index to see who has died and cross-reference the names against my list."

"Good idea," Vince approves. "If you do find some of these guys maybe we start by sending a formal letter of introduction or something. Just thinking out loud here. We'll talk more when you get back."

"Sure, sounds good." Brandon was already thinking ahead. "I'd better give Matt a call and update him." With that they both hung up and Brandon dials his immediate supervisor. Things had gone better than anyone had expected.

The attendants call to start boarding the plane, but Brandon's thoughts are consumed with finding other 1142 vets. Little does he know that as he flies back to Washington, D.C., George Mandel is leaving him a message.

It has been a week since Brandon stood on Fred and Lucille's doorstep where Cynthia now stands. She pauses for a moment and thinks of how that simple knock on their door has impacted their lives. The revelation about her father's wartime intelligence work is still sinking in. She had always admired her father and knew he was much too humble about his accomplishments. But now, to find out he was an important part of World War II intelligence and all the contributions he had made, only enhanced her admiration for him.

She slides the front door open and calls to her parents, "Mom, dad. I'm here!" and lets herself in. Her mom calls to her from the back deck. They're enjoying a warm, clear morning of summer breezes with a second cup of tea on the deck. The kettle was still hot for Cynthia.

Pouring a strong brew, Cynthia made her way outside. She gives her father a peck on the cheek and a quick hug for her mom, then settles into a cushioned chair as her mom talks about getting the family and grandchildren together this weekend.

The fact that her dad is sitting outside with them, engaged in conversation, is something. She realizes that talking about his past service, explaining some of his duties, and possibly finding his old Army buddies has renewed him. She wants to know more about her father's service during the war, but she knows to take it slow. This is something he is still getting used to talking about.

Last week after Brandon left, she and her mother talked a great deal about the war and her dad's life in Germany. She had to admit, she never realized how much her family's trauma in Germany affected her. After finding the old pictures, she revisited the war binder and found a paper trail of the family's movements from Landau to New York. There were letters to and from Aunt Tillie arranging their affidavit, some of her dad's and Uncle Rudy's academic accomplishments, and one of her dad's school sketches, a picture he had drawn in elementary school.

This was the picture he mentioned to Brandon, his childhood drawing of the book burning dated 30, March '33. In the picture, flames and smoke rise in a courtyard. Soldiers are standing on a balcony, arms raised as if you could hear them shout, "Sieg Heil!" The uniformed soldiers toss books into the burning flames, a red Nazi banner hangs from the balcony frame. *He even drew swastikas on the armbands of the soldiers*, Cynthia noticed. *He also left some of the courtyard archway unfinished, blocked out by the smoke.* She realizes what a traumatic image this is for an elementary school artist and is thinking about that picture when she sits down to talk to her father.

"I've been studying that picture you drew," she began.

"Oh?" her father looks over.

"The one of the book burning? It bothers me," she admits.

"It was a long time ago. As a kid you do what you're told. They say go to the square, we went to the square and watched them start a pile of books on fire."

"What did your classmates think? What did your friends say?"

"We really didn't know what to make of it. Then it happened a few more times." Fred remembers. "Unfortunately, it became more common and not just in Landau. Obviously, it happened in other cities and of course in Berlin. When the Frank's grandchildren came to visit, they mentioned it. You know the Franks? They lived in Frankfurt, but the grandparents, Otto's family, lived in Landau. They were our neighbors and good friends of my parents."

"Wait, the Franks, like Anne Frank?" Cynthia was stunned.

"Yes, Anne came to visit Landau with her sister Margot, who was closer to my age. Ann was just a young child, but we all played. My parents were close with her grandparents. They lived right around the corner from us." Fred said almost casually.

"But then Anne and her family...". Cynthia didn't need to finish the sentence.

"Yes, we all know what happened to them later. But as children, we had, what I thought, was a perfect childhood.

Then, of course things changed. It became more dangerous. That's why we left."

Cynthia had read The Diary of Anne Frank just like every middle schooler in America and connected with this young girl who was at the time about her age. The story frightened Cynthia and at the same time, steeled her heart. As with most children in middle school, she had a deep-seated fear and loathing of Nazis. How ironic, she thinks as she glances at her father, he ends up interrogating his tormentors.

"But even after the war, after all these years, why didn't you tell mom or any of us about interrogating Nazis? That's a big 'would've been nice to know." Cynthia was playfully baiting her dad.

"We took an oath of secrecy." Fred raised a hand like what was I supposed to do? This was intelligence work. We weren't to speak of it ever - even after the war."

"I understand, but I'm still surprised that no one, none of the soldiers you served with, have ever said anything." Cynthia still finds this incredulous as she sips her tea.

"Have you ever heard about Camp Ritchie, Fort Hunt, P.O. Box 1142 or World War II intelligence work?" Lucille asks her.

"Well no, but maybe I'm not the best-informed person." She half laughs, looking at her mom.

"Aside from knowing where Fort Hunt is, I never heard about all of this either," Lucille admits. "During the war you just didn't ask that kind of question. Afterwards, it didn't seem to be as important. We won the war, you know."

"Yes, I realize that." Cynthia rolled her eyes. "But after everything was declassified...well," she looks at her dad. "I guess you didn't know anything was declassified." Cynthia wants her father to open up more. "Dad, this stuff, the intelligence work you did, it was really important."

"Well, maybe now it's become interesting," was all he said.

"It led to some incredible advancements!" She wants her father to understand how important their intel had been not just in winning the war but afterwards. She had never heard of U-234 or that Germany was sending all its cutting-edge technology and leading scientists to Japan. She'd never heard of Heinz Schlicke. But she uses a microwave every day and understands remote controls and how submarines use sonar.

"All I can say is, what you guys learned really helped this country." Then she remembers to ask, "Have you talked to George Mandel yet?"

Fred sits up and brightens, "Yes, yes. After he called Brandon, the next day George and I had a chance to talk.

"That's great!" Cynthia is excited for her dad. She had been so consumed with unpacking and getting settled, she's missed a few days of the developments. "How is he? Did you pick up right where you left off?"

"We had a good conversation catching up," Fred reassures her. "We hadn't spoken for almost 60 years, and we certainly hadn't talked about the war. It was good to hear his voice."

He tells Cynthia of George's career, his years of teaching, his family, and that he has been living in Bethesda, Maryland the whole time. They both are eager to see each other.

"I told him I'd like to get together, and he agreed. We're talking about meeting in August. I thought we should go back to Fort Hunt....." And here he looks at Lucille for confirmation. Lucille made a career of deferring to her husband in almost every matter except for things like travel arrangements, which she realizes she needs to make.

"I can look into plane tickets, or maybe we could drive?" Lucille offers. "I might call Sandy. We can probably stay with her and Jon." She is thinking out loud and needs a calendar.

"Hey, let's make it a road trip!" Cynthia interjects. At the mention of flying, all Cynthia can visualize are her parents trying to navigate the airport, baggage claim and ground transportation. She wants to head this off. "I can drive. We'll all go. I'd like to see Sandy and Jon too!" she offers. "It'll be fun."

"You don't mind driving?" Her father looks over. "We should probably try and see your Uncle Rudy if possible." Fred's brother lives just outside Philadelphia. He has been battling cancer and it isn't looking good.

"Of course I can drive. Like I said, we'll make it a family trip," Cynthia reassures him. She hasn't seen her father this excited about anything in a long while. Now that he needs some assistance walking, she is glad to help orchestrate the reunion.

"I told Brandon I would find him some more names, a roster and anything else I thought might help." Fred tells Cynthia. "I should really look through my papers again." That is the cue to head inside, and Cynthia grabs the empty cups while Lucille assists Fred.

Once in the living room, Fred settles into his favorite chair and grabs the "war box." Cynthia rejoins her parents and notices the box of memorabilia is now permanently in the living room, open and readily available.

She kneels next to the open cardboard, then relaxes to a seated position on the floor resting her back on the couch close to where her mother is seated. Cynthia has seen these papers and read them with only a passing interest. Now she truly understands what they hold.

As she looks through various mementos, she remembers her father's first trip back to Landau which didn't happen until the '70's. He and Lucille were able to find Fraenz, Fred's nanny, who was then a grown woman with a family of her own. Their reunion was a happy occasion and had a healing effect on Fred, rekindling precious memories of Landau, his early childhood, and happier times. Still, even after she talked to her father about this trip, Cynthia personally never wanted to go to Germany. There were too many things she just couldn't get past.

She is lost in her thoughts when the phone rings and Lucille reaches to answer it. After a bright greeting she hands the phone to Fred, "It's Brandon."

Fred says hello and tells Brandon, "I found the picture I told you about, in fact Cynthia just had it," he looks at his daughter who pulls it out and lays it on the table. "It's right here, I can scan it. I'm still trying to locate other documents for you." Brandon and he had a comfortable rapport.

Then Brandon tells him, "I'm going to be interviewing George this week. He's driving over here to my office. I hear you two want to get together. We'd love to have that happen here at Fort Hunt. Everyone's excited about it."

"Yes, yes that would be fine," Fred is smiling. "Cynthia is going to drive us over."

"That sounds great!" Brandon is glad Fred and Lucille won't attempt the drive alone. They wrap up the conversation with a promise to coordinate arrangements.

Cynthia overhears the conversation and smiles at how Brandon can read her parents so well. They have emailed a couple times already, sharing resources and whatever information they've found. Next, she wants to investigate Werner von Braun and Operation Paperclip, something she still regards as confounding.

As she casually flips through plastic sleeves protecting various correspondence, she notes letters from Fred to her grandparents, her grandparents to Fred and Uncle Rudy, and other notes from her mother.

Years ago, she read a couple of her parent's letters, looking for something juicy. She was sorely disappointed. They were nothing short of boring, but now she knew why. Her father couldn't talk about what he was doing, and her mother was too reserved to write anything more than she missed him. Ultimately, she admitted her parents had the most lackluster courtship in the history of courtships! None-the-less, every letter was saved.

Then she sees a letter with the heading Office of U.S. Chief Counsel dated 2 November 1946.

"Hey, here's a letter from Rudy Pins. He was at 1142 with you, right?" She looks at her dad.

"Yes, we were at 1142 together. We corresponded for a little while after he left."

"He was at Nuremberg, right? Working on war crime interviews...." Her voice trails as she reads Rudy's letter.

"It looks like Rudy and two friends took a little trip to Prague, Czechoslovakia," Cynthia is picking an interesting passage. "Get this," she reads.

"Czechoslovakia is full of people in uniform, but otherwise it looks pretty peaceful. The Sudeten Germans who are left and who belonged to the Nazi party now have to wear a white or yellow armband, just like the Jews in the days when the Nazis were in power. They also get the same food ration that they gave to the Jews in the Third Reich days.

Anti-fascist Germans, on the other hand, are not molested and enjoy the same privileges as the average Czech."

"Looks like the Czechs gave the Nazis a taste of their own medicine," she muses.

"They were lucky it wasn't worse," Fred says wryly remembering that after the war there were reports of average people who had suffered greatly under the Nazis taking revenge into their own hands, exacting retribution on Nazi soldiers and Nazi sympathizers.

"Were you and Rudy close?" Cynthia is thinking about someone friendly enough to continue corresponding with after the war.

"Rudy and I got to know each other at 1142. He was there when I got there so he had more experience. But we became good friends and corresponded when he was sent to Nuremberg."

"What was his background, his specialty? What kind of scientist was he?"

"Rudy wasn't a scientist at all. As a matter of fact, his background was history and political science – and of course he spoke fluent German. But he was a very good interrogator, and he knew the Nazi party structure. That was important and maybe one of the reasons they wanted him at the War Crimes Tribunal."

"Ah, I see," Cynthia understands that would make more sense with his particular talents. Then she questions, "But you didn't keep up with him after that?"

"We did correspond for a while, during the trial, but not much after that."

Lucille notes the place where the letter came out and now Cynthia hands it back to her. As her father combs through documents and comments to Lucille, Cynthia decides to start her own search.

"I'm going to get on the computer and see what I can find," she announces and heads to the kitchen table. "I've got the promotion list," she says over her shoulder. She knows her mother has already marked the spot for its return.

GEN-MAJ REINHARD GEHLEN 3WG-1300   GEN-MAJ REINHARD GEHLEN 3WG-1300

Discharged   Fort Meade, Maryland July 25, 1946

223

Chapter 10

Discharged

Fort Meade, Maryland
July 25, 1946

Most of the soldiers of 1142 have been reassigned or
discharged. Finally, it is Fred's turn. Last month he was
transferred to Fort Meade and is now waiting to be processed
out. Fred thinks about the last couple of months of his service.
Was he lucky to stay stateside? Certainly, his parents think so.
But part of him would've liked to get into the fight, get back to
Germany and feel like he had done something, something
more. Intelligence work is singular and insular. Was it
enough? We won the war, he realizes. That will have to be
enough.

Things are changing in the country; he can see it and feel
it. There is a new energy he wants to be part of and get on with
his life. He made sure to have his recommendations in order
and letters of reference from his superiors before he left Fort
Hunt. He will need all the help he can get to quickly land a job.
He and Lucille want to start building their lives together. His
parents liked Lucille well enough, but she wasn't Jewish. He

told them this was America, he would make his own choices, and he chose Lucille.

Fred casually reaches to his left hand, feeling the newest addition to his wardrobe on his fourth finger. When the calendar heralded the new year, 1946, Fred and Lucille decided to tell their parents they intended to get married in April. Neither family was thrilled. Lucille had accepted a solitary diamond from Fred, and they made plans for a spring wedding. Lucille's father tried to make it logistically impossible for them to have the ceremony with family members present. Richard Barryman was a lawyer with the Federal Accounting office and was scheduled to leave in January for a large audit in Missouri. He planned on attending Lucille's brother's nuptials in June, but explicitly stated he would not make two trips back.

Fred's parents were equally upset because he chose to marry outside his faith. They registered their disapproval, but eventually softened.

If Fred and Lucille wanted to get married with both her parents present, they had just three days to pull this off before her father's departure. Once the decision was made, Lucille and her mother dove into wedding preparations.

Lucille's father had legal connections; they knew a Supreme Court Justice who was also a personal friend. Lucille's mother made the call and the Justice graciously agreed to perform the ceremony, in his chambers no less. With one call, they secured an officiant as well as a suitable location.

Lucille's cousin Nancy, who was like a sister, agreed to be her maid of honor, and Fred's brother, Rudy, would be the best man.

Lucille needed a dress, her cousin needed a dress, Lucille needed flowers, a headpiece, and a cake, not necessarily in that order. In lieu of a reception, Lucille's mother said everyone could come back to their home.

It was truly a miracle but in three days' time, Lucille, her mother, and cousin pulled it off. Luckily her mother and cousin had appropriate attire in their wardrobes. For Lucille, they turned to their sewing skills and made a lovely short, ivory sheath dress, accented with low shoulder pads, capped sleeves and a sequin-embellished belt that tied in a satin bow at her trim waist. She added ivory sleeve-lets with gloves for extra coverage since it was January.

Her mother made a hair appointment and Lucille's unruly tresses were swept into a stylish French twist adorned with a pillbox hat and birdcage veil. Lucille found a florist who could make a simple gardenia and rose corsage and boutonnieres; and a bakery that whipped up a traditional, white, two-tiered wedding cake.

Fred had held up his end by producing two classic gold wedding bands. His parents arrived from New York with his one and only, but dapper, navy suit.

Fred's brother Rudy was enrolled for his PhD in chemistry at Notre Dame and was in the middle of finals. The day of the ceremony Rudy missed his train from Indiana and scrambled to get on the next one. The judge jokingly said he was determined to join these two in matrimony and waited until Rudy's train arrived, which was after 5:00 pm. Even with all these obstacles, on January 3rd, with reluctant families assembled, they exchanged their vows. Rudy was pleasantly surprised to meet Lucille's cousin at the ceremony. He and Nancy hit it off immediately and from that day on, began writing their own love story.

Fred and Lucille had a brief honeymoon night at the Sheridan in Washington, D.C., then Fred headed back to Fort Hunt and Lucille went home. There was no available married personnel housing at Fort Hunt and Fred only had a few months left to serve, so they would just have to delay living together.

As he waits for his discharge papers to come through, Fred thinks back to the end of the war and the order to burn all the documentation, all evidence of their work. He carefully held back the Dictionary he and George compiled, as well as other papers he wanted to keep including a list of promotions with his name on it. He didn't want everything to be set ablaze in the steel drums. After the order came to burn all paperwork, he remembered seeing charred hairbrushes and singed playing cards in the piles of ashes. He thought those were strange things to burn, but he took it in stride.

Last fall, he had said goodbye to the prisoners who were his charges. Carl Hertz requested to be sent to the University at Uppsala in Sweden which offered him a scholarship to complete his doctorate. When he left, they shook hands as respected friends.

Heinz Schlicke was reunited with his family and transferred to Long Island. The other prisoners who were not scientists were sent to camps for processing and released to their home countries.

George was discharged at the end of December 1945, but he had some months before school started, so he decided to fill the gap by staying on as a civilian at Fort Hunt, leaving near the beginning of summer.

By mid-July, Fred is finally out of the Army. Moving in with Lucille at her family home is not an option, so he takes a room in a small boarding house in Alexandria and starts combing the classifieds. The challenge is finding a job in engineering. On the first Monday, he starts hitting the pavement and finds the only companies that need engineers are the power company, the phone company and a small engineering firm called Melpar which caters to government contract work. He goes to all three on the same day. The manager at Melpar calls him back and tells Fred if he has a drafting set to come down and start working tomorrow. By sheer luck and determination, he has a job. His plans for his future with Lucille are falling into place.

They quickly find a small apartment in Alexandria, but only temporarily because Fred wants to continue his education. After a few months, he transfers to Melpar's office in New York and enrolls in Columbia for a master's degree in engineering. They move in with his parents in Brooklyn until G.I. housing opens up in Bedford-Stuyvesant, and they finally settle into married life.

Back at 1142, Rudy Pins and a handful of soldiers are wrapping things up with the Reinhard Gehlen group. The spy master and his small entourage have been there almost ten months, longer than any other prisoner, hammering out a deal and working relationship with the newly formed United States Intelligence organization, the CIA. He will not be prosecuted for war crimes and in return, he and his small group will feed intelligence to occupying forces.

Gehlen and his men are being shipped back to Germany to set up and run the German Secret Service. He will specifically spy on the Soviet Union, share information with the United States and in return, the U.S. will fund his organization. Once he gets back to Germany, Gehlen will recruit thousands of the meanest, most despicable members of the Gestapo and SS, including Emil Augsburg who oversaw the murder of hundreds of Russians, Klaus Barbie, the butcher of Lyon, and Franz Six, who exterminated hundreds in the Smolensk Ghetto.

Also on the repatriate boat is another 1142 prisoner, Franz Gajdosch, a Slovakian German tank operator in the Panzer division. He was captured in France, interrogated at 1142, then spent the remainder of his time as a bartender, a skill he wanted to make his career.

Gajdosch ran into General Gehlan on one of the wooded walking paths at Fort Hunt. Gehlen immediately told him he was a general and made Gajdosch stand at attention in front of the higher-ranking officer. Gehlen made his blood run cold then, and now he found himself on the same ship heading back to Europe. Gajdosch makes sure to stay out of the General's sight.

When the group arrives at Camp King outside Frankfurt, Gajdosch is offered the chance to bartend at the Officer's Club. He takes the job. Even though he serves Gehlen, he keeps his distance, waiting to be released so he can return to his Slovakian town of Smolnik.

Meanwhile, the newly formed CIA continues to canvass 1142 interrogators for new recruits. One of the soldiers who expresses interest is Angus McClean Thuermer, a Chicago boy with an affinity for language. He worked for the Associated Press during college and was a stringer in Berlin before the war.

Angus experienced first-hand the developing Nazi machine and their aggressive activities leading up to the war. He filed chilling accounts with the Associated Press of each history-making event. By the time the CIA approached him, he'd already lived a war and then some.

Thuermer was in Berlin on Kristallnacht, November 9th of 1938 and had ridden his bike through the streets noting the destruction and damage to Jewish homes and businesses. He wrote an eye-witness account of the melee. Then the AP sent him to the Polish border two weeks before Hitler invaded. Thuermer was living through the rise of the Third Reich, continually reporting from Germany until the bombing of Pearl Harbor. When war was declared with the United States, he and other journalists were arrested and held for five months before being included in a prisoner exchange and allowed passage on a ship bound for New York. Once home, he went back to Chicago and the Associated Press.

Because he was eligible and had ROTC training in High School, he enlisted in the Navy and was commissioned as an Ensign. He picked up enough "street German" while abroad to be fluent, and because of his interest in intelligence work, offered himself up as an interrogator. The Navy obliged and he was assigned to 1142. He interrogated a U-boat captain who'd had the traumatic experience of being the lone survivor of his vessel.

"We sat in the grass and talked...and talked," he'd remarked to his new CIA boss. "I got plenty of information out of the U-boat captain, and we just sat in the grass and talked."

Angus spent only a short time at 1142 but would go on to have a 26-year career with the CIA. Rudy Pins joined him and would also enjoy a long career with the CIA.

Within days after Japan's surrender September 2nd, 1945, the MIS-X program was shut down and all records destroyed. Over that summer and fall, PWs were processed and repatriated.

By October of 1946, all intelligence personnel were moved out, and by November, the War Department declared Fort Hunt as surplus. The last troops were gone within a week.

World War II was over for a little more than a year when the War Department realized it was obligated to honor the terms of the special use agreement. They must return Fort Hunt to the Department of the Interior.

In early 1947, the US Army Corps of Engineers began the process of removing all temporary wartime buildings. The interrogation center, the barracks, the listening hub are all taken down and any semblance of those buildings removed. Only a couple of buildings, mainly the Officer's Quarters, are left.

In the years following the war, the area around Fort Hunt began to be suburbanized with a growing population. New neighborhoods demand more greenspace, parks and recreational areas. Fort Hunt slowly becomes the main recreational respite for the Alexandria area, and the clandestine purposes of its wartime usage all but disappear.

George Mandel   GWMP Offices, McLean, Virginia July 13, 2006

Chapter 11

George Mandel

George Washington Memorial Parkway Offices
McLean, Virginia
July 13, 2006

Brandon is getting ready for his interview with George Mandel. The transcription of Fred and Lucille's interview is proving to be a useful roadmap. Just like Fred building on one interrogation to be more efficient with the next, Brandon thinks, smiling at the irony. Reading over Fred's transcript really does help him see where he needs to tighten up some questions and be more direct when asking others.

Brandon remembered how reluctant George was to talk about Fort Hunt, just like Fred. His first conversation with George was the same tug of war. "The reason I was speaking with Fred is because of his military service," Brandon had tried to explain. "And I want to talk to you for the same reason. You were both at Fort Hunt."

"Brandon I can't talk to you about that." George cut him off. "That's military intelligence."

"Yes sir, but now it's declassified."

"No, no, I don't think so." George was very reluctant. "We took an oath never to disclose this information."

"Yes sir, I know about the oath, but I had someone from the DIA at the Pentagon inform Fred it is now OK to talk about this. Your experience with interrogation would be most helpful to our training programs today."

"You and Fred talked about this already?" George had been surprised.

"Yes sir, and he mentioned among other things the dictionary you two wrote together."

With that George was a little taken aback. He started again slowly, "Fred told you about writing the dictionary together? Why do you still need to talk to me?"

"Sir, I'd love to record your memories of Fort Hunt and anything you can tell us to better explain what went on there during the war."

"Well, if Fred has talked to you, then I think you probably know quite a bit." George was still hedgy.

"Yes, but your perspective would be important."

George was mulling it over, then finally said, "Alright. I would be happy to talk to you."

Brandon didn't realize he'd been holding his breath till he relaxed, and his lungs slowly exhaled. That was almost two weeks ago. Now he is getting ready for George to come to his office in McLean, Virginia. Brandon enlists the help of his summer intern, Sam Johnson, to set up and monitor the recording device and tapes so he can focus on the interview.

Brandon discusses with Vince the importance of asking George the same background questions about family, their childhood and leaving Germany. Those stories alone are worth documenting. Vince indicates he wants to be more involved and plans to attend the initial interview with George. Brandon's boss, Matt Virta and Ranger Sam Swersky also want to sit in.

It is a bright, warm July morning when George arrives on time at the park ranger's office. George is a balding, bespectacled professor, relaxed, personable, and good natured. Brandon ushers his guest in with a quick introduction of his team, all genuinely excited to meet him.

Once inside the conference room, Brandon offers George a seat across from the recorder and takes out his notes. Since Brandon and George have already spoken a couple of times, George is up to speed on Brandon's project, the permission to speak and Brandon's conversation with Fred. George is also getting more comfortable telling his story.

George speaks first. "Before we start, I wanted to let you know that Fred and I have spoken a couple of times," then he pauses, "It's been a long time." He shakes his head hardly believing so many years have slipped by.

"It was good. We both want to get together, so he's coming back to Alexandria for a visit." George explains. "We're still working out the details, but we tentatively set a date in August."

"Fantastic," Brandon knows of their plans and is anticipating park ranger involvement with the reunion. "I'm assuming you would like to meet at Fort Hunt. It would be great to walk the grounds with you and Fred."

"Yes, we talked of meeting at 1142. Thank you for offering to walk us around."

"I'd like to arrange for a reporter from the Washington Post to come and do a story on you two," Vince offers. "That is, if you don't mind being interviewed." Then he adds, "I think I can speak for the whole Cultural Resources team when I say we would all like to meet you guys."

George is mildly flattered at the attention and smiles a humble response. "Sure, sure, that would fine." He and Brandon will coordinate their efforts, and Brandon realizes he has about a month to pull this together.

Sam announced the tape recorder is set up and ready to go. Brandon starts with his usual slate of time, place, and attendees, then begins, "George, can you start by telling me a little bit about where and when you were born, your family and growing up."

"I was born in Berlin in 1924 and my parents were Jewish." Then George guides Brandon and Vince through a course of events similar to Fred's culminating with the family fleeing Germany in 1937.

George graduated from High School in Scarsdale, New York and attended Yale. Once they were aware of his language skills, instead of being inducted into the Army, George was fast tracked through his chemistry major, graduating in 2.5 years at the age of 19. He was drafted in 1944.

Like Fred, he was singled out and spent three months in intelligence training at Ohio State University. He thought he would be shipped out to Europe but instead found himself at Camp Ritchie where he met Fred and went through further interrogation training. He tells Brandon about arriving at 1142, the secrecy oath everyone took and that he never spoke of his activities.

"Of course, most people knew 1142 was Fort Hunt," George mused. "But everyone knew not to ask about what we did."

Brandon asks about his interrogations. "What were some of the things you talked about with prisoners?"

"One of the first people I questioned started talking about jet engines," George began, "which was new at the time. The Messerschmitts had jet engines, our American planes did not. Our pilots couldn't figure out why they, the Germans, were suddenly so much faster than we were. So, we grilled them on jet engines." He thinks a minute, then says, "There was something called a proximity fuse I was told I should ask about. We discovered it's a device that blows up near an airplane without hitting it, and the explosion would bring it down."

"Wasn't that something Heinze Schlicke was developing?" Brandon remembers the scientist Fred mentioned.

241

"Yes, the proximity fuse had limited use towards the end of the war, and we acquired new prototypes of different kinds of fuses from the submarine U-234," George confirms. However, he admits that details surrounding the rest of that incident elude him since he was not directly involved with those interrogations.

"And then there was the atomic energy project," George comments. But after sixty years, the details surrounding that topic also elude him since he was not directly involved. "You know, I wasn't crazy about physics, so I didn't get into it too deep, and I didn't know a lot about what other people were doing. Besides, this was highly secret." This is George's explanation for his lack of detail.

"I do remember talking to this one professor who I think was a biochemist. He talked about what the Germans had done on the atomic project and that it had failed because they bet on the wrong course for the spectrums and how they characterized uranium isotopes. They relied on heavy water to be brought to Germany. The British got wind of these transports and bombed the ships. Without heavy water, the program was dissolved."

George can recall that this was just one of numerous programs the Nazis were working on. But when Brandon mentions rocketry, George comments, "We wanted everyone, and we wanted them because we just did not want those experts to go to Russia." Brandon nods as he is now familiar with this strategy.

Through George's recounting of interrogation techniques and protocol, Brandon understands that some prisoners were interrogated one-on-one but more likely they were interviewed by a team, interrogating from a chemistry perspective, then an engineering perspective. It would all depend on the prisoner.

Brandon asks about the rocket scientists. George remembers going to Boston to interrogate Werner von Braun and his team before they were transferred to Texas and points beyond. He recalls being in Boston for only a month before getting transferred to Maine in December. "That was cold! I couldn't wait to get back to 1142," he chuckles.

"I was discharged in late 1945, December. At that time the idea of the CIA began to develop," he explains, "and many officers thought this would be a good opportunity to get into a new government department. But I wanted to finish my Ph.D. I came back to George Washington University to teach and start my professional work. I got continuous calls from the CIA. 'Now that you have your degree, we really want you to join the CIA," he recalls the conversation lightly.

Over the past 60 years, George established himself as a beloved teacher and mentor. He created learning programs for all levels at George Washington University, from first year med students to seniors, while also making significant contributions in his field of study.

Brandon did his research on George, and knew one of his students, Julius Axelrod, who earned his Ph.D. under George, received the 1970 Nobel Prize in Medicine/Physiology for his work with neurotransmitters, leading to a new class of antidepressants and the development of drugs like Prozac.

George has already received numerous teaching and service awards and was very well respected at the university. But Brandon keeps thinking, a grateful nation would also like to show its appreciation to George, Fred and any other 1142 veterans he can find.

As the interview wraps up, Brandon asks about a story George mentioned earlier. It concerned interrogation techniques, which George assured him were non-violent and more cerebral in nature. They got their information without physical violence, that fact was verbally underlined. Then Brandon asks, "For the recording can you tell me that story about Paris?"

"Oh, sure, sure," George is affable and takes care to set the scene.

"It was my first international conference in Paris, this was in the 70's, and at one of the parties there was a fountain of champagne. I thought this was wonderful. As I approached, I saw somebody that looked familiar. I looked at him, he looked at me, and in that moment, we realized we had met at 1142. The fellow turned to his wife and said, 'My God, there is my former prison warden.' And we had a good laugh. This fellow had become a professor of biochemistry at Heidelberg. We stayed in contact afterwards off and on." George finishes.

This story could never have been told if there was torture involved, Brandon thinks.

Then George mentions, "As a scientist I was asked to participate in conferences all over the world. This one time, after a lengthy trip from Poland to Russia and Moscow, I got a call from the CIA after I returned home. They wanted to know what I thought was going on in Russia and my impression. They knew I had been at 1142 and I thought this was very impressive that they would keep tabs on me."

He stops for a moment and says in earnest, "Brandon, I want to give you and your colleagues tremendous credit for following up on this story. It's an incredible story that should be told. As a soldier, you go where they tell you to go and do what they tell you to do, but I hope we were productive. I hope it all meant something," he looks directly at Brandon. "I hope we did our part."

Brandon knows these men are humble, but they really have no idea of their impact. "George, what you guys accomplished made a difference. You made a difference. From the space program through the Cold War to scientific and technological advancements, all these accomplishments came from 1142 information. So, yes, you did your part, and more."

George nods and the tape runs to an end.

The next day Brandon is back at his desk with a new tape to transcribe and more names, courtesy of George. Brandon is cross checking and verifying each name, then trying to find contact information. He is knee deep in it when the phone rings.

"Hey Brandon!" Cynthia's enthusiasm pours through the phone. "Got a minute?"

"Hey Cynthia, sure, what's up?"

"You know since you were here, George and dad have been talking, which has been great. We're getting these guys together in August.

"Yes, we're all excited to have them here."

"I'm going to drive them. The thought of them navigating an airport and car rental – well, that's not happening," she laughs. "Besides, I really want to be there. Mom's arranging everything so we can stay with Sandy and Jon. Is it OK if they come too?"

"Yes, that's fine and the Cultural Resources team is planning on showing them around." Brandon realizes as he's talking, he needs to check in with Vince.

"Vince has a contact at the Post. We'll try and get a reporter to cover this," he says as he scribbles a list to himself. "We're thinking that if other vets see this in the paper, they'll contact us."

"Great idea!' Cynthia is impressed then asks, "Was George helpful?"

"Yeah, what a nice guy," Brandon can't say it enough.

"Good, good. I'm looking forward to meeting him," Cynthia says thoughtfully. "You know I looked him up, he's had quite the career. Graduated from Yale, doctorate in organic chemistry, Professor of Pharmacology at George Washington University. He's still teaching! Can you believe it?

He researches cancer-causing environmental toxins – and he's still teaching!"

"Yeah, he's accomplished, plus talking to him is like talking to your dad."

"I'm glad you said that cause I really want to find more of these guys. I looked up some other names. We gave this list to you, right? You should have the same names." She grabs for the browning, aged list she's claimed from her father. On another page were her scribbled notes.

"Were all these guys over-achievers?" she asks rhetorically. "I mean, everyone I looked up has a story. Like Henry Kolm. I found a Dr. Henry Kolm, a physicist professor at MIT, involved with the space program, inventor, innovator, named Entrepreneur of the year in 1981, built the first electromagnetic aircraft catapult for the Navy, I mean who does this?"

Brandon is smiling and has no words.

"Then there's John Dean, John Gunther Dean. Escaped Germany in 1938, family name Dienstfertig, but they shortened it to Dean, graduated from Kansas City High School at 16, went to Harvard then served in the Army from 1944-1946 in Military Intelligence. So, this has to be the guy, right?"

"Yeah, John Gunther Dean, I have his name."

"After the Army he went back to Harvard, finished his degree graduating Magna Cum Laude in 1947 and got a doctorate in law from the Sorbonne. This guy was a diplomat and served as Ambassador to the Khmer Republic, Cambodia,

Denmark, Lebanon, Thailand, and India. And he's just one of the people I found!"

"This is turning out to be an impressive group. If we can find these guys and get them together, boy, the stories!" Brandon muses out loud, then remembers, "Oh, and George's wife, Marianne is coming with him in August. You know she never knew anything about this either."

"You gotta be kidding me!" Cynthia thought her strait-laced father is the only one who would follow this rule so intently.

"No, not kidding. He told her some story about talking to scientists, but never mentioned Nazis or interrogations. She got the same surprise you did."

"Well, I'll be."

With that, she and Brandon ended the call promising to touch base closer to the reunion date.

Cynthia sets her papers back down and thinks about who to search next. After a minute she types in Werner von Braun. Might as well search for a name much has been written about, she reasons.

At first, she finds the cleaned-up biography which highlighted almost everything her father had said. German American aerospace engineer and space architect. "Space architect" she thinks, was a little inflated but she reads on.

The V-2 rockets and Peenemunde are mentioned, his brother Magnus and their surrender recorded with the same events her dad mentioned, even the fact von Braun had a broken arm at the time of surrender. But then she reads something different.

Newly declassified information confirming von Braun had been a member of the SS, only now it has been revealed he used prisoners from the Buchenwald concentration camp when he needed technicians and laborers. This hits Cynthia like a bolt.

Von Braun's trip to Buchenwald during the war is well documented and this recently released information verifies his use of prisoners to build his rockets. As she lets this information sink in, she realizes, this is what the Paperclip initiative would have erased, or re-written. Then she thinks about this country in 1945 and doubts many Americans would have found von Braun's use of concentration camp prisoners palatable. But wouldn't this kind of activity also have constituted a war crime?

She sits back in her chair, takes a deep breath, and tries to look at this with a longer lens. She contemplates the weight of the decision to erase Nazi war-crimes over the impending cold war and the space race. Apparently, the United States government felt that what von Braun brought to the table outweighed his past. But Nazi activity, concentration camps, forced labor and extermination sat in the pit of her stomach and caused anxiety on a level she was now starting to recognize. She could never brush aside these crimes and knew there were not two sides to these facts. She felt in her heart what was right, and she knew what constituted a crime. No amount of re-writing could erase that history.

She sits back up and focuses on the computer screen. She learns von Braun became the brains behind the space program and NASA. He even collaborated with Disney – yes, Walt Disney, on making films to excite kids and educate them about space. Then von Braun found religion, ending up in the Episcopalian church. *Maybe he was atoning?* she thinks, *who knows?*

Once again this brings up the moral dilemma of how to win a war and what winning looks like. All this information buried for so many years is becoming the responsibility of her generation, the next generation. Somehow, she will have to make sense of decisions that still make little sense.

Reading about von Braun's life also brings up a larger question, forgiveness. This is more complex than she realizes. She isn't ready to forgive because the information is still too fresh and the edges quite sharp. The knot on her stomach seems to tighten.

However, she feels less animosity towards other scientists her father mentioned. She understands the dilemma many of them faced. They could either work for the Third Reich or end up in a labor camp alongside other political prisoners, that is, if they were even given a choice. She lets out another long breath and again tries to focus.

She begins to understand what her father had been ordered to do. They had to be nice to their prisoners to get them to talk. Simple, right? Her father had done his job well. She respected him for that. Why was she so conflicted? All she wants to do is honor her dad's contribution and those of his fellow interrogators. She must keep her feelings under control and maintain perspective. This isn't new to her father, but it is new to her. She tries to remember that.

Back in Washington, Brandon is discussing his next moves with Vince. Brandon found the original oath clearly stipulating the need for silence before, during and after a soldier's tour of duty. He contacted the DIA and requested clarification in the form of a letter that allows soldiers to speak with him about their war time activities, releasing them from that pledge. It took about three weeks, but he finally has the response. He and Vince compose a cover letter, explaining the Parkway's Heritage initiative.

Brandon mails out ten envelopes hoping they won't be returned "not at this address," or worse, ignored. Once they are gone, he turns his attention to the growing list of other responsibilities calling for his attention.

Sixty Years in the Making   Fort Hunt, August 19, 2006

Chapter 12

Sixty Years in the Making

Louisville, Kentucky to Fort Hunt, Virginia

August 18-19, 2006

Cynthia closes her suitcase, glances at her watch then calls out to the rest of the house, "OK this is it. We need to get on the road. Almost 7:00!" It is a nine-hour trip, and they are driving straight through. Cynthia wants to get to Alexandria by dinner. With an hour stop for lunch, they should be fine. Her time calculations preoccupy her as she heads to the garage.

She lifts her suitcase in the trunk, then goes back inside for the other two. Her parent's suitcases stand together like heralds announcing the important journey. She grabs both and heads to the car as her mom packs drinks in a cooler.

"Almost seven!" Cynthia calls again over her shoulder, as a reminder they need to get going.

Lucille arranged for them to stay with Sandy and Jon. She is looking forward to the reunion with her close friend almost as much as Fred's reunion with his.

Her parents climb into the car as Cynthia slips into the driver's seat. It is a beautiful, clear August morning as Cynthia pulls out of the driveway and grabs for her sunglasses. She loves driving through the Smoky Mountains in summer. This is absolutely the best time of year, she thinks, except for fall when the colors are spectacular. That's great too, she admits to herself. But today, she is in the moment.

Even in late summer she sees haze lingering at the higher elevations. The mountains are majestic as they leave Kentucky and head east. Cynthia's calculations are nearly perfect as they hit very little traffic outside of Alexandria, now considered a bedroom community of Washington, D.C. Having grown up in Arlington, she still considers this whole area home turf. She maneuvers through traffic with ease, something her parents greatly appreciate.

When they pull into Sandy & Jon's it is almost five thirty and the hosts come out to the driveway to warmly greet them. There's nothing like old friends to welcome you back home. Sandy and Lucille embrace as Jon and Fred clasp hands. It has been a while. Cynthia is welcomed into the reunion as the two reunited neighbors walk arm-in-arm into the house.

Jon grabs suitcases with Cynthia's help, since her father is now navigating with a cane. Once the luggage is placed in the appropriate bedrooms, everyone finds their way to the back patio which has lemonade, iced tea, and shade. After everyone has something cool to drink, Jon turns to Fred.

"Fred, tell us about the friend you're meeting." He hasn't been privy to the numerous conversations Lucille and Sandy have had and quite frankly, he couldn't keep up. Fred gives

Jon an abbreviated version of meeting George in the Army, training together and being stationed at Fort Hunt.

"And you haven't seen each other in all these years?" It was a question, but more of an amazement they'd had no contact.

"They did write for a while but then lost touch," Lucille explains, not wanting to add further details her husband might want to hold back.

"The Park Service wants to talk to you about Fort Hunt?" Jon was trying to get more of the story.

"Yes, they wanted to know more about activities there during the war." Fred let out information in small drips.

"What *did* go on there?" Jon asks.

"We conducted intelligence work and interrogations." Fred starts. "Prisoners were brought to us for questioning."

"This was very hush-hush." Cynthia jumps in to explain. "Since dad speaks fluent German, he was useful in interrogating German prisoners. And the amount of information they got from Fort Hunt was important to the war effort." She feels she summed that up nicely.

Jon and Sandy both seem impressed and take all of this in stride. Living near the nation's capital, and next door to many military and political families means they sometimes run into intelligence topics when discussing people's jobs.

"Tomorrow we're meeting everyone about ten o'clock at Fort Hunt," Lucille informs the group. "Brandon and his boss, Vince Santucci will be there to give Fred and George a tour."

She smiles at Fred. "We'll see if you can tell Brandon where some of the old buildings used to be."

"I'm afraid he's going to have to tell me!" Fred admits. "The last time we were at Fort Hunt it was hard to recognize where anything had been."

"You never know, Dad, it may come back to you with George there to help." Cynthia is trying to be positive. By the time they finish their drinks it's time for dinner.

Sandy rises, "I hope you're hungry," she teases.

Dinner conversation is happy and relaxed. Of course, everyone marvels at the serendipity of Sandy and Jon being at Fort Hunt on the day Park Ranger Dirks made her plea.

"Brandon said she's going to be there tomorrow. The whole team is going to be there to meet us," Cynthia confirms.

"I'd like to know what else they learned about 1142," Fred says thoughtfully, "but mostly I will be glad to see George."

The conversation drifts from kids to the rest of the plans for the trip and heading to see Fred's brother Rudy in Philadelphia. Rudy enlisted before Fred, did a stint at Camp Ritchie and spent the remainder of the war in Europe. Once he got back, he attended Notre Dame and earned a Ph.D. in chemistry before landing a job with Dupont. He had a good career, highlighted by various promotions and his one major accomplishment, the creation of plastic grocery store bags, which Cynthia would wryly refer to as the family's blessing and curse.

Since Rudy married Lucille's first cousin, their two children were "like double cousins" Cynthia would laugh. Now, Rudy is hospitalized battling cancer. Unbeknownst to any of them, this visit will be the last time they see him alive.

The friendly conversation on the patio propels the gathering well into the evening and when the lights along the path flicker on, they reluctantly go inside.

The next morning there is an air of excitement and anticipation. During breakfast Lucille recaps some of Fred's interrogation stories for Sandy who is completely engrossed. Lucille adores and respects her husband and is immensely proud of his achievements, which does not go unnoticed by Cynthia or their friends.

After breakfast, the Michels pile into their car and head to Fort Hunt, followed by the Grays. It is only a twenty-minute drive. Cynthia has never been to Fort Hunt, but easily navigates to the front of the entrance, clearly identified with a large wooden park sign. Just off to the left is a refurbished white house they think might be an officer's quarters or caretaker's house. She drives past a picnic area where a family reunion or party of some kind is just getting underway. She sees balloons, a grill being fired up and kids running to catch a frisbee. Cynthia pulls up in front of an older, white two-story building, the Grays park next to her.

Cynthia glances down the sidewalk and spots an older couple standing with a group of park rangers. Just then Brandon turns and waves to Cynthia. As each car door opens, the group of people on the sidewalk turn to see who is joining them. Lucille takes Fred's hand as they head towards the group, but Fred has singular focus on one distinguished, older gentleman.

George Mandel clasps Fred's hand with the other landing on top. This is the most outward show of emotion men of that generation usually show, but Cynthia can see in their eyes what this reunion means.

"George, it's been too long," Fred is genuinely overcome with emotion. Then he turns to introduce Lucille who George vaguely remembers. George follows etiquette and introduces his wife, Marianne. Cynthia is then brought into the group, finishing with Sandy and Jon Gray.

Brandon takes the lead and introduces the rest of his team. Brandon's immediate boss, Matt Virta, his boss Vince Santucci, and Dana Dierks the park ranger who had started the whole line of discovery; and finally, Petula Dvorak, a reporter for the Washington Post who will interview each veteran. Her photographer has begun subtly snapping a few pictures of their initial meeting.

Lucille and Marianne quickly engage in conversation while George and Fred catch up.

Brandon and Cynthia are watching with smiles, awed by the moment. Vince, Dana and Matt are listening and absorbing the exchanges. When asked about the buildings, Vince gives the group some background on what's still standing.

"This wood framed structure was built in 1904 and was the NCO or non-commissioned officer's quarters. It's one of the only buildings left standing after the war. I thought we might end up here if you'd like to take a little walk first?" he suggests.

"If we go down this way," he motions for the group to follow as he navigates across the well-manicured grounds, "we'll walk past where the barracks were positioned."

The group follows him down a path, past the picnic pavilion to the parade grounds. As they walk, Cynthia strikes up a conversation with George about his memories of 1142, prisoner interrogations and keeping silent all these years. He tells her about some of the same events her father told Brandon, questioning prisoners on specific topics of interest, interviewing scientists in Boston, finally bringing up the dictionary assignment.

"Dad told us about the dictionary and made sure Brandon understood it was created by both of you. He wants to make sure you are also credited."

"Yes, we worked together well," George admits with a fondness Cynthia can hear in his voice.

She asks about his family and his grandchildren. Their conversation flows so easily she feels George could have been her uncle. He is relaxed, very well educated and well-spoken, yet makes her feel included. She can tell he must be a good teacher because he is not speaking down to her, which she appreciates. She likes George immediately.

Cynthia falls back while the group gathers around Vince who is pointing out landmarks. She thinks about George, her father and all the years that passed between them. George built a good life, has a strong marriage, excelled in a distinguished career, is respected and loved. George and her father were very much alike. As she watches her father and George reconnect, it strikes her how fortunate they were.

George and Fred are asking questions, reminiscing about their duties, and trying to identify where buildings had been so many years ago. Vince tells them, "The old barracks and the interrogator's quarters stood over here," he points across the path. Fred and George talk about arriving in the bus with the windows painted over and their initial impression after being deposited in the middle of nowhere.

"This is where the mess hall was." Vince is facing a flat grassy patch, "and right in here…" he points, and Fred finishes his sentence, "… were the other barracks." Fred recognizes the open area, now part of the flat picnic grounds.

"Yes," George confirms, now seeing it all with younger eyes. "The prisoner barracks were just down over there," he says pointing down the road, "maybe too far to walk today."

"Right, yes, they would've been down that way, "Vince confirms.

"Where did you do interrogations?" Cynthia asks as she looks around.

"They were conducted in the main building on this road." Fred says as he moves to the grass.

"And we're about where the mess hall was," Brandon says, which brings humorous comments about German vs U.S. Army cooks.

Vince points across the field, "When you came in, if we had turned away from the Non-Com building, that area was where the hospital stood. It was called the Creamery."

"Remember we talked about the other military intelligence operation that was conducted here?" Brandon jogs Fred's memory.

"Yes, yes, I remember you telling me, but we didn't know anything about it at the time," he says, glancing at George.

"What's this?" George turns to Brandon and leans into the conversation.

Brandon briefly explains the other military initiatives conducted from "The Creamery" and "The Warehouse." George is just as surprised as Fred to learn what went on literally under their noses, however they both remembered the constant line of trucks and daily mail runs.

"Where was the pool?" Fred asks and Vince points on ahead and urges the group to keep walking, making a loop.

As they make a turn following the asphalt road, Vince points to an open area across the way. "The swimming pool was just over there, and beyond that were the Officers' quarters or maybe the huts for special prisoners like Heinz Schlicke."

"And wasn't there a fence, like a holding yard too?" George asked as he did a 180 pivoting from his vantage point.

"Yes, as we head back to the NCO house it was that open area beyond the building."

Brandon and Vince are trying to pass on as much information as their research uncovered. The fenced in yard was beneath one of the guard towers, an open area they would've passed on their way in. The listening station or bunker was near the battery. Farther down was the administrative building where they were first initiated to Fort Hunt.

As they stand in the warm August sun, they marvel at how young they were when they arrived and all the responsibilities they had. Fred looks around again. There are no familiar buildings left. The swimming pool has been filled in, the guard towers and fenced yards removed. Even the drive where they first stepped off the bus and dropped their duffle bags has all changed, paved over years ago and expanded for group parking. There are no poles with speakers, no jeeps with servicemen, no MPs, no PWs.

Brandon and Vince seem to be the only ones who can locate where wartime landmarks once stood. After so many years, the transformation back to a natural park is complete, hiding all semblance of the war initiatives in which Fred and George participated.

Vince leads the way back and the group easily slips into their own conversations. Ranger Dierks is the first to speak to Cynthia. "You must be tired of hearing all the war stories by now," she jokes.

"What war stories?" Cynthia asks. "We never heard any of this!" she glances at Lucille.

Marianne is talking to Lucille but stops to interject, "We never knew any of this either. George just never talked about the war and if he did, he would dismiss it as no big deal."

"I knew Fred was doing something important, just from the hints he would give," Lucille adds, "but the stories I'm hearing now are quite something."

"I had no idea he interrogated anyone, let alone Nazis," Cynthia admits.

"And had I known Nazi prisoners were this close to my house..." Lucille shakes her head at the thought, "well, I would've wanted to move!" was all she could think to say.

"You know it's a shame their secrets kept them from talking to each other." Marianne reflected. "Now, hopefully, that will change." The women continue walking slowly behind the others. Brandon and Vince meander along beside George and Fred. The photographer snaps a photo here and there while Petula listens, taking in details of their conversations.

George and Fred talk about some of their interrogation activities; dressing up as officers, the ruse of pretending to be Russian Generals, playing softball and chess, bits of conversations and information remembered that proved to be vital to the war effort. Occasionally, the name of a fellow interrogator or a PW long forgotten, now suddenly seems relevant. Some of the details escape them, but the weight of their responsibilities floods back.

They come up to a picnic table area and decide to rest. Fred gingerly lowers himself to sit with George. Brandon takes a seat and Petula sits, taking the opportunity to ask questions.

"So, when was the last time you two saw each other or spoke?" she asks.

"It was after I was discharged, Spring of 1946. "George offers first. "I came back to 1142 to work as a civilian before starting school. Once I was discharged, we kept in touch a little, I think I wrote you a letter," he turns to Fred.

"You were going back to Yale to get your Masters," Fred remembers. "I wasn't discharged till summer, July of '46," he clarifies.

Petula asks them to recount some of the stories they told Brandon. They summarize a list of intelligence topics ranging from the submarine schnorchel to sonar to infra-red technology, atomic and molecular studies, jet engines, and the revealing conversation George had on enriching uranium.

Fred tells her about the shift to rocketry and how the U.S. wanted to retain numerous scientists towards the end of the war. He mentions the space program and Operation Paperclip.

Petula is not familiar with Operation Paperclip but quickly realizes what it accomplished. This is a topic she feels could fuel a completely different article, so she tucks it away for later. Then she asks about their backgrounds, and each recounts the highlights of their childhoods in Germany, fleeing the Nazis and immigration to the U.S.

It was not lost on Petula that, by the time they had grown up, gone to school, enlisted, and landed at Fort Hunt, they were still young, in their early twenties. She appreciates their cunning and ability to go one-on-one with top Nazi scientists. Maybe it was the boldness of youth that allowed them to perform so brilliantly, confirmed by the quality of the intel they gathered. Even more unbelievable was that all of this happened in a little-known fort sitting along the Potomac in pastoral Virginia.

Brandon is listening intently and feels a need to reinforce the fact that this story would never have come to light had it not been for the historical markers project. "The chance encounter here at the park between Fred's neighbors and Ranger Dierks is what brought these two veterans here today," he says. He sits for a moment wondering how Petula is going to boil this story down to a few lines in an article for the Washington Post and is relieved it's not his job. Then he offers to show George and Fred some of the pictures and documents he's found in the National Archives.

The veterans carefully rise and follow Brandon and Petula into the frame building trailed by the others. Before he goes through the door Fred stops and turns to take in the expanse of the lawn, the trees, and the calmness of the park.

"It's good, it's very good to talk about all of this at last," George admits and both men turn to enter.

Cynthia takes the opportunity to present an idea to Vince. "Brandon and I were talking, what do you think about a real reunion?" This has been burning inside her for weeks now. "I mean if Brandon can find more soldiers, could we do some kind of bigger reunion?"

"Actually Cynthia," Vince laughs as Matt walks up, "We were just talking about that. We'd like to do something for these guys, but of course we'll have to see if we can find them and if they are able to travel."

"Brandon is the contact," Matt explains, "and he's having some success. There's this one fellow he's been calling who literally will not talk to him about Fort Hunt. I think it's the cryptologist guy."

"Bedini," Vince knew exactly to whom Matt was referring. "He may come around if it's a larger, more formal ceremony to honor the men of 1142. All we can do is keep trying."

Cynthia nods. It was anyone's guess how many 1142 vets are still alive. "Even if it's ten people, I would still like to do something to recognize them," Vince admits.

Cynthia is relieved. She knows what her father's service means to her and she can see Vince understands. "I'm tossing around some ideas for a reunion with speakers and even a memorial to these men," Vince offers. "Let me work on that." Then he motions towards the door, "Shall we?"

Brandon is showing Fred, George, and the others the spread of documents he's collected. There are copies of interrogation transcripts, a brief about the other intelligence departments and a copy of On the River Potomac. This is a historical study Matt commissioned from a Cultural

Researcher, Dr. Matthew Laird which is now his team's historical reference bible.

George and Fred leaf through the materials with interest. Fred recognizes an interrogation transcript as one of his. The photographer snaps a shot here and there while Petula asks Brandon if she can lay out some of the research on the table.

"Sure, here you go," Brandon pulls a couple of photos and forms from a folder.

Fred looks on curiously. There is a U-boat captain he recognizes in one photo on top of an induction form. Seeing the papers splayed on the table immediately brings him back. He sways slightly and steadies himself on the edge of the table. This is a lot to take in.

Lucille, ever vigilant of her husband, suggests they sit someplace, and the group heads to some picnic tables. The past couple of hours have been emotional and wearing for both Fred and George. Their spouses know it and realize they need to wrap this up.

Lucille is the first to thank Brandon and the staff for their kindness and hosting them. This is the signal to bring the reunion to a close. Hugs are exchanged, heartfelt handshakes grasped, and each family slowly makes their way to their respective cars with the promise to keep in touch.

Once on the road, Cynthia is very much aware her father is fatigued and just needs to sit and rest. She's glad for the drive to give everyone a chance to take in the events of the morning. George and her dad had a familiarity and seemed to speak the same language. She could see there was a comfort in that.

They drive in silence for a while as Cynthia maneuvers around Washington traffic heading to Uncle Rudy and Aunt Nancy's in Philadelphia. Cynthia knows seeing her relatives will also be emotional, which is a lot to go through in one trip.

As they head out of the worst traffic, she realizes it's inching past lunchtime, and they could all use something cool to drink. There's an exit ahead with plenty of choices.

"Who's ready for lunch?" she brightly asks with a smile as she turns off the highway.

Lost, Now Found   GWMP Offices, McLean Virginia August 2006

Chapter 13

Lost, Now Found

GWMP Offices, McLean Virginia

August 29-31, 2006

Brandon sits at his desk piled with park projects, correspondence, and responsibilities that need his attention. He needs to pack for his trip to Georgia tomorrow to interview Wayne Spivey, and marvels at how quickly things are happening.

He and Vince found the original secrecy oath with numerous signatures and requested the Pentagon send a letter releasing the soldiers from their prior commitment to silence. The two men are much more confident, reasoning that this official approach would bring more veterans into the open. Brandon had mailed the letter to his list of vets, and all but forgot about them as he focused on Fred and George.

Petula's article about their reunion ran on the front page of the Washington Post the very next day, a Sunday. It proved to be one of the most effective advertising vehicles Brandon could have hoped for. Veterans and the children of veterans started contacting him.

It was literally a couple of days after the article when his phone rang. On the other end was someone he had not been able to locate, but who had found him. His voice was deep with a pronounced German accent which reminded Brandon of Sergeant Schultz from the old TV show, *Hogan's Heroes*.

It was Rudolph Pins. Rudy had heard Brandon was interviewing people about 1142, got his number and called. Rudy was living in New York and was willing to talk about his service. Brandon mentioned Fred Michel and that brought a flood of warm memories. Brandon was planning a trip to New York in September and now, he wanted to add Rudy to the list.

As they chatted Rudy told him about being sent to America while his brother was sent to Israel and that he lost his parents in a concentration camp. He told Brandon that he ended up at 1142 because of his language skills, just like everyone else. Brandon was anxious to hear and record his story. "I'm planning a trip to New York in early September, and I'd like to interview you if that's OK?"

"Certainly, certainly." Rudy was easy going and seemed ready to talk about his family's history and what he did during the war. Their interview was set for September 14th and 15th. Brandon figured he'd need as much time with Rudy as he'd had with Fred.

Brandon thought for a minute and asked," Did you know Reinhard Gehlen? Is that name familiar? He would have been at Fort Hunt towards the end of the war."

"Yes, Gehlen, Reinhard Gehlen was the head of the *Fremde Heere Ost* or the Foreign Armies East. He had been German military intelligence, the security service of Himmler's SS and senior intelligence officer on the Eastern Front. He was an expert so to speak on Russia and Eastern European Armies. He was interrogated about Soviet capabilities, their organizations, their personalities, etcetera, etcetera."

"Really? Did you interrogate him?"

"Only tangentially," Rudy was playing it close to the vest. "I was the morale officer. I escorted him to movies."

"In Washington?"

"No, no, on the post." Rudy clarified.

"But we wanted him because of his Soviet knowledge, right?"

"Yes, he knew a great deal about the Russians, and he was eventually set up to run the equivalent of a German CIA after the war."

"We seemed to shift to Cold War tactics pretty quickly after the war," Brandon realized out loud. "Was he an important Cold War expert at the time?"

"Gustav Hilger. He was probably more important from a diplomatic standpoint," Rudy assessed a prisoner with whom he had become close friends. "You know Hilger was a civilian, never a soldier. He was the number two man in the German Embassy in Moscow for almost twenty years, sort of a career diplomat. He is sometimes considered more valuable than Gehlen, because of his specific Soviet knowledge."

"You interrogated him?"

"Yes, he was at 1142. Bill Hess interrogated him too. Bill had never interviewed a foreign service person."

"But you got to know Hilger well?" Brandon again was amazed at the friendships that formed.

"Yes, until I left for Nuremberg. After the war we reconnected and became good friends and stayed friends over the years. We came back to visit Fort Hunt a couple of times."

"Really?"

"Yes. We would have a picnic."

Then Brandon remembered Fred's comment about keeping in touch. "While you were in Nuremberg, Fred mentioned you wrote to him."

"Yes, we corresponded for a while. I left in the middle of May, '46 because I was recruited by the War Criminal Tribunal in Nuremberg to do interrogations."

"So you went right to Germany," Brandon assumed.

"No, no. Because of the usual Army bureaucracy and screw-ups and so forth, it took until August until I finally managed to get to Nuremberg. I did spend some time in Czechoslovakia."

"When you finished at Nuremberg and came back, did anyone try to recruit you for intelligence work?" Brandon couldn't help but ask because of his Nuremberg experience.

"There was some attempt, some consideration," again Rudy was playing coy. "I did work for the government," was all he would say.

"OK, so you did intelligence work for the government?" Brandon pressed.

"Yeah."

"Really?" Brandon thought he was getting somewhere. "And what was that?"

"I don't intend to go into that," Rudy politely shut him down, and that part of the discussion was closed.

Their phone call ended amiably and the date for their interview was set. What Brandon didn't know is that neither he nor anyone would ever get Rudy to talk about the years in between the war and the present. Few if any knew what he did after the war, his career or where he had worked for the last few decades. He never married or had children. Perhaps the work he did was intelligence, which he would hint at but never confirm. Later, the only conclusion Brandon and others could come up with was CIA, or some other secretive branch of the service. They could only guess.

Brandon got off the phone marveling at Rudy. Of the 1142 vets he'd talked to, all were friendly, intelligent, and underneath it all, very tough. He admired them.

In the weeks after the article and after Brandon's query letters, first three, then five, then seven positive responses came trickling in. Brandon started to follow up on each one. He felt it was important to do a pre-interview, a process where he could break down any lingering barriers and set the tone and guidelines for an in-person interview. Brandon would also be able to get a general idea of each vet's experiences, their responsibilities at 1142 and their availability.

One of the response letters was from Angus McClean Thuermer. That was quite a name and Brandon had a feeling there was a bigger than life personality attached to it. He wasn't disappointed.

Brandon had a number for him and dialed. He wasn't quite sure where he got this name, maybe from a list of transfers. At this point it didn't matter. The no-nonsense Midwesterner on the other end answered and confirmed he was indeed Angus Mclean Thuermer. As they chatted Brandon recognized a different kind of war story taking shape. This veteran's tale started right here at home.

Angus was born in Quincy, Illinois, raised on the south side of Chicago and attended Illinois University in Urbana. He had an affinity for language, and although at the time he didn't speak fluent German, he could read and understand most of what he read. He wanted to be a foreign correspondent and he also wanted an advanced degree. It was arranged that he would spend six months at the University of Berlin or the Kaiser Wilhelm University and six months at the Alliance Francaise in Paris, but he never made it to Paris. He had landed a job with the Associated Press as a stringer in Berlin.

Angus told Brandon about being in Berlin the night of Kristallnacht, being sent to Poland and watching firsthand as the Nazi army invaded.

"I could report until Pearl Harbor, then I was taken into custody with over a hundred other journalists and detained for about five months. Once I got home, I enlisted and volunteered for intelligence work and that's when I ended up at 1142. But I wasn't there long. I did interrogate a U-boat captain, though."

Brandon is duly impressed with the history this one man had lived but wanted more Fort Hunt information. "At 1142, were you ever given specific topics to investigate?"

"No, but we did learn interesting facts about how the Kreigsmarine functioned that we could use later. For example, if a boat was captured, the first thing you do is separate the officers from enlisted men and take their clothing. In the hip pocket of enlisted men is a card used to register what Wehrmacht bordellos they'd visited on leave. They track this in case a sailor gets sick. Then the ship's doctor can look at his card and see, 'Oh, you were with Maria last.' So, he'd make a call and take Maria out of business."

"We'd use that information to start a conversation and ask, 'Is Maria still on the job?' and they'd be amazed!" he laughed. "They thought we knew everything already, so if we asked them about a detonator or new torpedo, they thought we had the information anyway and they'd open up. Worked beautifully," he finished.

"Can I ask you if you knew Jack Alberti?"

"Alberti! Sure, yes, my gracious. Alberti was always in civilian clothes, a nice looking fellow."

"What we understand," Brandon begins, "is that Alberti was a civilian who may have been commissioned by the Navy but was essentially a direct link between the Pentagon and Fort Hunt interrogations. He was assigned to Heinz Schlicke. Do you know anything else?"

"The name certainly rings a bell, but that's it." Angus had no more to offer.

After the war Angus joined the CIA and had more experiences than Brandon wanted to cover in this initial conversation like spiriting Joseph Stalin's daughter Svetlana out of New Delhi. Brandon arranged to meet at Angus's home in Middleburg, Virginia near the end of October.

"That's going to be some interview," he thinks. Vince Santucci and Park Ranger Sam Swersky think so too and say they want to join him.

Last month, after Fred and George's reunion, Brandon and Vince quickly realized it would be too much for many of these vets to travel for an interview. Vince felt if they were going to continue the project, he needed a budget to send Brandon and maybe Sam to the veterans' homes.

Vince went to Robert Sutton, the Chief Historian who was not only interested in the oral history project but was committed to capturing these interviews for posterity. Sutton pooled dollars from every budget line he could spare and gave Brandon the go-ahead to travel. Tomorrow, Brandon is flying to Marietta, Georgia, to talk to Wayne Spivey, the librarian of 1142. He'd gotten Wayne's name from George.

As Brandon packs his tape recorder and notepads, he thinks back to his phone conversation with a gentleman who had a classic southern drawl complete with relaxed, elongated vowels. At first, Wayne was reluctant to talk about 1142 and needed to check Brandon out.

"Why thank you for cawlin' but ah don't know if ah can tell you much, son." Wayne started out.

"But sir, I do have permission to talk to you about your activities at Fort Hunt, as I've explained. Besides, I have spoken with the DIA at the Pentagon, and they allowed Fred Michel and George Mandel to interview with me."

Wayne said he had a faint recollection of the names and remembered seeing them printed on the transcripts. "Then ah guess we can have a go at whatever you want to talk about. You say you know about the PWs we had there?"

"Yessir," Brandon replied. "Fred and I had quite a talk about many of the PWs that came through 1142. It was quite remarkable to say the least. As I understand it, you were the one who kept all the paperwork and the transcripts organized."

Wayne smiled on the other end. "You know we had over thirty-four hundred PWs come through 1142. That's a lot of interrogation and a lot of transcripts." Wayne started to relax, and things were coming easier. Yes, he remembered some of the interrogator's names. Kolm, Pins, Hershberger and a few others. He talked about the volume of interrogations which had to be transcribed, catalogued, and cross-referenced.

Then Wayne paused and said, "You know, Brandon, ah would love to talk to you more about all of this. I haven't spoken of the war or 1142 since – gosh, probably never. It felt good to tell you these things. Thank you."

Brandon was deeply touched and for the first time, really felt the impact of releasing these soldiers from their oath.

They set a date for the interview then Wayne ended the conversation with, "And now, son, ah need to go and tell my wife what ah did during the war." With that he hung up.

Brandon remembered sitting there with the phone still in his hand, letting the impact of what Wayne had just said, thoroughly sink in. He knew he was getting emotionally invested, but he didn't care. Maybe that's the thing. He did care and was starting to care more deeply than he thought he would. He was both proud and eager to talk to these men and give them the thanks they deserved. He knew he had to find as many men as he could as quickly as he could.

The next day Brandon flies to Atlanta and finds his way north of downtown to the growing bedroom community of Marietta. When Brandon gets to Wayne's house, he is welcomed by Wayne's whole family who has eagerly gathered to hear this story. Wayne's three children, spouses and some grandchildren are scattered around the living room, dining room and throughout the house.

Wayne starts with, "I was born in Centerville, Georgia, next to the last of seven children." He had volunteered before

Pearl Harbor, then when the U.S. entered the war, things changed quickly.

"Ah kept seein' all these German American boys, the Italian American boys and they were shippin' us all to a place called Fort Hunt. It was July 13th, 1942, and they were gettin' it ready for us."

Wayne knew of the Creamery but said they never let him go near it. He was too busy with the volume of interrogations and transcripts he was charged to manage.

"Tell me about your archiving system," Brandon asks.

"Well, it was born out of necessity, I can tell you that!" Wayne begins. "We had, as ah said, a voluminous number of interrogations and excerpts to keep track of and any of the officers might call back a portion at any given time. Usually, Major Szlapka and Sergeant Sharp would go over all the interrogations and flag some of the most important materials for the Pentagon," Wayne explains.

"One day the Major came in and told me he had a hard time findin' things and I should get this organized. It was Saturday and I had to have it done by Monday!" Wayne laughs. "Well, ah got it done with a cross-referencing system too."

"The Major had to be happy with that." Brandon comments.

"Well, he was so happy he made me Chief Clerk!" Wayne laughs again, "and that kept me pretty busy."

Wayne explains how he catalogued transcripts but there were also PW drawings, sketches and diagrams of weapons and technologies he couldn't identify, but nonetheless, he carefully logged.

"And there was this one interrogator who came back with these atomic symbols and molecules and such. The next day the Major says, 'Stamp that stuff confidential and send it off to the Pentagon today. So ah did! Ah didn't know what it was, but it was hot. Ah think it was related to the atomic energy."

Since he had been there so early on, Wayne could identify many buildings like the Creamery, the Warehouse and the Sugar Mill, but maybe not what each was used for since his area was interrogation and they all stuck to their own areas.

"And they didn't have a chapel there," he adds.

"No?"

"No. If you wanted to go to church, there was ah truck on Sunday mornin' to take you up to Fort Belvoir." Then Wayne starts to laugh. "There would be about three Protestants and twelve hungover Catholics! Those boys would be out carousin' all night, but they'd get up and go to mass the next day, even if they were all slumped over!"

Everyone enjoyed the story, then Wayne recounts the games they'd play like baseball, football and volleyball which became very competitive. He remembers a team of Mormon boys who played them in volleyball and "stomped us into the ground."

Then he says, "George Frenkel," which caught Brandon by surprise. "George was another interrogator who was there early on, then they transferred him to Fort Ritchie. That's all I know, but George was a fine fellow. We got along real well."

Brandon was jotting down the name of George Frenkel when Wayne ends with the story of his younger brother Harry who was a flier and was shot down in the South Pacific. He parachuted out, was injured, and captured. Wayne knew his brother was tortured before he was executed. The family finally recovered an urn with his ashes after the war.

"He's interned up here in Marietta National Cemetery."

"I appreciate you sharing that," Brandon says.

"I just wish ah had better recall." Wayne admits. "They were a fine group of men and ah feel they made a great contribution to the war. I'm proud to be part of them. It was an honor to be included."

Once the interview is wrapped, the family surprises Brandon with Braves tickets. Wayne is taking his grandson and Brandon to a game sitting 5 rows behind the dugout. Brandon feels like a celebrity.

After such an eventful weekend it should have been anticlimactic coming back to work. But Monday morning Brandon walks into Park Headquarters with more leads and a fresh interview to transcribe. Then he realizes he has Sam the intern to help. Relieved, he passes along the tapes and turns his attention to tracking down more vets.

He slides into his desk chair with a fresh cup of coffee and reaches for the top envelope on his stack of responses. It was from Eric Kramer, and includes a phone number, so he dials.

An older gentleman with a New York accent answers. After the initial introduction and pleasantries, Eric is eager to talk about 1142 but questions, why now?

Brandon explains declassification and the chain of events that has led to 1142 and asks Eric about his memories of Fort Hunt. "I understand you served with Fred and were transferred there about the same time."

"Yes, I remember Fred. We were at Camp Ritchie together and we went to 1142 together," Eric confirms. "We did intelligence work, interrogations. We had similar backgrounds." Eric has a very matter of fact way of summarizing information.

Eric recounts growing up in the Bavarian Palatinate and living in Munich. "When Hitler and Nazism began to rise, well, that's what forced me to leave. I couldn't go to school to get an education, so I left. I was 17 and my parents sent me to the sister of my grandmother in New Jersey. I lived on their couch in the living room!"

"She was your sponsor?"

"Yes. It wasn't ideal, but I was lucky to get out, come here and find a job."

"What about your parents?"

"They made it out through Italy. I got them tickets on an Italian ship. They lived into their 90s." Eric was proud he was able to give his parents a long life.

"How did you end up at Fort Hunt?"

286

Eric said he enlisted, then describes his confusion of having no orders. "I thought I was getting shipped back to Germany, you know because I spoke German. But then I end up at Camp Ritchie for intelligence training. That's when I met Fred. We all had to ride this painted bus over to 1142."

"I heard about that bus." Brandon says with a smile.

"You know, the whole place, all of 1142 was bugged," Eric says casually. "So we could hear conversations and make transcripts of everything."

"Yes, Fred and I did discuss that," Brandon recognizes the same information. "Do you remember who you interrogated?"

"We talked to German officers, some U-boat personnel. Towards the end of the war everything was about rockets. You know, Werner von Braun and Magnus von Braun, a couple of East Prussian aristocrats," he says with a slight disregard.

"But they were great scientists and there was a lot of them. Towards the end of the war, they had all tried to move south to Bavaria. They wanted to surrender to the Americans, not the Russians," something else Brandon was used to hearing.

"For von Braun and his scientists," Eric concluded, "what I did was more custodial. We had to go to New York, I guess they were in transit from Boston, and my job was to process and transfer some of them to White Sands, New Mexico."

"I see," Brandon understands the process of transferring these scientists. "Eric, there's a lot more I would love to talk to

you about, but I want to record everything, in an interview."
Brandon goes on to explain that other 1142 soldiers live in the
vicinity of New York City, and he is planning a trip in
September. He asks if September 12th works for an in-person
interview.

They agree on the date and will meet at Eric's home.
Brandon hangs up and adds Eric's name to the calendar, then
opens another letter. The respondent is Peter Weiss who
includes his address and phone number in Manhattan.
Brandon dials.

"Hello, Mr. Weiss? This is Brandon Beis of the National
Park Service."

"Oh, Mr. Beis," an older, seasoned voice of a New York
City dweller answers. "I've been waiting to hear from you. I got
your letter about Fort Hunt and found it quite interesting."

"Yessir," Brandon is looking for a way to launch into his
appeal, but Peter does it for him.

"So let me get this straight. You are gathering
information about Fort Hunt or 1142, for a historical project.
Certain information has been declassified and you have
already spoken to someone about our intelligence work at
1142. Is that right?"

"Yes, sir, that's it in a nutshell." Brandon finds himself
relaxing. "And to that point, I was hoping to interview you
regarding Fort Hunt and your time there. I have already
spoken to someone you served with, Fred Michel."

"Yes, Fred. I was at Camp Ritchie with him and then we were sent to 1142. Yes, I do remember him. You want to talk to me as well?"

"Yessir."

"You know I came to this country as a Jewish refugee and ended up interrogating Nazis." Here he surprises himself at the irony. "It's quite a story actually, but one I have never fully told."

Brandon assures him the information surrounding Fort Hunt is declassified and he has a permission letter to prove it. Peter is affable, quite friendly, very well spoken but direct. When Brandon finds out he is a lawyer, the tone of their conversation starts to make more sense.

Brandon learns Peter came from Vienna and that his whole family luckily made it to the U.S. in 1941, settling in New York. He was in college when war broke out and was drafted in '44.

"I was stationed at Fort Sam Houston in Texas when my CO, my commanding officer, asked if I spoke German. I said yes and he said, say something in German. So, I recited a line of a Goethe poem, and he said stop! Good enough. And I was shipped out to camp Ritchie," he quips with a short chuckle.

"Did you know it was an intelligence training facility?" Brandon asks.

"Yes, we knew it was intelligence," Peter confirms, "While I was there, we learned how to interrogate, ask the right questions, there was some counterintelligence training and things like photo interpretation, which I found quite interesting."

"Do you remember anyone else at Camp Ritchie with you?"

"Arno Mayer was there too. There were a lot of German speakers in my section but there were probably other languages there too." Peter was struggling to remember details.

"How long before you went to 1142?"

"I wasn't there very long. I got some kind of diploma that I graduated from Camp Ritchie and then we went to the Pentagon, from the Pentagon to 1142. Of course, no one told us anything. We had no idea where we were going."

Brandon notes the similarities in Fred's and George's transit stories. Brandon could have gone on for hours but realizes, "I'd like to set up a time to interview you."

"Sure, we can set something up." Brandon hears Peter reaching, maybe for a calendar. "You know the whole place was bugged," Peter adds as an afterthought.

"Yes, so I've been told." Brandon is again smiling.

"And that was one of my jobs, monitoring," Peter offers. "We listened in on PWs cells. There were two PWs to a cell. If they started to say something interesting, we would turn on the recorder. That was one thing." Peter finishes. "So what dates are we looking at here?"

Brandon is visualizing a soldier with earphones listening to a conversation in a World War II barracks and has to snap back to his calendar. "Yes, let's see, I'm planning a trip to New York in September so if we could look at the 13th, that would be great."

"Yes, that will work." Peter confirms. "Come to my office. It's in Manhattan. It might be more comfortable."

Peter gives him the address and they confirm a time. Then he adds, "And we never laid a hand on anyone."

"Excuse me?"

"We never used force or torture or any kind of violence to get information."

"Yessir, I've heard that as well."

"Not like this waterboarding business, what we're hearing in the news now."

Brandon can hear the disdain in Peter's voice, then comments, "Fred mentioned that although you listened in on conversations, most of the intel came from interrogations. Did you find that to be the case?"

"Yes, for the most part, but..." Peter is clearly setting something up. "This one time we had a guy, a PW who was from the German embassy in Madrid. When he came in, we put him with another PW who was also captured in Madrid, and we listened to them to see if any good information would come of this pairing. The second guy starts telling the first guy about this German woman he had picked up in Madrid and had this wonderful affair with. Well, it turned out to be the embassy guy's wife!"

"What!" Brandon couldn't help but let out a laugh. "I'd love to see that transcript!"

"After that there was a lot of screaming – we had to get someone in there to separate them," Peter finishes, relishing the twist.

Brandon is enjoying the stories and tells Peter he is looking forward to the interview. Then he casually asks what kind of law Peter practices.

Peter quickly sums up his law career telling Brandon he became a lawyer after the war and mentions almost in passing his work at Nuremberg. He was involved with preparations for the trials of German business leaders who had funded the Nazi party to win elections and financially supported the Nazis so they could maintain power.

He went on to practice commercial law, but in the 1950s pivoted to advocate for civil and human rights. Peter mentions an important case in 1966 where he advised the victims of the massacre at My Lai, an incident during the Vietnam War.

Brandon was familiar with it from history studies, and if he had not been impressed before, he was now. As a human rights lawyer, among other things, Peter was instrumental working with a group of international lawyers against nuclear arms. Their work led to the handing down of an opinion by the International Court of Justice in the Hague in 1996 stating that the use of nuclear weapons would violate international law. The man was an international justice icon and Brandon had an interview set up with him, in his Manhattan office, for September 13th.

After he hangs up, Brandon takes a moment to let the whole conversation sink in. This was becoming larger than the Park Service and the accounting of one location's history. Brandon can see the impact of the story of P.O. Box 1142 interrogators is turning out to be bigger than anything he had imagined.

Just then Vince comes in and pulls up a chair. "How's it going?" he asks.

"Good – almost too good." Brandon admits. "I'm finding these guys and I have a couple of interviews set up. I'm planning a trip to New York. I have four people I can interview up there," he says adding, "thanks for the travel money. I'm going to use it!"

"Thank Bob, he's the one who found it!" Vince laughs. "This is all we've got so let's get the most out of it! At least until next year and we'll see if we can build more into the budget." He pauses. "What else is on your mind? You looked a little shell shocked when I walked in." He is starting to know this kid well.

"Yeah, it's the larger picture, I guess. The enormity of World War II, the Nazis." Brandon feels himself rambling and sits up. "Vince, these guys have a story to tell. One that has never been told – at least as far as I can see. No one, and I mean no one knew about this interrogation center. And if they did, they've said nothing for 60 years. We're sitting on something big."

"Yeah, I have to agree with you on that," Vince says. "I think you're going to find more of these guys than you think." Vince squares his chair to Brandon. "Maybe not all of them but a good number. I think we should start canvassing vets as we talk to them about coming to Fort Hunt for a reunion. We'll see how many would be willing to travel and then we can pick a date. I'd like to honor them for their service, maybe invite the media, get some coverage, and let their story be told. What d'ya think?"

"I think that would be great!" Brandon admits. "I'll start asking these guys. Getting Fred and George back together was a good trial run. How long do you think we need to pull this together?"

"Definitely until next year. Give everyone time for arrangements. We'd need a reception or a flag ceremony, or something," Vince was spit-balling ideas. "By the way I got a call from Congressman Jim Moran. One of his staff saw the story about Fred and George in the Post. He wants to talk about how many vets we've found, but he mentioned sponsoring a House Resolution Bill honoring these guys. We just started talking so we'll see where this goes." With that he leaves, and Brandon turns back to his desk. Things are happening.

Over the next weeks, Brandon makes it through all the response letters. The last one is postmarked California. It is from Arnold Kohn who is in Pacific Grove, California. Brandon knows California is a 3-hour time difference. He glances at his watch, does the time-zone math, reasons it isn't too early out there and picks up his phone.

A pleasant older woman answers, and Brandon introduces himself.

"Why, we have been talking and talking about this since we got your letter. I'm Helen," Arnold's wife introduces herself with a refined Virginia accent. Then she calls over to her husband to pick up the other line and commences a 3-way call.

After the niceties of their introductions and Brandon's pitch for Fort Hunt information, he finds both Arnold and Helen agreeable and eager to talk about their activities during the war. As it turns out, both spent time at 1142.

"So, you were brought in as a secretary?" Brandon now can't believe his luck.

"Yes! Don't ask me how I managed that but somehow it happened," the good-natured Helen charmingly jokes.

"Actually, I chose her specifically because of her typing skills." Arnold interjects. Helen explains she worked at the Pentagon with top-secret clearance when Arnold needed someone to come to 1142 for document processing and clerk typist duties.

"Helen did the typing of the Fragenbogen, the questionnaire. It was a screening document," Arnold clarifies.

"Let's back up a minute," Brandon needed more foundational information. "Arnold, I'm guessing you speak

German. What were you doing at the time, and did it involve prisoners at 1142?" Brandon asks.

Arnold, it turned out, is another unique story. He tells Brandon he was born in Boston of German parents. His father's job brought them to Europe when he was very young, and he ended up learning kindergarten German and kindergarten French, he quips. But his linguistic skills are what helped him in intelligence work.

Arnold went to officer candidate school and reached the rank of major. In Algiers he oversaw prisoners, so by the end of the war he was a good candidate for 1142. Arnold became the officer in charge of the scientific section and was tasked with processing PWs as a precursor to Operation Paperclip.

"I needed a typist, and they sent me to CPM," he states.

"CPM was Civilian Personnel Management," Helen interjects. "I was a civilian working in that department."

"They said I could pick someone to help me," Arnold goes on. "When I got there, I was handed a list of over 200 names, so I literally chose the name with the best typing score!"

"Well, as fate would have it," Helen picks up the story, "Arnold brought me back and forth to work on a daily basis."

"Nothing happened for a while," Arnold assures Brandon, but Brandon can't care less. He is very entertained at the re-telling of their courtship. "But then we had a retirement party for General Vandenberg who was director of intelligence and was leaving to take over the Air Force. We were at the party and Helen wanted to dance with someone handsome, so I asked her to dance!" He adds with a laugh.

"You know, he was quite handsome," Helen teases, "so you can guess the rest of that story!"

Brandon was smiling and now eager to get their 1142 memories recorded. Helen especially offered a unique take on what Fort Hunt was like, commenting on the layout of buildings and the environment which seemed quite relaxed for a PW camp.

"A prison camp in a pastoral setting is a better description," she says.

"Were you there long after the war?" Brandon asks, wondering when the buildings had been taken down.

"We processed the scientists, then they brought in Gehlen, Reinhard Gehlen." Arnold remembers. "He was a big deal. He was a German spymaster type. But by the time he and his group came, we were winding down."

"Did you interview him?" Brandon was intrigued.

"No, no, I just heard his name."

The fact that Arnold and Helen were in California poses a unique geographic problem for Brandon. Luckily, a past coworker had relocated to the west coast. He would arrange for the Kohns to talk to her.

The call ends and Brandon quickly looks up Karen Kinsey. Karen had been a historian for the Cultural Resources team of the Park Service who was now in California. He calls her and once he explains the project, she is immediately on board. She will do the interview and send the recording back to Brandon.

Over the next few weeks Vince gets Sam Swersky permanently assigned to the project. Sam will accompany Brandon to New York. Brandon and Vince are talking about expanding the budget to include a camera and lights for the interviews.

The trip to New York went better than expected. Each veteran is still sharp and eager to tell their stories. Their insights on the intelligence operation helps paint a more detailed picture of how this intelligence branch impacted the course of the war.

Brandon, Sam, and Vince now understand how 1142 intelligence supported all branches of the military. Early in the war, 1142 intel had provided the order of battle and German military insignias and ranks, which helped the D-Day invasion.

Interrogators from 1142 identified a strategic ball-bearing plant; they found out the Germans were loading and unloading trains at road crossings, not rail yards; that the Germans were masking submarine pens by building fake coverings and that Japan and Russia had been secretly laying plans to join forces against the United States after Germany surrendered.

The result of this significant intelligence was the bombing of the ball-bearing plant, more accurate curtailment and bombing of rail shipments and submarine yards. The vast amount of intelligence accumulated through interrogation at Fort Hunt also provided information on how to beat the U-boats' sonar-proof skin, the use and effectiveness of infrared detection devices, the German Flamingo omnidirectional infrared warning system used against heat radiation of infrared searchlights on airplanes, the U-boat schnorchel underwater apparatus, infrared homing devices, cloaking devices, amplification of high-speed messages to submarines, remote control steering of a boat explosive using radiolocation heat from ships and applying infrared technology to steer rockets.

Adding that to the information they already heard about infrared and microwave technologies, jet engines, rockets, detonation devices and laying plans for the Cold War and the Space Race, it came to quite a list of accomplishments.

Brandon understands why the government wanted to keep this quiet. The interrogators of 1142 were, in fact, our own secret weapon, and now it was time to acknowledge them.

It is now fall and the leaves outside Brandon's office are starting to arrange a colorful palette for display in the coming month. He can feel a brisk hint of the changing season in the breezes swirling around him on the way into work. He bounds through the front door, navigates down the hallway to his office and settles into his chair when the phone rings. An older gentleman with a definitive New York accented greets him.

"This is George Frenkel, I hear you are looking for veterans of 1142."

Brandon is thrilled to hear from George and wants to know how he knew about the research project. Frenkel had spent his career in the Army, working as a military historian so news of a historical project involving Fort Hunt seemed to find him. He quickly confirms that yes, he had been at 1142 for a short time during the war.

"Do you remember Wayne Spivey?" Brandon asks.

"Yes, we got to 1142 about the same time and served together till I was moved."

Brandon asks about his background and what George tells him is akin to how many soldiers arrived at 1142. He was born in Berlin to a solid middle-class family but the financial collapse in 1930, "destroyed the middle class and pushed them into the arms of Hitler," he explains to Brandon.

His father, like Fred's, had seen the writing on the wall and made efforts to get George out. Then in 1937, just like Rudy and Peter, his family decided to send him, alone, to America. He was just a teenager.

George was reluctantly sponsored by a distant relative who didn't want him as a financial burden. Even though Frenkel was well educated and had come from a well-off family, he lived a meager existence, taking any job to support himself. He survived by the kindness of others and attended school at night.

His parents were lucky enough to get out in 1939 but Frenkel would learn after the war, he'd lost many other relatives to the Holocaust, specifically the concentration camp of Theresienstadt in Czechoslovakia.

In May of 1941 Frenkel was drafted. The Army needed linguists and Frenkel was sent to Camp Bullis in Texas where he learned interrogation techniques. He became a good candidate for the MIS-Y program. Like Wayne Spivey, he was one of the first to be assigned to Fort Hunt, arriving in the summer of 1942. Frenkel monitored and translated interrogations, then was transferred to Camp Ritchie to become a recruit instructor.

"Instructing new recruits kept me on my toes, but I got my real experience when I was sent back to Europe as a prisoner-of-war interrogator. You know, on the spot interrogation. That's different," he explains. "That experience made me a better interrogator," he adds. "I have to tell you, during my interrogations I never laid a hand on anyone. We extracted information in a battle of wits."

Brandon asks, "Do you remember anyone else who was there at the start of 1142, with you and Wayne?"

George was thinking, then came up with "Lucky, Lucky Moritz. I think his name was Werner, yes, Werner Moritz. If you find him, he'll have some stories to tell."

That certainly piqued Brandon's interest and they ended by setting up a formal interview for early December.

As he gets off the phone, he looks at the growing list of names. Each name has a unique personality and a story that is now part of his life. He has been on quite a journey, but he knows it isn't over. This history has fallen into his lap, and he feels a duty to tell it well and accurately.

Those park signs, those wayside park signs started it all, he laughs to himself. Of all the projects in all the locations of the whole National Park Service, I ended up at Fort Hunt with this project, he thinks. What, luck, what sheer dumb luck.

As Brandon marvels about the strange turn his life is taking with these veterans, Vince Santucci is researching interrogation techniques and military intelligence. He's run across a thesis paper written by Lieutenant Colonel Steve Kleinman, U.S. Air Force Reserve career intelligence officer doing his military master's thesis on strategic intelligence. Kleinman is a recognized expert in the fields of human intelligence, strategic interrogation, special ops, and survival training. His paper and theories intrigue Vince, especially considering everything Vince is learning about interrogation. He makes a note to reach out to Kleinman who he thinks might be interested in what 1142 vets have to say.

SECRET

Information received ~~Item~~ #608   13 September 1945
P/W Dr. SCHLICKE, Heinz.   Maj. Hershberger
Korv. Kapt. U-234   Sgt. Michel
SRG- 1265

                                        18 SEP 1945 -0800

Development of the Infra Red Detector (Bildwandl

        Research completed August 1944.

                    fra-red detector.

                 the current model.
                 detectors in series (Dopp
                 rror or infra-red detector
                 ector with secondary multi
                 -red detector.

              um Infra-Red Detector.

              e current infra-red detec
              oto-electric layer, the b
              ing potential of the cath

                                   an be u

        cesium, the   ct-
        part. A hig   of
        ral sensiti
        the infra-

        The photo
        energy   t
        sensitivi   tor.
        sensitivi   ive
        the ener   . It
        photo-el   e-
        can be a   out
        electric   face

Unsung Heroes   Louisville, KY Spring, 2007

layers, to be separated from the photo

                    - 1 -   SECRET

Chapter 14

Unsung Heroes

Louisville, KY
Spring 2007

Cynthia and Lucille are excited about the arrangements for the very first Veterans of Fort Hunt, P.O. Box 1142 Reunion, which is now planned for early October. Everyone at the Park Service is well aware of how much they are asking of these eighty and ninety-year-olds, but so far, the response has been enthusiastic. Cynthia assures Brandon the Michels will be there.

Brandon mentioned to Cynthia that many of the veterans' wives and families learned about their loved one's war experiences for the first time after he contacted them. Even if the veteran was reluctant, Brandon found their children and grandchildren were quite eager to hear more of their father's or grandfather's achievements and to pay tribute to all the veterans.

Cynthia is looking forward to meeting other family members and comparing notes. She is also thankful the activity generated by the event has kept her father busy and he is looking forward to reuniting with his Army buddies. As

Lucille noted, "He still has his moments, but overall, he seems to be doing better."

Cynthia was glad for the change in her father's temperament but still worried about his depression. One night she and Lucille had a long talk about her father's career, the pressures of his various jobs, the ups and downs, finally coming to what may have sent him into a tailspin.

"When he took the job at Melpar, all contact with his Army buddies just seemed to stop."

Lucille was walking down memory lane. "Melpar was a good company until that awful scandal."

"I was in like sixth or seventh grade when that happened," Cynthia laughs.

"You probably don't remember all the details, and some of this is unsavory," Lucille cautions, "But after your dad was with them a while, Melpar got caught up in a contract scandal with Bobby Baker who was the Senate's Secretary to the Majority leader. It was called influence peddling which is just plain bribery," she says definitively.

"Baker was arranging sex for votes on awarding government contracts, overpricing goods on government contracts and God knows what else. This all broke in 1964 but by 1968 the damage was done." Lucille is referencing a scandal that stained the Lyndon Johnson administration and spawned Senate investigations that went on for almost three years.

"That's when he went to Westinghouse?" Cynthia interjects.

"Yes, it was Westinghouse Maryland at the time, and he developed weaponry for the war – we were embroiled in Vietnam. But you know the Army always wanted your father and even though it took a few years, they created a position only your father could fill."

"I remember, but he was still a civilian, right?

"Yes, a civilian position that gave him the equivalent of 4-Star General clearance. I think he was quite happy with that job."

"That was the *lean company-automation* stuff?"

"Yes, it was quite revolutionary at the time and your father was in demand."

"Do you remember that trip Dad took to Poland? When was that, 1977?"

"Yes, I think it was. The Polish government requested he come to speak on how to implement *Lean Company* techniques."

"All I remember was how sick he was, but he couldn't refuse; he had to go."

"When a foreign government asks for you to come and speak on your technology, you go, sick or not." Lucille stated. "But that trip affected him. It wasn't being sick or being in Poland. It was the trip to Dachau. That experience stuck with him." Lucille remembers.

"Is that when you got involved with the Holocaust Museum?"

"Yes, it was around that time, during the Carter administration. You know your cousin Werner and his wife Joan helped us and other supporters raise almost $200 million in private donations to build that museum. Remember I showed you the Washington Post front page with Werner's mother's passport in the middle of the Museum's announcement?" Cynthia is slowly nodding, recalling the image. "Anyway, your father's depression started in earnest well after that, after he retired from the military and started doing consulting work."

"One day he had a meeting with someone at DOD and they told him something. He never told me what, but I can only imagine. He fully retired after that and then the depression set in. So, I can only draw the conclusion that for some reason he was out. They didn't need him or want him. Maybe they were cleaning house? Maybe he was too old? Maybe he wasn't up on the latest technology - whatever it was, they no longer wanted him as a consultant and that's what deflated him. It was then that this depression set in."

Cynthia was mulling over all these possible explanations. "It sounds like he just wanted to be needed, feel useful. You know his whole identity was wrapped up in his career. Not doing something he felt was important would've been a low blow. But dad is so much more!" She saw so many other qualities, his wisdom, his love for his family and his duty to his country. This seemed so one dimensional. "Maybe I'm grasping here, but I'm hoping the reunion will give him some of that back, give him some kind of validation. You know he did ask Brandon that very question. Did it all mean something? What they did – did it matter? Maybe that's what dad is looking for?" Cynthia is replaying his conversation with Brandon on her head. "I wonder if the other soldiers have gone through this?"

It was a conundrum she feels is unique to her father, but maybe reconnecting with other veterans would somehow substantiate her father's role at 1142. She is hanging a lot on the power of these friendships and their shared experiences, but maybe this reunion would help her father find answers.

Cynthia's mind wanders beyond George Mandel to Rudy Pins to Eric Kramer to Peter Weiss to all the other faceless names on her father's roster. Would he be able to reconnect after sixty years like he did with George? Will being honored and thanked by the Park Service or whatever Brandon and Vince are cooking up, validate his service? She doesn't know for certain it will bring him out of his depression, but she sure hopes it will.

At GWMP headquarters, Vince is calling Colonel Steve Kleinman. Vince tells Kleinman he is intrigued by his paper on interrogation, and they chat about current and past techniques, and what these 1142 soldiers accomplished.

Steve Kleinman is an intelligence officer and recognized expert in this field who advocates against the use of torture. Non-violent techniques are something the 1142 soldiers used successfully and aligned perfectly with Kleinman's philosophy, expertise, and training.

Kleinman cut his teeth in Operation Just Cause, Operation Desert Storm and Desert Shield. He was assigned as Director of Intelligence of the Personnel Recovery Academy which is responsible for Survival, Evasion, Recovery and Escape – SERE – a product of the WWII program of Escape and Evade.

In 2003, he was involved with the questioning of Iraqi insurgents and halted the use of coercive interrogation tactics citing legal, moral, and ethical grounds, concluding torture has no place in American intelligence programs.

Recently he testified before Congress to call attention to abusive treatment of detainees and called for the interrogation manual to be replaced. However, his proposal, for the most part, was ignored,

Vince is bringing Steve up to speed on some of the men of 1142, their intelligence accomplishments, their training and how they interrogated Nazis prisoners.

"We have an interview set up in a week with someone we've talked to before, but maybe you'd like to join us?" Vince offers.

"Yes, I'd like that," Steve responds. The interview is in Silver Springs, Maryland at Bill Hess's home. It would include Brandon, Vince and now Steve.

Steve asks for any materials they already have on Bill Hess and Vince obliges with his transcript and some information from the first interview.

A couple weeks later, Steve finds himself in front of the WWII vet with the two park rangers who are chatting comfortably.

Brandon quickly has the recorder set up and once everyone settles, hits record. Brandon begins with his standard opening introduction of names, date, and place, then asks Bill about training at Camp Ritchie, to get Steve up to speed.

Bill talks about intelligence training and conducting reconnaissance exercises in the farmland of western Maryland. After a while Brandon tries to home in on specific WWII information asking about three areas of interest Bill mentioned earlier: ball bearings, rubber and petroleum.

"Well, petroleum was important because Germany made synthetic petroleum with IG Farben. And ball bearings because there were few resources. They were made in Frankfurt."

Steve learns that 1142 intel contributed to the bombing of a ball bearing plant at Schweinfurt, just east of Frankfurt.

"At the end of the war did you ever hear comments about atomic weapons or nuclear weapons?

"Yes, we did hear about atomic weapons, and something was going on near the Hohenzollern castle. There was a little town in the mountains near that castle. That's where they stored the heavy water, stuff like that."

Brandon goes on to ask about Operation Paperclip, but Steve is thinking a map would have been helpful to nail down where Hohenzollern castle was and further interrogate on the location and importance of the atomic weapon information. He can't help but feel an opportunity just passed.

Vince then asks Bill, "If you can take yourself back to 1947, '48, '49 and since then, do you have any sense of how important the MIS-Y program was?"

Bill thinks then shrugs and says, "I really don't know, except it's interesting to my family. But I guess the two important things I can mention are the schnorchel, you know, for submarines, and the magnetic torpedo, the homing torpedo. That was the first time I understood that something was very important. The rest? I really don't know how important it was."

Here Steve needs to explain, "I've done some research into the program, I looked at materials in the archives and I can tell you without hesitation that your program was indispensable."

Bill looks pleased and says, "Thank you, that's good to know."

Back at headquarters, Vince is moving forward with reunion plans. They have located over a dozen veterans who have committed to attend, and those vets are contacting others.

Vince, Brandon, and Matt are tossing around ideas for the event; maybe have speakers from each branch of the military the interrogators were drawn from, Navy and Army. They are thinking about giving each veteran a certificate of appreciation for their service, have a flag presentation or dedication of some kind. Vince suggests he and Brandon put their archeological skills to the test and locate the WWII Fort Hunt flagpole. He is thinking they could construct a new flagpole base with a plaque honoring the veterans. "Once the weather is nicer," he tells Brandon. "We'll get out there and get started."

More immediately, Vince needs to check back with Congressman Jim Moran's office. Someone on his staff is calling wanting more information on the veterans. They are surprised at the depth and scope of the military intelligence conducted at Fort Hunt and are impressed with the fact that none of the veterans ever spoke of their service afterwards.

That was all Representative Moran needed to hear. He was writing House Resolution #753 honoring and thanking the soldiers of "Post Office Box 1142," and hoped to have it signed and passed by October.

Brandon is deep into his mission of finding more vets, especially before the reunion. The stories and anecdotes he hears from these soldiers are amazing. At Nuremberg, Rudy Pins interviewed Hermann Goering over a game of chess. Angus Thuermer was one of the last vets to ride on the heavy German cruiser Prinz Eugen which the US Navy got as a war prize. Peter Weiss became an international human rights lawyer. He could only imagine the stories that would be told when these veterans got together.

Brandon is confirming his headcount. Helen and Arnold Kohn, the charming couple in California said they unfortunately would not be able to make the trip across the country. Just the same, Brandon is glad to have their unique perspective recorded by his friend.

Brandon turns back to the task at hand and continues down the list of names. He finds himself staring at the name George Frankel had given him, Werner Moritz. Brandon locates him in Charlotte, N.C.

He dials the number and waits. A low, slightly gravelly voice with a distinct German accent answers. Brandon introduces himself and explains the reason for the call, mentioning the intelligence work of P.O. Box 1142.

Werner was a little reluctant at first, but once Brandon assures him of declassification and at the mention of George Frenkel's name, Werner relaxes. He starts by telling Brandon his nickname was "Lucky" and it's a moniker that would prove to be well earned.

As a kid, he lived with his widowed mom and siblings in Frankfurt. But in 1933, when Hitler started to rise, his mother saw what was coming and in 1935, sent him to his uncle's home in England. Werner lived there working in his uncle's fur business sewing pelts, but he didn't get along with him. Werner tried to persuade his mother to leave and take his brother and sister out of Germany, but she was reluctant, so he decided to return to Germany and try to convince her.

"You were in England, but you went back to Germany?" Brandon asks.

"I made the mistake of going back on Nov 9th of 1938." Werner explains.

He reminds Brandon that was the night German Jews suffered Kristallnacht. Brandon understands the danger Werner put himself in. During the Night of Broken Glass, many Jews were rounded up and put into concentration camps, including Werner. He was sent to Buchenwald, then released after 4 weeks with horror stories of the treatment he experienced. He returned to Frankfurt, but now he couldn't get his family out. They had no papers or sponsors, but he did. He could still return to England.

"Saying goodbye was awful, a terrible scene, you can't imagine. But when I got to England, I didn't want to stay with my uncle. I wanted to get to America, to New York. I had an American friend who knew someone at the Consulate and got me a sponsorship, an affidavit. I made it to New York and found work in the only business I knew from my family, the fur business."

"What about your family? Your mom?"

"The camps. My sister and mother were gassed in one of the camps outside Berlin. My brother, I am not exactly sure what happened, I never found him. But I did hear from someone who said they were in a camp together and that he was killed."

Brandon understood and went on. "Once you got to the United States, you were working and then how did you enter the war?"

Werner told him when Pearl Harbor was bombed, he made the decision to enlist. He had to report to Camp Upton and did so on the same day Jerry Lewis and Mickey Rooney arrived. "There was some press and a lot of fanfare with those two." Werner remarks.

After that unusual start, he was one of the first soldiers to be identified as a German speaker and assigned to 1142.

"You were one of the first to arrive at Fort Hunt?" Brandon can't believe his luck at finding someone who could give an earlier perspective of Fort Hunt, different from vets like Fred, who arrived near the end of the war.

"Yes," Werner confirms. "When I came to Virginia to report for duty, the Pentagon was still being built! There was confusion about where we were going but we finally made it to Fort Hunt." He laughs and then tells Brandon that a lot of the buildings were still being built. Their barracks were rudimentary but adequate.

"Did you receive any training when you got there?"

"We were trained by Brits on interrogation techniques." Werner explains. He was also sworn to secrecy for the work they were doing and told to remain silent about his service even after the war. He knew they would be doing intelligence work and became aware of coded letters being sent to American PWs. When talking to one of the CO's, he suggested using certain German words spelled backwards as a code.

"I'm not sure they used my suggestion, but I thought it might help."

"But you interrogated prisoners *and* knew about the coded messages?" Brandon starts to realize that as one of the first soldiers at 1142, he would have been able to do a little bit of everything. Things hadn't started out so compartmentalized. "What else did you do?"

"One thing 1142 offered were patrols to help find Nazi units or sympathizers in this country, in the United States."

"I didn't know we did that."

"Yeah, this was a service 1142 provided. I was sent out a couple of times; but this one trip I was on a train riding through Texas looking for listening posts and Nazi sympathizer cells. We found one sixty to seventy miles outside of Houston. This was a German-speaking spy cell. We would triangulate the signal to locate them. We found out they had actually been contacted by the Germans."

"How did you handle that?"

"Turned the location over to the FBI. It was important enough to arrest some of these people. We had nothing to do with arresting people. We just located them."

"What else did you do back at Fort Hunt?"

"Maybe the biggest contribution I think I made was when Frenkel and I and a guy named Kreuger overheard two PW Naval officers talking about Peenemunde."

At this Brandon perked up. "The rocket production plant?"

"Yes, yes. We discovered where the V1 and the V2s were being developed and built before they were even fired. We knew of the test firings in the North Sea, but at this point, none had landed in England yet. These two officers were speaking so quietly, so hushed that Frenkel and I really had to listen hard to their words and sometimes we even argued with each other about what the words were. But we listened and listened until we got the words right."

"What happened to the information?" Brandon knew the Brits had bombed Peenemunde but only after England had been pummeled.

"So, this is important," Werner prefaces his next remarks. "This information was forwarded to the officers involved. They were supposed to take our information then disseminate it. It turned out two weeks later the V1s and V2s pummeled England and the top echelon didn't know anything about it!" The lapse in proper communication still irritates Werner. "The information was not disseminated. The top echelon got so pissed off and they said, 'Clean out 1142!' and we were all sent overseas on short notice."

"When was this?" Brandon was taken aback as the whole operation had been in jeopardy.

"Well England was bombed in June of '44, so right after that, late July or August 1944," Werner states. "We should not have been sent overseas because it was not our fault. We did our job. We predicted the V1s and V2s. We knew where they were. We forwarded the information, and they dropped the ball." Brandon could still hear bitterness in his voice over sixty years later. "Then the General in charge of 1142 was relieved of his duties."

"Wow, what happened to you?"

"We also got relieved, and we ended up meeting overseas. The officers right above us? They held their jobs because of who they were. But they were not qualified to keep their positions." Then he thinks for a minute, "Is that too strong?

"No, actually," Brandon admits, "You aren't the first person to say this."

"They may have been nice guys, but they were not qualified. And we didn't find this out until we all got canned."

"What happened to you and the other men?"

"I was sent to Europe and attached to George Patton's headquarters. Before we shipped out, they sent us to Camp Ritchie for field training and new weapons training. It was tough training, but after I got to Europe, I was glad we had it!" he admits.

"Once I got to Europe, I was dispatched with a group to locate German bigwigs. We're out in the countryside on the outskirts of Nuremberg. It's late in the afternoon, getting dark and we see three guys marching toward us, one with a white flag. I go back to my guy with the phone, and I say we need orders, what should we do? I think these guys want to surrender. So, this guy from the Third Army says, 'Tell 'em to drop their weapons and come forward.' I did, and they told me they're from a division and the division wants to surrender."

"The whole division?"

"The whole division. Here I am taking possession of a division! So, I call the Third Army and ask what should I do with these guys? We manage to get this division in a field and they send soldiers to put wire around that division and call it a prison camp!" He laughs at the haphazard solution.

"I asked their general why he gave up? He said, 'There's no place to go. We're finished. We're done.' I wanted to question him more, but he wouldn't talk to me because I wasn't an officer. To tell you the truth I should've been made an officer after capturing a whole Division!" he says with emphasis.

"What did you do after that?"

"We were given orders at that point to roam around and find Nazis. We were a team of four riding around in a jeep near Waldering, Bavaria. So, we're out in the countryside, it's hot as can be and this kid comes running down a hill yelling at us. I talk to him, and he tells me Julius Streicher is in this farmhouse. We have four MPs and four interrogators so when we get in there, I go through the house and what do we find? Julius Streicher in bed with a 15-year-old girl. I get him up, tell him to get dressed and I take him into custody."

Julius Streicher was part of the Nazi propaganda machine and was the editor of the maliciously antisemitic newspaper, Der Sturmer, which made him very wealthy and deeply reviled. Brandon is somewhat familiar with the name but not the deep impact his name has on Werner.

"We take him out of the farmhouse and put him in a hut. Before I go in, I tell the MP, 'Listen, this guy is a guy of great importance. He hates everyone. He hates Jews. He hates Blacks,' and you know three of the four MPs that were with me were Black. But I tell them, 'I would kill this guy right now because he doesn't deserve to live, but I'd be court-martialed. I'm going to do what I have to do.'"

"I went inside the hut, I had Streicher undress. I took out my penis and I pissed all over him, his head, everywhere. He started to move, and I said, 'Don't move.' I told him to keep his hands on his head. He was going to sleep like this, naked on the hard floor. I had my pistol and I told him I'd shoot if he moved. Later we handed him over and he stood trial at Nuremberg."

Brandon is taken aback by the act and Werner's candor in telling it. He will never really get used to shocking war stories. "When was this? When did all this happen?"

"Towards the end of the war. Germany had surrendered, so, May of '45."

"Then what did you do?"

"We wandered around and found a Waffen SS who wanted to surrender. He was hurt. He wanted to bargain for medical treatment to save his eye in return for information on some of Goering's riches. He was Prussian and he said he lived just down the road in a Chateau. We had heard that Goering had hidden some of his stolen loot all over in this region."

"Did you help this guy? This Waffen SS officer?"

"His story sounded intriguing, but I was skeptical. But yes, we helped him. We had Medics come and they saved his eye. Once he was a little better, I said 'Let's go see what we can find.' I told him he should show me anything concerning Goering."

"I know Goering was a notorious art thief," Brandon says, a little skeptical of this story. "What happened next?"

"They assigned a Lieutenant to me – which pissed me off because I wasn't an officer, as if I couldn't handle it. But no matter, the Lieutenant was a nice guy, Lt. Brown from New York."

"The next day we had a truck, a 4x4 and two jeeps, the second one full of MPs. I told the MPs to bring shovels, everything we might need, even a jack. We got to this place and it's a pretty big chateau. So that night we slept in the chateau, the next morning the guy took a metal bar painted blue on one end, red on the other and counted out steps from his front door to a spot in the lawn. He turns to me and says, 'Tell your guys to take this metal rod and drive it into the ground until they hit something.' So that's what our guys did. They drove the red part into the ground till it stopped. Then we started to dig."

"We dug for 2 hours and then found there was a massive, massive vessel down there. It was made of steel. It took the guys another hour and a half to dig the dirt out around it and six guys to get it out. We didn't have cranes or anything, but we got it out. We opened it and inside were royal possessions, crowns, gold inlays with pearls, a genuine massive amount of what looked like monarchy jewels. We tied it all together to protect it and they brought burlap to cover it all up. Then we found three boxes full of American bonds, corporate bonds. We sat there for hours that night guarding it - all night and into the next day. There was a couple of million dollars' worth."

This was war plunder Brandon will have to corroborate later but for now he just listens.

"We also found dollars. The MPs helped us count. Another million, million and a half in big denominations. A $100 dollar bill was the smallest and there were $1,000 dollar bills. I'd never seen one of those before." This also seemed incredulous but, considering everything Brandon knew of Goering and Nazi self-preservation, a large cash safety net was certainly within the realm of possibility.

"Our Waffen SS guy says, 'Now we go,' and he measures off more steps from the front door to a different location on the lawn. He tells us to take the blue side of this rod, drive it into the ground till it hits something, and dig. So, we did the same thing. We found another container but had to stop because it was nightfall."

Brandon wasn't sure if any of this treasure hunt was true, but he was in too deep to stop Werner from telling his tale. "What did you do?"

"We ended up getting it out the next day and it was full of bonds. Most of them were in Pennsylvania Railroad bonds, loads and loads of bonds. That's what Goering stashed away. So Kubala might have captured Goering, but we got his loot!" Werner laughs again.

"We let our guy sleep with his wife and see his kids that night and the next day we hauled the stuff back to the Third Army. They were going to turn it over to the 12th Army Corps. When they took possession, they gave Lieutenant Brown a receipt. And I never got credit for it, for capturing this loot. I was promised a second lieutenant's commission. That's all I'd wanted before I die," he finishes.

Obviously, Brandon understands this still sticks in his craw, but without being able to offer a resolution to this sixty-year-old slight, he decides to move on.

"Werner, I'd like to set up an interview with you so I can record our conversation and have an oral history of your memories."

"Sure, sure, when would you like to do this?"

They set up the interview for mid-May, giving Brandon and Sam a few weeks to make travel arrangements to Charlotte, where Werner and Florence live.

"By the way, I also want to let you know we're planning a reunion of 1142 veterans at Fort Hunt in October. I'm not sure how you feel about traveling, but please think about it."

"Yes, that would be something!" Werner seems genuinely excited about the prospect of seeing Fort Hunt and other vets. Brandon ends with confirmation of their July 24th interview.

After he gets off the phone, he sits back not sure he fully believes the shocking and incredulous events Werner described. Did all that really happen? Who was he to doubt this veteran. Quite honestly, Brandon must take his word for it because he has little time to research or corroborate this story even if he could trace Goering's stolen treasures. He realizes his immediate responsibility is to these veterans and the growing list of 1142 soldiers he still wants to find.

John Gunther Dean, a name that had come up with Fred and Rudy Pins and one name Cynthia had researched, was printed on a transcript of an interview he'd gotten from the Jimmy Carter Presidential Library. Cynthia had found the right person. Dean served as an ambassador under four administrations, Carter being one. In the transcript there is a mention of 1142. Brandon is now wondering where to find John Gunther Dean.

He gets up and wanders over to Vince's office. Vince is making a list of available park rangers he can pair with each vet to make sure each soldier and their families have travel arrangements, transportation, and hotel reservations for the event. Vince looks up "What's up?"

"John Gunther Dean." Brandon answers. "Not sure how to find him," then Brandon summarizes Dean's bio.

"Maybe a department of Foreign Service, like the State Department?" Vince offers.

"Good idea, I'll start there. How are you doing?" Brandon asks, noticing the scrawled notes of who might need a wheelchair and the word transportation with a question mark next to it. "Are we still doing the flagpole?"

"Yes, that's another thing, but I think we have time. I still need to get a program together. I think I'd like Steve Kleinman to speak. He's got a perspective these guys will appreciate."

"And Congressman Moran. Is he still working on the House bill?"

"Yeah, his office will let me know when it's done." Vince says almost as an aside. Then he sits back and thinks, "But I also think it would be good to present the history of Fort Hunt, you know what we've already learned through our research. I think I'd like to explain what else went on at Fort Hunt, the MIS-X program."

"I wouldn't mind talking about the oral history project, to keep it going as long as we find more vets," Brandon offers.

"That's good. That'll show them how important their interviews have become. I think Tim Mulligan might be good to include too." Tim is a researcher they all know and has extensive knowledge of Fort Hunt and its military history.

"Ah, Tim's great. He's retired but he was a big help at the National archives. He'll be on board."

As they brainstorm events for the program, the first Fort Hunt P.O. Box 1142 reunion is taking shape.

P.O. Box 1142 Reunion   Fort Hunt, Virginia October 5-6, 2007

Chapter 15

P.O. Box 1142 Reunion

Fort Hunt, Virginia
October 5-6, 2007

Cynthia wakes in a room at the Hyatt in Arlington, Virginia. She can see through slightly parted curtains a clear sky, signaling a beautiful October day. It is Friday, the day of the reunion.

The park service has flown Fred, Lucille and her to Washington and put them up in Arlington. It was maybe a twenty-minute ride to Alexandria and another five or ten minutes to the park. Today's reunion was the one she, her father, mother, Brandon, Vince and the whole Cultural Resources team had worked so hard to orchestrate.

She lies in bed for a moment thinking about the journey it has taken to get here, seeing her father's transformation and her mother ever supportive and eminently proud. She is savoring the anticipation of the events planned for today.

Her mind drifts over the faceless names that populated hers and Brandon's lists. Today she will get to put faces with those names, fill in the gaps and complete the stories. She will finally get to know the personalities of the men who were the backbone of Army intelligence. Now she can look them in the eye and thank them for all they did.

Over the past months, she has watched her father's excitement grow as he engaged with Brandon. Cynthia and her mom couldn't help but notice Fred was fueled by Brandon's enthusiasm. Brandon and Fred talk so frequently Cynthia joked to her father, "He's becoming the son you never had!"

Fred made it his mission to find soldiers from 1142. Ever the methodical engineer, she was not surprised but amused that he kept a private stash of 1142 paperwork tucked away in his "Army" binder. These were rosters, transfer lists and various papers he had rescued from the post V-J Day fire bins.

Fred privately scoured his resources and fed the names to Brandon in batches. Then Brandon used all the tools at his disposal to locate veterans. As word got out, more and more veterans were contacting Brandon.

Cynthia is lost in her thoughts when she happens to glance at the clock. She can't lie around because she knows her parents will be up and hungry. The schedule clicks into her head, *I need to get moving.* She quickly showers, dresses, and applies light makeup, then knocks on her parents' door. She isn't surprised to find them ready to go so they head down to the restaurant.

At Fort Hunt, Brandon is walking to the check-in table, taking a deep breath of fresh morning air. Today couldn't be more perfect. High, light cloud cover will shield everyone from getting too hot. Temperatures are projected in the low 80's, not too warm but comfortable. He glances up as he walks across the clearing and notices the speckled leaves are just showing hints of orange and yellow around the edges, not fully turning even though the calendar proclaims October has arrived. He can't help but think this might be the start of a pleasant *second summer.*

Brandon is exhausted but excited. He, Vince, Matt, their Supervisor Dave Vela, and the whole GWMP team have been working for months, contacting veterans, getting them to commit to the reunion, making travel arrangements and following up on every question. Vince assigned a park ranger to each veteran to help manage travel and logistics. They have thought of every detail to make sure today will run smoothly.

Brandon sidles up next to Vince and picks up one of the programs from the table. Vince is glancing out at the WWII vehicles they'd managed to procure to help set the mood. "I think they turned out pretty good," he says, drawing Vince's attention to the cover.

Vince takes the program and appraises the pictures he and Brandon carefully chose. The black and white shots of soldiers posing near the mess hall, the 1142 correspondence room with typewriters lined up, the penned in yard. On the top right corner is the Fort Hunt Park and National Park Service logo giving subtle but well-deserved credit to the organizers of the event. They have done it. They have managed to make the P.O. Box 1142 Veterans Reunion a reality.

Vince smiles when he sees the clip art of a flagpole with a fluttering flag printed at the top of the schedule of events. During the summer he and Brandon used their archeological skills to find the original WWII flagpole base. Once they located it, they moved five feet forward and had a new base and flagpole erected, this time with a plaque for the 1142 veterans.

Vince spots the reporter, Petula Dvorack, who is thrilled to return to cover the rest of this amazing story. He promised her access to any veteran who agreed to talk for her article and built time into the schedule for those interviews. He waves and moves towards her.

Brandon turns to see a bus pulling into the parking lot. *It's starting*, he thinks. *Time to welcome everyone and get them checked in.* Brandon is on the move.

There are twenty-one veterans and their families attending, fifteen more they have spoken with who could not come. Vince and the team have wheelchairs for those who need them and park rangers to assist getting them where they need to go. Brandon is keeping an eye out for Fred and the family. Finally, he sees Cynthia and heads over to welcome them.

People are lining up at check-in, grabbing name tags, the program and schedule. They start to gather in small groups, slowly recognizing each other as they carefully approach. Brandon watches as veterans come up to one another, have a moment of recognition which then gives way to a hand clasps, and broad smiles.

Various introductions could be heard; "This is my wife," "This is my oldest son," "This is one of the guys I interrogated with," and the conversations wove among each group.

Vince is busy moving through the crowd, watching the soldiers, their families, and his team of park rangers. *The rangers seemed to be as excited as the veterans*, Vince notices, trying to keep his own emotions in check. He is very proud of his team and the herculean task of pulling this reunion together. Vince knows each and every park ranger who has been involved not only gave 100% of their time and energy, but also their hearts. That was worth everything. Vince spots George and Fred standing together, flanked by Brandon, Marianne, Lucille, and Cynthia. He waves and walks over to join the group.

"You made it!" he proclaimed the obvious, as everyone beams, happy to be among the crowd.

Fred and George chat comfortably, looking forward to mingling among other veterans. "We haven't kept up with anyone for a number of years," Fred begins, "I hope we recognize each other!"

"There's a few people here you should know," Brandon says with a smile. "Two fellows, George Weidinger and Dick Kleeman both contacted me after they saw the picture of you two in the Post!"

"So people did see it!" Fred says, a little amazed.

"It *was* on the front page." Brandon reminds them.

"We're just too good looking to pass up," George jokes.

"I'll say!" Cynthia plays along. *Thank you Petula*, she thinks and makes a mental note to speak to her later.

Brandon and Vince move on to greet others who are just arriving. Between them, they had interviewed just about everyone who was here and were anxious to greet families and say hello.

"Let's move in closer," Cynthia suggests and gently maneuvers her group towards the check-in line. A bespectacled man, a little plump with sparkling eyes and cropped gray hair comes over.

"Fred?" he asks. Fred turns. "Rudy!" It was his friend, Rudy Pins. Cynthia recognizes him as the man who had written from Nuremberg. George stands there for a moment then Rudy turns to him, recognizes him, and extends a warm handshake. In a moment all three men are simply Army buddies, ready to reconnect.

"What have you been doing with yourself?" Rudy enthusiastically asks. The gap of a lifetime of experiences was hard to boil down. But Fred, being a man of few words, simply said, "Engineering, mostly factory automation," then he turns and says, "This is my wife Lucille, and this is one of my daughters Cynthia."

Rudy had a round face and a charming German accent that hasn't diminished over time. He shakes Cynthia's hand then turns to Lucille and says, "From the USO! I remember!" which brings up old stories and laughter.

Cynthia wanted to talk to everyone all at once, but feels she needs her father to pave the way through this crowd. As she stands there, another man, obviously a veteran, approaches George. He is diminutive with neatly groomed silver hair and kind, intelligent eyes behind silver framed glasses. It is Henry Kolm, now *Dr*. Henry Kolm of the Massachusetts Institute of Technology.

The MIT professor and the George Washington University department head exchange a cordial greeting, then realize they remember each other from Fort Strong in Boston Harbor where they interrogated the Peenemunde scientists. Almost immediately, Henry and George start talking about their careers, the higher learning institutions where they work and what was on the horizon in their fields. Looking backwards to the war just didn't seem as important as finding out what they had accomplished with their lives. For Henry, George, and the other veterans, it was how they used the opportunities offered in America, getting and using their education to do something meaningful. That's what seemed to matter now.

Cynthia listens, absorbing everything, amazed at the achievements of some of these men. Her father shakes hands with Arno Mayor, now a European history professor at Princeton; Bill Hess, who they discovered worked with Uncle Werner at the Pentagon; Werner Gans, who was a documents translator and interrogator at Fort Strong in Boston, and Eric Kramer, who had trained with her dad at Camp Ritchie. She is now meeting all of them.

Conversations flow easily and soon the group is directed towards a large bus for a tour of the grounds which Brandon and Matt plan to narrate. *Boy, these guys are old*, Cynthia admits to herself as she watches her father and others gingerly navigate the steps up into the bus. *It's a good thing the reunion happened now.*

Fred and George board and find seats across the aisle from each other, their wives seated near the windows while Cynthia lands behind her father. As the bus slowly pulls down the tree-canopied road, Brandon and Matt take turns identifying where the barracks, interrogation center, prisoner barracks and non-com quarters once stood. The bus makes a turn to where the pool had been, then drives past the guard station where the fenced yards used to be. Fred and George are talking about the listening post which was built into a berm, and Peter Weiss offers where he thought it was. After all, listening was his main contribution.

The bus returns and deposits everyone at a pavilion for a quick break. Cynthia is amazed how well her father is holding up but may take Brandon's offer of a wheelchair for the rest of the events. There is talk among the veterans about the war in Iraq and how interrogations are now being conducted. Before long, recent stories of atrocities committed in the Baghdad prison dominate the conversation.

"We never would have done it that way," Peter Weiss states. He is passionate about defending the 1142 method of interrogation and separating themselves from what is happening now in Iraq. His comments bring swift and strong agreement from many of the aged interrogators.

That discussion, however, must be tabled because it is time to gather around the new flagpole for the dedication ceremony. A semi-circle of white folding chairs is set up across from the flagpole and there is a podium with a microphone to the right. The check-in tent is behind the podium, and now houses various dignitaries scheduled to speak. The grass is still green and soft beneath Cynthia's shoes as she turns to motion to Brandon for a wheelchair. Fred is grateful for the ride, and the group moves in closer with everyone else.

Once the crowd quiets down, Vince welcomes everyone and explains the point of thanking these men for their service at Fort Hunt. Vince introduces the GWMP Superintendent, David Vela, who gives an impassioned and heartfelt recount of all the interrogators accomplished and how it contributed to the victory in WWII. He also asks for help in finding more veterans to complete this story.

Then the Regional Director of the National Park Service, Joe Lawler offers his thanks, and the Park Service Honor Guard presents the flag. Vince has timed the presentations, so the Honor Guard starts at 11:40, then, at exactly 11:42 am, Wayne Spivey comes forward to raise the flag. A bugler crisply plays Reveille as the flag unfurls over Fort Hunt. Soldiers fire off a cannon which is on loan from Arlington Cemetery and Cynthia jumps at the sound.

The plaque on the base of the flagpole is revealed. Cynthia can only make out a couple of words from where she's standing but takes a minute to appreciate the entire scene. The attendees place their hands over their hearts as a recording of the National Anthem plays. Once it is quiet, Wayne goes back to his waiting family.

Vince walks up to the podium and explains Congressman Jim Moran could not attend, but one of his aides will read the newly passed House Resolution Bill 753. "This bill serves to honor and thank the soldiers who served the top-secret units for the United States Military Intelligence Service under the project name P.O. Box 1142," he begins. After the reading, there is a spontaneous and courteous applause in appreciation of what the Congressman has done for the group.

Vince again addresses the crowd explaining there are representatives from both the Navy and the Army to make presentations to the veterans. He introduces Rear Admiral Ann Gilbride who then extols the accomplishments of the 1142 soldiers adding her voice to their praise. "Their work helped defeat the German U-boat fleet in the Atlantic and provided information which served as the basic foundation of Naval Intelligence in World War II." She knows the wealth of intelligence these men provided touched every part of the war effort and impacted the actions of the United States for years after.

She tells the crowd, "Today these details are too numerous to mention, but all 1142 veterans are special because their purpose had to be kept secret, even from their families, some who are learning about their accomplishments for the first time. Their satisfaction for the job they were doing had to come from within. Now, I am proud to honor their contributions." With that she calls the first recipient, Angus Thuermer, now 92.

As Angus walks up to receive his certificate, Brandon can't help but remember their conversation. It was exactly a year ago this month he, Vince and Sam interviewed Angus at his home in Virginia. *The stories that guy told – Berlin, Kristallnacht, Hitler. He's a living almanac - and still a character*! Brandon thinks with a smile. Angus accepts the award, shakes both officer's hands and stands while someone snaps a picture.

One by one each Navy veteran is called to accept their commendation. Then the Army representative, Colonel David Griffith takes the podium. He will present each interrogator with a Freedom Team Salute and Commendation for outstanding service.

The first person called who is present is the Honorable John Gunther Dean who has flown from Paris to be here. A pin is attached to his lapel, and he is handed his commendation.

Then the others come forward as their names are called. They are now old men, some with canes, some struggling to manage the award and handshake, but each is smiling and proud to be here.

When Fred's name is called, he rises with the help of a park ranger and makes his way to accept his award. Cynthia's eyes tear. She can't help it. She glances over and her mother is the same. They each acknowledge the pride and love they feel and break into wide smiles. Fred reaches for the award and shakes the hand of the Colonel who turns to the crowd and mentions, "Had it not been for this man, none of you would be here." There are subtle laughs from the crowd. Fred is a little embarrassed at the attention, but he accepts the award.

"As I understand it, we owe Fred a debt for shedding light on this chapter of our history." Then he turns back to Fred and simply says, "Thank you." A light applause supports his sentiment and Fred, smiling now, stands for a quick picture then returns to his seat.

Lucille takes the award as Fred lowers himself into his chair. Once he is settled, Cynthia doesn't miss the opportunity and leans into her father's ear, "I think you're blushing," and he waves her away with a little shake of his head. "Congratulations, dad," she adds with a small grip to his shoulder. Lucille is on the other side of Fred, looking at the citation in a thick, padded document holder. Only a piece of paper but the message of gratitude behind it means a great deal.

Each veteran is called up, congratulated, and handed their certificate. Then Peter Weiss' name is called. Peter approaches the Colonel but does not take the citation. He has a conflict he must vocalize, and he knows this group above all others, will understand.

He steps around the Colonel to the mic and explains. "I am deeply grateful for this honor, but I want to make it clear that my presence here is not in support of the current war." His comments are respectful but direct, and there are nods of agreement and support from the crowd. Then Peter politely accepts the commendation and pin before returning to his seat.

There's gonna be a lively discussion at lunch! Cynthia thinks as she watches Weiss move back to sit next to his wife, Cora.

Once the awards are given out and a group picture taken around the flagpole, the veterans have time for interviews from local news outlets. A handful of reporters are covering the event including Petula from the *Washington Post* and Chuck Hagee from the Mount Vernon Gazette. Cynthia waves to Petula who acknowledges her but is making a beeline for Peter Weiss who is already talking to Chuck.

"I find it almost incomprehensible that our moral values and our abhorrence of war has deteriorated so far. It would not have even occurred to any of us serving here during WWII to do what is being done today to gather intelligence," Peter is explaining to Chuck.

Petula joins the interview and gets the second part of his reaction. "We were proud to serve in the Army at that time.

The tactics employed today are unconscionable and I don't think they produce good intelligence," Peter finishes.

Petula is about to ask her own question when another veteran of 1142 comes over to shake Peter's hand, thanking him for speaking out. "Thank you for making that point," he says to Peter. Then he turns to Petula, "We all feel the same way. We extracted information in a battle of wits. I'm proud to say I never compromised my humanity."

Cynthia is introduced to John Gunther Dean, the foreign diplomat who Brandon tracked down in France. Fred is talking with Eric Kramer who trained with him at Camp Ritchie, then processed the Peenemunde scientists at Fort Strong. Lucille has struck up a conversation with Peter Weiss' wife and all seem to be deep into their conversations. Just then the park rangers approach and remind people it is time for lunch. They head towards the Pavilion.

Cynthia understands Peter's need to make a point of their treatment of prisoners. She knows these men would have conducted themselves with the highest integrity, mostly because she knows her father and what he would do. Now, she was beginning to know his fellow 1142 interrogators and the type of men they are. These men were all cut from the same cloth.

As the group moves into lunch, she ends up sitting near Ambassador Dean and is fascinated hearing stories of the positions he held, the countries he lived in and the Presidents he served. Now he is settled in France with his wife and has made the long journey back for this reunion. Cynthia asks about his responsibilities at 1142 and he tells her he was the morale officer for Heinz Schlicke.

"The U-boat scientist?" Cynthia remembers.

"Yes, your father was his interrogator, but I had to get his family out of Germany."

"For Operation Paperclip."

"That's right. The agreement was to get their families out safely and Germany was a mess after the war." Then John goes on to tell Cynthia how he collected Schlicke's wife and children and brought them to the U.S.

Cynthia is still struggling with her feelings on "Paperclip," but she would litigate that later. There were more stories to hear and veterans to talk to.

After lunch a park ranger helps wheel her father up to the front of the pavilion where a small dais and microphones are set up for a veteran's discussion. Fred is flanked by George on one side and Peter Weiss on the other. This panel is set up as a "meet your fellow veterans" opportunity and remarks are supposed to be contained to remembrances of Fort Hunt.

Matt Virta is still making his way to the dais as Peter continues explaining to George, "I felt I needed to clarify that my presence should not show support for this administration's tactics. That's not the way we conducted our interrogations."

Arno, who was on the other side of Peter can't help himself and pipes in, "I feel like the military is using us to say, 'We did spooky stuff back then, so it's OK to do it now,'

Then George Frankel leans into the conversation, "I conducted many interrogations, many. And I never laid a hand on anyone. None of us did." His voice firmly hit the last word. George and Fred agree.

Cynthia is watching the mini discussion from the audience, wondering what they are talking about as Matt approaches the mic and asks the crowd to quiet down. He then invites each man to introduce themselves, starting at the far end of the table away from Fred. Cynthia strains to see Dominick Marletto stand and take the mic. Dominick was the only guard they interviewed and recounted the events surrounding the only prisoner who was killed at Fort Hunt.

"It was June of 1944 and Werner Henke, a U-boat Commander who believed the British wanted to try him as a war criminal, didn't want to be handed over. He instead decided to rush the fence. We had two barbed wire fences. He was ready to go over the second one when the guard ordered him to stop. When he didn't, the guard shot him. They had to have a trial because a man was shot and at the trial he was fined about the price of a pack of cigarettes. He paid the fine and they gave him the cigarettes. This happened all on the same day."

There were slight chuckles and rumblings because some were not aware a prisoner had been shot there during the war. Marletto went on to recount how they set up a primitive dark room so he could dabble in photography, snapping pictures around the fort.

Here Matt interjects, "I have to tell you how important those pictures have become. The pictures he took gave us the only physical documentation we have of Fort Hunt at that time, something we were most grateful for."

Marletto wraps up with his sentiment, "There was a job to do, and you do whatever is asked of you."

Moving down the line different veterans recount harrowing abuse at the hands of Nazis before escaping to the United States. Then, when war broke out, they willingly enlisted to fight for their new country.

Werner "Lucky" Moritz retold how they had learned of the V-1 rocket production at Peenemunde.

Wayne Spivey, in his gentlemanly southern drawl could only sing the praises of his compatriots. "These men, with their high academic level and advanced linguistic abilities, well ah was in awe of the caliber of men ah was able to work with." Then he adds, "It was a great pleasure and great honor to serve with these boys."

George Frenkel turns out to be a charming character with a disarming wit who lightens the conversation.

Werner Gans, a Ritchie Boy like Fred, references his training and emphasizes, "We never used force of any kind," which brought supportive applause.

Then one of the veterans, Heinz Lychenheim reveals he has remained friends with two of his fellow soldiers, Bill Hess and Norm Graber. It looked like they were the only ones who kept in touch since their days at Fort Hunt.

Rudy Pins used his time to credit their Commander, Colonel John Walker, who told Pins, "Prisoners are people too and we must obey the Convention rules. That guided me through my time at Fort Hunt and afterwards," he finishes.

Ambassador John Gunther Dean declares, "At only nineteen, I learned that serving others is very satisfying and can lead to a very fulfilling life. We led by example, followed the Geneva Convention rules, and lived up to our reputation." He talks about U-234 and getting Heinz Schlicke's family out of Germany. "We did what we did with respect. What I learned at 1142 is to stand for honesty and justice."

Heartfelt applause supported his sentiment. Cynthia understands how deeply these men feel about non-violent interrogation and never resorting to the use of torture.

Then Peter Weiss tells a story about hitchhiking with Arno Mayer and landing up in a very nice car driven by Mamie Eisenhower, which brought laughs. As soon as he finishes Arno Mayer takes the mic and the opportunity to contradict Peter's memory saying it was he and Leslie Wilson who were hitchhiking, and they had a letter from General Eisenhower to prove it! Cynthia just laughs to herself, looks at her mom and says, "I'm sure there was a lot of hitchhiking going on, Mamie Eisenhower or not."

"It's been over sixty years; do we really have to argue about this?" Lucille playfully asks as she chuckles along with the crowd.

With that, the formal program is over, and everyone rises to head out to the buses. Cynthia helps her mom up and moves to the dais towards her dad. Fred carefully makes his way to the waiting wheelchair. Cynthia uses the opportunity to meet Peter Weiss and Arno Mayer. She can't help but razz them about the discrepancy in the hitchhiking story which they eventually laugh off.

Cynthia walks over to the flagpole on the way to the bus. Brandon and Vince did a great job, and the new plaque is especially moving. It is dedicated to the veterans of P.O. Box 1142 and reads in part,

Their top-secret work at Fort Hunt not only contributed to the Allied victory, but also led to strategic advances in military intelligence and scientific technology that directly influenced the Cold War and space race.

Cynthia absorbs the impact of the dedication, the efforts of her dad and the contributions of all these soldiers. She breathes in deeply, feeling appreciation for her dad and now all the other soldiers. Her parents have quietly come up next to her. She brushes a tear away and smiles. They understand. It has been a day filled with smiles and tears.

"We'd better keep moving if we're going to get on that bus," she says, then laughs, "I'm not sure you want to hitchhike back to the hotel!"

The next morning Cynthia, her mom, dad and the rest of the attending guests arrive at Fort Hunt by 9:30 am. There is a more collegial atmosphere, relaxed conversations, and familiar joking after breaking the ice the day before. George and Marianne gravitate to Fred and Lucille, and they easily hang together in their own group.

As Cynthia looks around, she now sees the faces of new friends and dear older gentleman who, like her father, have found a place in her heart. She understands their bonds with Brandon and he with them. She feels the connection between these men and the Park Service. *The park rangers are the other unsung heroes*, she thinks. *They've brought the whole story together*.

She spots Vince who seems to be everywhere all at once, guiding, managing, shaking hands and supporting his large team while playing host to the speakers and dignitaries who make up the reunion's roster.

As Cynthia casually walks behind her father's wheelchair, leading their little group to the pavilion, she thinks about the veterans who spoke yesterday. What a powerful reminder of what was at stake in World War II and how adeptly these men, then so much younger, handled each challenge. She smiles at the stories of the two Alex's who were US -Russian speaking soldiers, and the "play-acting" they did as Russian generals. There was the irresistible southern charm of Wayne Spivey, the succinct yet kind Rudy Pins, the cavalier Werner Moritz and their dear friend, George Mandel.

It strikes Cynthia at that moment how her heart has opened wide, and a new family has come in. She glances at her father and wishes so hard this reunion had happened when he was younger than his 85 years. As they settle into their seats inside the pavilion, she takes in the room and finds a new appreciation for what each soldier had willingly given to this country. Their youthful boldness is what helped win the war. *If that was hutzpah*, she thinks, *they had it.* No matter the challenge, they figured out a way to get the job done.

Her mother hands her the schedule for today's presentations. Lucille leans over, "It looks like Matt Virta will talk about Fort Hunt and P.O. Box 1142, probably what Brandon had told us in the living room," she comments to Cynthia.

Cynthia looks down the program she only briefly glanced at, "Brandon's talking about the oral history project. He told me yesterday more vets have been contacting him once word got out. Petula's article in the Post was a big help."

Overhearing the conversation, Rudy leans into their row and says, "There was an article in the Post today about the reunion. That should help find a few more people."

"Petula is amazing," Cynthia says with a smile. Then she tells her mom, "We need to get copies of the articles." Lucille agrees but she also knows her friends are clipping the article for her as they speak.

Cynthia continues down today's agenda and sees Vince is scheduled to talk about the other program, MIS-X, aiding

American POWs. And then there is Colonel Steve Kleinman. Brandon has mentioned him. As Cynthia understood it, Kleinman was the expert on interrogation. He is talking about applying lessons learned from MIS-Y to the challenges today. She leans back over to her mom and says casually, "I bet this Steve Kleinman agrees with dad on interrogation tactics. He should be interesting too."

After a brief welcome Brandon again takes to the podium and sings the praises of Fred whose interview began the whole project. "We will be forever grateful to Fred Michel for opening the door to this incredible story of 1142, leading us to Dr. George Mandel and eventually to all of you." Light applause follows. Fred is beaming, warmed by the gratitude of the soldiers, their families, the Park Service and especially Brandon.

Brandon recounts his many fact-finding visits to the National Archives, combing through lists of soldiers, transcripts of interrogations, pulling prisoner files with veteran's names on them and trying to piece it all together. Once he found Fred, they worked together to actively find other soldiers of 1142.

"It was instructive to find there was no physical violence of any kind used. Maybe some mind tricks," he said with a wink, "but the interrogators relied on conversations and room monitoring." Here he showed a slide of an enormous bell that was the *listening device* of the 1940's which brought a few sniggers from the crowd. "This was cutting edge!" he playfully defends.

"Of the information that was gathered, there were three events that stuck out," he says. "The capture of U-234 and the technology we learned about through interrogation. The collection of Werner von Braun and his Peenemunde team which were processed by 1142 soldiers. And the spymaster, Reinhard Gehlen." Here he shows a mug shot of the German who was then an expert on Russia.

"Our job now is to preserve history and this story for the public. We are working closely with the CIA, DIA, local veterans' organizations, the Washington D.C historical conference, Holocaust Museum, groups involving classification of documents and the media." He ended with, "we found about thirty-five soldiers, and we are looking for more. With your help, we'll find them."

With that, a huge applause goes up for Brandon who has given so much to these men. Since Brandon has interviewed or will interview everyone in the room, he has a special connection to each veteran and their families. They appreciate all he has done to tell their story.

Next, Vince Santucci takes the podium and, as Cynthia expected, describes the MIS-X program and the fact they had only found three people living from that division, and one recently died. He also mentions the book, *The Escape Factory* and the movie, *The Great Escape*, tying in the activities of Fort Hunt to each. He mentions the *Creamery* which housed coded communication and the *Warehouse* where clandestine packages were assembled to send to American POWs.

Then he posed an interesting question. "I always wanted to know where the number 1142 came from. We always thought it was the P.O. Box number of Alexandria, Virginia. But when we checked with the Post Office, the numbers jumped." Here he shows a slide of postal boxes jumping from 1139 to 1150. "And the Post Office isn't offering an explanation." The crowd laughs.

"I then obsessively Googled *1142* and found a British bedtime story that was told to children around the turn of the century." Vince recounts the story of Empress Matilda who was Queen of England in the year 1142 and was held against her will in Oxford Castle.

"Legend has it she fashioned a disguise and was able to escape and evade her captors, slipping past enemy lines to freedom. She eventually regained her throne. Is it coincidence the British MI-9 program that helped design the escape and evade program helped set up a program named 1142?" Vince asks. "We'll never know," he teases, "but it's interesting and fun to think about." With that tidbit to mull over, Vince steps down and yields to the last speaker, Colonel Steve Kleinman, Senior Intelligence Officer in the Air Force Reserves, at Air Force Special Ops Command.

Colonel Kleinman is a tall and lean man with close cropped hair touched ever so slightly with gray at the temple. Cynthia likes his voice because it's authoritative and knowledgeable. She relaxes back in her chair. She thinks she could listen to him all day.

Colonel Kleinman cuts quite a figure in his Air Force uniform with shining medals on his left breast. She knows this is a uniform that commands respect, yet he seems very approachable.

The Colonel begins with some background. He has extensively studied combat interrogations and wrote his thesis on the MIS-Y program's interrogation techniques. He was a huge advocate of never using physical force, a stand which seems unpopular with the administration during the current war.

"I started at the National Archives thinking this information from WWII will be, at best, 'quaint.' I was truly humbled at what I found. MIS-Y was a world-class program, well-designed and efficient. You were tasked with getting information from hardened Nazi prisoners and you did so with your wits, your command of German knowledge and language, conforming to Geneva Convention rules while maintaining a humane approach. The volume and more importantly the quality of information you obtained was both broad and deep. You were incredibly creative, incredibly insightful, and incredibly successful."

Yes, Cynthia decides, *I like this Colonel Kleinman.*

The Colonel goes on, "Let me just recap some of the intel gleaned from Fort Hunt interrogations. Because of your work," he states as he motions to the men seated before him, "We were the first to learn the Germans were changing their metallurgy used in building bombers. How did you do that? By looking at and analyzing the crashes of our own B-17s.

"You identified the names and government positions of Gestapo members working undercover throughout the German government. Your intel was immensely important in getting a true assessment of bomb damage inflicted by Allied raids on Germany.

"You were the first to report the deteriorating morale among the German people and waning support among the military for the failing Nazi regime. You were instrumental in piecing together the intricate understanding of the German scientific and technical communities, information which proved indispensable to Operation Paperclip at the end of WWII and setting up the Cold War."

Then Colonel Kleinman pauses to make sure this information sticks.

"The consequences of what you did cannot be overstated so let me make this point. America's lead in technology from space and aviation to chemistry and computers can be traced directly back to your accomplishments here at Fort Hunt in identifying the scientists that would join our side and help us in these efforts."

There it is, Cynthia realizes. The explanation to what she had been conflicted over was clearly laid out. There was reason, a purpose, and a definite benefit in the outcome of

Operation Paperclip. She felt herself relax into the explanation with a new understanding.

"Let me qualify this information with an example. During WWII, there was the Enigma Project, a secret program which allowed Allies to intercept key German communications. That program was significant in turning the tide of the war. My research shows that by the end of the war, information produced at Fort Hunt was on par with the intelligence produced from the Enigma."

The crowd was murmuring and taking in not only the breadth and scope of what these men had accomplished but also the lasting impact.

What didn't these guys find out about? Cynthia thinks to herself. She hadn't heard a lot of this, and she was riveted.

Colonel Kleinman continues. "What I learned is that interrogation is a complex and dynamic process. MIS-Y was made of a collection of individuals with impressive academic credentials, knowledge of language and culture who were able to produce results in an environment marked by chaos and ambiguity. Your streamlined approach started with a multi-tiered screening process that began in Europe. Once they got to the U.S. you kept for interrogation only prisoners that had critical and valuable information, the rest you sent on.

"You also put the work in. There was exhaustive preparation and research for each interrogation, between three and six hours of prep for each one. As a resulting benefit, the interrogator became an expert in that particular area or field.

Let me say again, you are the gold standard of how to conduct a strategic interrogation program. In essence, what you taught us was how to do good and therefore, be great."

Cynthia couldn't have said it better and with the pride on her mother's face, she knows every family member here feels the same.

"I'll wrap up with a little something you don't know but probably should. I am the son of a hero. My father served in WWII and flew B-17s. He was shot down, captured, interrogated, escaped prison camp and evaded recapture. After the war, he never wanted to talk about what he did. Like all of you, he remained humble as part of the greatest generation. So, I think I know what heroes look like," here Colonel Kleinman's voice catches in his throat, but he looks up and pushes on. "....and I'm looking at a room full of them."

Wild applause breaks out and those who can, rise to their feet in grateful ovation.

"There is only one thing I can do now to show my appreciation. I salute you." With that he steps to the side of the podium and raises his right hand in a crisp and heartfelt salute to an emotional crowd.

There are returned salutes and more applause while the room floods with emotion. Cynthia's eyes fill and her chest tightens as she fights to control her need to let out a sob.

It was the ending she hoped for. This is the recognition she wanted not only for her father but for all the soldiers. She is clapping along with everyone else and in the moment, slowly finds absolution for her own conflicted feelings. The soothing words of this expert untangled the complicated political and moral dilemmas that now make sense.

She is feeling many emotions, but as she looks at her parents, she sees only love. Lucille's eyes are also moist, and she is cradled into Fred's arm, to give support as well as get support. *They are holding each other up*, Cynthia thinks.

Slowly the clapping dies down, and people finish dabbing their eyes. The crowd begins to rise, there is a rumble of conversation and even laughter as people move to the next area to have lunch. Fred sits back down in the wheelchair; but before the park ranger starts to push, he looks up at his wife and daughter. "That was really wonderful. I appreciate what he had to say. I never really understood that all the information we gathered amounted to so much."

"It's impressive, dad, that's for sure." Cynthia assured him.

"You played an important part in this," Lucille's hand rested on her husband's shoulder. "You know I'm so proud of you," she said as she looked at her husband. The gratitude in both of their eyes said more than words ever could and Cynthia's heart was once again bursting. Just then the park ranger slowly begins to wheel Fred towards the dining area with Lucille alongside, her hand still on Fred's shoulder.

Cynthia lingers a moment, finding herself drawn to the crowd around Colonel Kleinman. People are shaking his hand with a comment of thanks, and then they move on until she is alone standing in front of him.

"Great presentation Colonel," came blurting out, then she realizes she is coming on a little strong.

He is unflappable and replies, "You can call me Steve. And you are?"

"Oh, Cynthia," she regains her composure and thrusts her hand forward. "Cynthia Michel. I'm Fred's daughter." Her nerves seem to jump, and her heart starts pounding while she smiles and tries to look relaxed.

Steve takes her hand and returns the vigorous grip. "Oh, your dad's the one!" He realizes. "He was the first soldier Brandon talked to!"

"Yes, that's him, that's us!" She corrects, not sure why she is suddenly so nervous in front of him.

"I'd love to talk to you about the project and Brandon finding your dad. Can I walk you into lunch?" he offers, motioning to follow the remains of the crowd.

Cynthia laughs and accepts the kind gesture. She is blushing for some reason as they walk unusually slow.

Steve is casually telling her how he enjoyed talking to the older veterans and hearing their stories and she is looking at his eyes thinking how much she'd like to know them better. His voice is soothing, and she is lost in the vibrato. He is asking her about Fred's service, and she has barely registered the question.

"You know it's kind of loud in here." She feigns deafness instead of distraction.

"Maybe we should have dinner, a nice quiet dinner where we can talk," he suggests.

"I'd like that," she turns and looks right into those blue eyes. "Dinner sounds great."

Epilogue

In the years after the initial reunion, Fred and George kept in touch, rekindling their friendship, which was a comfort to Fred.

Cynthia, true to her word, cared for her parents for the rest of their lives. However, within a few years, Fred's health took a turn for the worse. On May 30, 2009, literally 3 years to the day of Brandon's first interview, Fred passed. Brandon is asked to speak at the funeral. As a last gesture of gratitude for all Fred meant to this country and to the Park Service, Brandon presents Cynthia with the flag flown at Fort Hunt.

After Fred's death, Lucille and Cynthia pack up Fred's uniform and selected mementos, including the partially burned book from U-234, given to him by Heinz Schlicke. The National Park Service gratefully receives these items and creates a *P.O. Box 1142* display honoring the veterans of Fort Hunt. It is located inside the Arlington House which is the Robert E. Lee home located inside Arlington Cemetery, part of the George Washington Memorial Parkway. The items are still on display.

Lucille writes a touching letter to her friend, Sandy Gray, thanking her for all she did to help her husband regain a sense of purpose in his final years.

Over the next four years Brandon, Vince and members of the Cultural Resources team continue their interviews and pursuit of Fort Hunt veterans, eventually locating and interviewing over seventy. They will also find a German prisoner who was a tank operator in the Panzer division, captured in France and brought to P.O. Box 1142. This prisoner worked in the mess hall, and sixty years later validates the humane treatment cited by his interrogators.

They locate and interview two retired majors who were pilots, shot down in North Africa and used their Escape & Evade training to elude capture, citing the program's effectiveness.

The Cultural Resources team realizes they have priceless information and first-hand accounts of a unique period in our nation's history. They organize and transcribe each interview and create a website for the Fort Hunt Oral History project, which is still available to the public.

As more of the Fort Hunt veterans pass, Brandon is asked to give the eulogy at some funerals, most notably at Wayne Spivey's.

Cryptographer Silvio Bedini never attended the Fort Hunt reunion, but his children did. He was literally on his deathbed, dying of cancer, when his children convinced him to talk to Brandon. Bedini was interviewed on Oct 15, 2007, by Brandon and Matt Virta. The P.O. Box 1142 Reunion was held Oct 17th and Bedini died November 14, 2007.

George Mandel's health held for the next few years but on July 15 of 2011, he passed.

Brandon Bies and Vince Santucci have done such an exemplary job with this project, they are each promoted and reassigned. Once they leave Fort Hunt and the George Washington Memorial Parkway, the project is considered complete, and no further interviews are conducted.

At the end of World War II, it is estimated that of the roughly 9,500 U.S. servicemen captured by the Germans, the MIS-X operation helped or aided over seven-hundred prisoners to escape. This is not a large percentage but there is no way to know how many were able to evade capture because of their preventative training and the E&E items. It is also hard to estimate the positive effect the *loaded* packages had on prisoner's morale and survival.

As a last postscript, it was noted by Brandon Bies that included in the collection of papers from Lucille and Cynthia were Fred's discharge papers. Brandon and Vince would confirm that Fred's military service included a citation for intelligence work at Fort Hunt and something they were surprised to see, "assistance with the Manhattan Project."

They now regret never asking him about this.

Acknowledgements

It was an honor to tell the story of Fred Michel and all the veterans of P.O. Box 1142. Their service to our country went unrecognized for too many years. I sincerely hope my efforts pay ample tribute to their memory. I could not have told this story without the generous help of Brandon Bies, Vince Santucci, Bob Sutton, Steve Kleinman, Dana Dierks and Tim Mulligan.

Many soldiers at Fort Hunt were German Jewish refugees like Fred; others came from various European countries and from across the United States. They had diverse language skills and talents which contributed to the war effort. Their activities were conducted under a cloak of secrecy which lasted over sixty years. Their story could not be told until all documentation and records of their work were declassified. Now that we know their story, we owe these veterans a debt of gratitude for their service.

The men of P.O. Box 1142 interrogated prisoners and gathered intelligence without the use of force, physical violence, torture, or harmful psychological methods. Many of them, like Fred Michel, who fled the violence of Nazi Germany, when given the opportunity, chose not to use violence against their enemies. They were smart enough to understand torture doesn't work. Because of this philosophy, their intel could be trusted. This is the real legacy of P.O. Box 1142.

As I was researching this story, I recognized another group of secret heroes, the men and women of our National Parks Service. Their diligence and straight up tenacity in researching, interviewing veterans, and documenting the intelligence activities at Fort Hunt should be commended. Little was known of what happened at Fort Hunt until Brandon Bies interviewed Fred Michel. That meeting led the Park Service on a journey through the rich and exciting history of American intelligence and counterintelligence during WWII. They worked tirelessly to find and honor the secret heroes of P.O. Box 1142.

The entire Cultural Resources team including Brandon Bies, Vince Santucci, Bob Sutton, Dana Dierkes, Matt Virta, Sam Swersky, and numerous others who helped with the 2007 Fort Hunt veteran's reunion, should all be thanked. The result of their efforts is an informative, and in some cases jaw-dropping account of Fort Hunt's impact on the outcome of WWII. This is a small way to say thank you to Fred and all the men who served at P.O. Box 1142.

Made in the USA
Columbia, SC
29 June 2024

37747474R00221